WICHITA
FALLS

*Delaney Vineyards
& Winery*
DENTON   *Hidden Springs Wineries*

*La Buena Vida
Vineyards*

FORT
WORTH   DALLAS

TEXARKANA

TYLER

NACOGDOCHES

WACO

TEMPLE

*Alamosa
Wine Cellars*

*Fall Creek
Vineyards*

BRYAN   *Messina Hof
Wine Cellars*

*Spicewoods
Vineyards*

EDERICKSBURG   AUSTIN

*ecker
Vineyards*   *Texas Hills
Vineyards*

*mfort
ellars
Winery*

*Sister Creek
Vineyards*   *Dry Comal Creek
Vineyards*

SAN ANTONIO

BEAUMONT
PORT
ARTHUR

HOUSTON

*Haak Winery
& Vineyards*   GALVESTON

VICTORIA

FREER

AREDO   CORPUS CHRISTI

G U L F   O F   M E X I C O

BROWNSVILLE

D1087496

Compliments of

TURTLE & HUGHES INC.
Houston, Texas
(713)923-9004

FIRST IN THE LONG RUN

Your #1
Crouse-Hinds Distributor

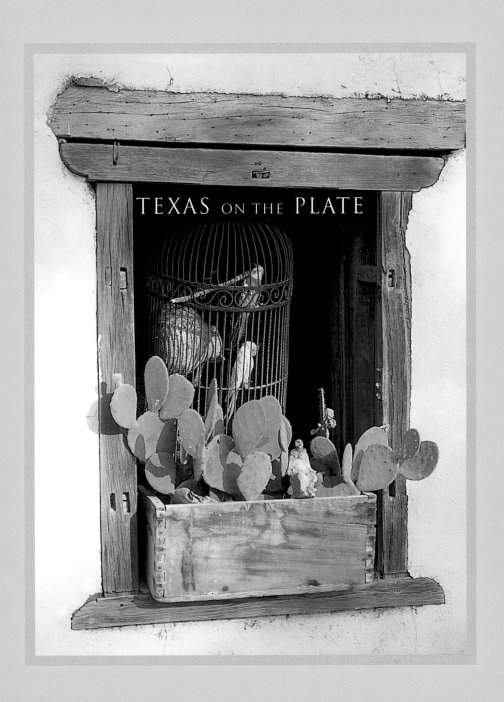

TEXAS ON THE PLATE

TEXAS ON

FOOD PHOTOGRAPHY BY RALPH SMITH

LOCATION PHOTOGRAPHY BY BOB PARVIN

SHEARER PUBLISHING
FREDERICKSBURG, TEXAS

THE PLATE

by Terry Thompson-Anderson

Library of Congress
Cataloging-in Publication Data
Thompson-Anderson, Terry, 1946-
Texas on the plate / by Terry Thompson-
Anderson ; food photography
by Ralph Smith ; location photography
by Robert Parvin.
p. cm.
ISBN 0-940672-72-3
1. Cookery, American—Southwestern
style. 2. Cookery—Texas. I.
Title.
TX715.2.S69 T557 2002
641.5979—dc21
2001057630

Published in 2002 by
Shearer Publishing
406 Post Oak Road
Fredericksburg, Texas 78624
www.shearerpub.com
800-458-3808

Book Design by Barbara Jezek
Editing by Alison Tartt
Food Styling by Julie Hettiger
Prop Styling by Janice Blue
Map Illustration by John A. Wilson

Production by Phoenix Offset
Printed in China

CONTENTS

ACKNOWLEDGMENTS

I am who and what I am because of the people I have learned from and the people who have given me chances to prove my abilities. I feel that I have been richly blessed because there have been so many of those people in my life.

Although my mother didn't teach me to cook, she loved to eat good food at good restaurants, so she exposed me to a profusion of ingredients and cooking styles. She always believed in my abilities when even I doubted that I had any.

My daughter Cory spent her whole life eating experiments and being thought of as somewhat strange by her friends because she willingly ate things like fish eggs and snails. As a grown-up, she now has the curse of a palate that is not cheaply satisfied.

My sister Sandy, her husband Steve, and my niece Kelsey are my most valuable recipe evaluators. Steve provided the impetus that led to this book and will always have the seat of honor at my dinner table.

My husband Roger is my rock. He was a middle-aged bachelor when I landed in the middle of his life with all the chaotic trappings of my career as a chef and cookbook author. He taught me how to fish and a new appreciation for every exciting aspect of this great state. He's the best cowboy of all.

Nathalie Dupree, my mentor, instilled in me a profound love of good food and a boundless passion for creating it. She also provided much encouragement and advice over the years. Francois Dionot, president of L'Académie de Cuisine, taught me to strive for perfection and was my role model of a professional chef. Shirley Corriher taught me about the science of food. Rose Beranbaum demystified the world of baking, pastry, and chocolate.

My association with Sharon Tyler-Herbst goes way back to the early days of the International Association of Culinary Professionals (IACP). She made the contacts that ultimately led to my first book contract.

Virginia Elverson is a very longtime friend, both through IACP and the Houston food scene. I am grateful to Virginia for referring me to Shearer Publishing Company, publishers of her great and enduring book, *Gulf Coast Cooking*.

Bert Greene molded me into a food writer. He painstakingly waded through my first voluminous manuscript and patiently helped me turn it into a book. My friend Lee Barnes gave me my first chance to teach cooking at her legendary school in New Orleans. The world of food lost much with their deaths, and I lost two beloved friends.

Blake Swihart has been a longtime and steadfast friend who always believed in my capabilities. His friendship and support, both professional and personal, have enriched me.

Paul Prudhomme will always be very special to me. He was my friend and encouraged me when I was struggling to build a career in food. His joie de vivre for everything, especially food, served as an inspiration to me.

Chuck and Lil Sheldon have been in my life for over twenty years. They now own one of Houston's best cooking schools, Sheldon's Taste of Hospitality, and I am privileged to teach there.

Last, but never least, I owe my great staff at Maner Lake Lodge enormous gratitude for their tireless efforts on behalf of this book. They measured, timed, tested, tasted, critiqued, then tested and tasted again many, many times. And they endured my periods of stress. Thank you, Cecilio, Roger, Fantine, Susan, and Rosa. You're the best staff in the world.

Bald cypress, Comal County (right); Nopal window planter, San Elizario (frontispiece); Rolling Plains farmland near Canadian (title page); Dunes, Mustang Island (pages 4–5); Shackleford County Courthouse, Albany (page 6); Skyscrapers, Houston (pages 10–11); Volcanic ash flats, Presidio County (pages 12–13); Workover rig, Iraan (page 14); German-Texan farmhouse, Fayette County (page 15).

TEXAS CUISINE—
THE EVOLUTION

TEXAS! *Just say the word and it conjures up a vast array of images: cowboys, ranches, beaches, the Gulf Coast, fishing, hunting, cattle, the citrus industry, rice growing, cotton farming, Dallas society, Houston's big business, NASA, the Golden Triangle's Cajun Connection, oil riches, East Texas timber, the Alamo, Hispanic culture, the Hill Country and Highland Lakes, German settlements and culture, wide-open spaces, border towns, Tejano music, country music, and great country music stars. Just imagine the variety of cultures and lifestyles existing simultaneously in this vast state.*

And vast it is. Texas is larger than the area encompassed by the states of Michigan, Wisconsin, Iowa, Illinois, and Indiana combined! The state covers over 267,000 square miles. The Texas border stretches for more than 3,800 miles. Texas has mountains reaching 8,000 feet and hundreds of miles of beaches. Texas has more than 80,000 miles of rivers, a portion of the largest desert in North America, tropical valleys, marshlands, and millions of acres of prairies and canopied woodlands. The state actually contains ten distinctly different ecological regions. Now, you ask, "Do we brag in Texas?" The answer is, "You bet." As John Steinbeck once observed, "Texas is a state of mind, Texas is an obsession. Above all, Texas is a nation in every sense of the word."

The history of Texas is a rich tapestry woven by the diverse people who inhabited the state as natives, or those who came here to conquer and seek riches and fame, or to forge new lives from the rough frontier.

These people used many colorful threads in the making of the tapestry: exploration and expansion, conflict and conquest, tragedy and tumult, adventure and accomplishment, discovery and diversity, pride and perseverance. But one of the most noteworthy threads woven into the tapestry was the amazing variety of foods introduced by each of the ethnic groups that came here.

Texas, as a unified entity, has existed under six flags: Spain, France, Mexico, the Republic of Texas, the Confederate States of America, and the United States of America. In addition to these six major influences on the state's culture, twenty-eight major ethnic groups settled in various parts of Texas where native Indians had inhabited Texas for thousands of years. Each brought their skills at preparing the foods of their native homelands. In many instances, they introduced new food items to the area. They also developed new ways of preparing the native ingredients that they found in Texas. These dishes formed the basis of an ever-evolving "Texas Cuisine."

As the Texas Cuisine progressed into the era of the range cowboy and later the giant cattle ranch in the late 1800s, chuckwagon cooking created such dishes as chili and other one-pot dishes built around beef. Texas became known as the land of thick steaks and barbecue, which, in Texas, means beef brisket. In the past twenty-five or so years, however, the evolution of Texas Cuisine has gone into overdrive. Innovative chefs have reached into the larder of all the ethnic groups that formed Texas, taking an ingredient here and

an ingredient there, to create ever more exciting dishes. The cuisine has focused on its strongest components—cowboy cooking and Mexican cooking with the use of chilies, both dried and fresh. It's not the food of the state's founders, but it draws on the sum of all those flavorful parts, expanded on with trendy ingredients introduced by savvy chefs. Some of these ingredients have actually been around for eons, but only recently have they been "rediscovered" by curious chefs and food writers poking around in our culinary history. Here they've discovered wonderful chilies from remote Mexican villages and ancient varieties of beans and grains such as quinoa. Some delicious foods, like rutabagas, were simply rediscovered in Grandmother's kitchen!

The evolution of a typical dish might go something like this: East Germans brought the weinerschnitzel, a breaded veal cutlet that was quickly pan-sautéed. In Texas, beef round steak was substituted. First the tougher cut of meat was pounded to tenderize it, then it was breaded and deep-fried, creating the classic chicken-fried steak with the addition of a thick, milk-based gravy spiked with ground black pepper. Today's upscale interpretation of the classic consists of a rib-eye steak breaded in Japanese breadcrumbs and deep-fried, then served with a chili-spiced version of the cream gravy. At my favorite Vietnamese restaurant, Hu-Dat's, in Rockport, the ubiquitous Gulf Coast fried shrimp is robed in a Japanese-style tempura batter, coated with sesame seeds, and deep-fried to golden-crisp perfection.

Our thriving citrus industry in the Rio Grande Valley has added a tropical note to Texas Cuisine. The recent influx of Thai and Vietnamese people has brought yet another tier of exotic ingredients heretofore unknown in Texas cooking. Lemon grass, coconut milk, fish sauce, spicy chili pastes, fresh ginger and galangal, jasmine rice and red rice—all have found their way into mainstream Texas cooking. In Houston and Dallas, Thai and Vietnamese cuisines have become major forces in the restaurant industry.

Today in Texas cooking, the grill and barbecue pit are no longer the domain of just beef. Everything gets grilled in Texas—from veggies to pizza to fish and shellfish. And they'll likely get marinated and basted with ingredients borrowed from four or five ethnic food groups.

As the executive chef at Maner Lake Lodge, a large hunting and fishing facility owned by Halliburton and located outside West Columbia in coastal Brazoria County, I have a wonderful opportunity to experiment with the best and freshest produce, meat, and seafood available through my purveyors. I am passionate about the food I create, and this book is written for other "foodies" like me who enjoy their lives through their palates. I find it a very exciting time to be a food professional in Texas. In fact, it's an exciting time in Texas for any of us who love to cook and eat great food. Our small rural towns are still alive and kicking in the twenty-first century, but they are isolated enough to retain the cooking customs of their ethnic roots. Our cosmopolitan cities like Dallas, San Antonio, and Houston present delicious and innovative combinations of the ethnic ingredients that have come to our state in the past 300 years, with new influences arriving constantly.

So all we have to do is pick a direction from wherever we are, and we can sample a vast array of great food and drink—everything from a heaping plate of bratwurst and sauerkraut in the Central Texas Hill Country, to a platter of perfectly boiled crabs on the Gulf Coast, to a fiery Thai curry in Houston or seared foie gras with truffle shavings in Dallas or slow-smoked brisket with a fine smoke ring in Lubbock or, of course, a fine grilled steak just about anywhere! Micro-breweries are producing hearty, European-style beers with a Texas twist.

Included in the back of this book are resource sections that will be helpful to all types of cooks. The section titled "Basics" gives some easy-to-use directions for preparing staple ingredients used in many of my recipes. Another section, "The Texas Cook's Pantry," lists sources for ingredients with which you may not be familiar.

There is also a section on Texas wines and wineries with tasting notes and a glossary of wine terms. Our state's rapidly growing wine industry is still in its infancy, but it is producing some great, award-winning wines. Wines are being produced in areas where the scoffers predicted that drinkable wine could never be made. Each year, new wineries open and new varietals are planted. In Texas, we never listen to scoffers! Winemakers from my favorite fifteen Texas wineries have paired their wines with most of the entrées in this book.

Intricate, this tapestry that is Texas. Intricate and enticing. It's a growing, constantly evolving weave. Explore Texas. Travel. Talk to the locals. Eat out in small towns and big cities. Visit a German town or go to a Czech Fest. Stomp grapes at a winery harvest. Go to a rodeo or the State Fair in Dallas. Catch a fish. Set out a crab trap. Throw a backyard barbecue. Climb a mountain. Just be real sure that you sample all the great and wonderful food and drink in every corner of the state. Texas has it all; become part of it, even if you're just visiting.

FOODS FOR GRAZING

I'd be hard-pressed to say when the first party was held in Texas. It's a generally accepted fact that Texans like to have fun. We also like to celebrate "occasions."

It can be a celebration of a historic occasion, like San Jacinto Day, April 21, when the whole town of West Columbia, the first capital of the Republic of Texas, celebrates right down the middle of its main thoroughfare for the whole weekend. Or it can be a true celebration of our heritage, like Fiesta in San Antonio each spring. New Braunfels celebrates its German heritage with an annual Wurstfest. We celebrate fishing tournaments in Freeport, with barbecue pits blazing at every bait camp. Dallas turns itself into a giant celebration for the Texas State Fair each fall. Houston celebrates its cowboy heritage each February at the Houston Livestock Show and Rodeo. We celebrate football games with tailgate parties in stadium parking lots—from high school stadiums to Texas Stadium, home of the Dallas Cowboys. El Paso residents celebrate many special occasions with festive, traditional Mexican dances performed by folklórico dancers in traditional costumes or at lively meriendas, where dozen of dishes are served with tequila drinks and sangria.

Why, we've been celebrating occasions since the state was just a baby. Back in the early days in

Soda fountain, Bastrop; San Saba River hay meadow, Menard County (pages 18–19).

Abilene, New Year's Eve was a big occasion for celebration, but the town needed a way to remind the revelers in the saloons when it was time to go home. So John C. Clinton, Abilene's chief of police, would step into the street on the corner of South First and Chestnut every New Year's Eve for thirty-seven years and empty his pistol into the air precisely at midnight, decreeing that it was time for the saloons to close.

But the common thread to all these celebrations is food and drink—and plenty of it. There's a washtub full of iced-down beer and soda pop, probably a spigot-cooler full of iced tea. There are tables piled with meats or barbecue and all the "fixin's"; pies and cobblers and somebody's pound cake; salads of every description; and loads of bread. You grab a plate and just start drifting around, picking up a bite here, a fat helping there. Top it off with a slice of bread set right on top of the whole thing, grab a cold brew, and find a place to sit and eat. That's pretty much the way we give parties at home, too. Lots of goodies arranged on the bar, around the living room, or stationed around the patio or pool when it's warm. Because when it's warm, we like to party outside. More room to kick up your heels and not have to worry about spills. We "graze," moving from one munchie to the next, stopping to chat when we come upon a fellow grazer. It's Texan—and it's fun.

Serving pan de campo *near San Isidro; Riverwalk, San Antonio (pages 22–23).*

CHILI CON QUESO DIP WITH HOMEMADE TORTILLA CHIPS

Gooey, drippy, spicy chili con queso was most likely served at the very first party that was held in the state of Texas. Maybe they even served it at the victory celebration when Sam Houston beat General Santa Anna at the Battle of San Jacinto to win Texas its freedom from Mexico. Don't even think about having a party without it, or you might be mistaken for a Yankee. Another tip: don't try to fancy it up by using some gourmet variety of real cheese. It just won't be chili con queso if you do. Just use plain old pasteurized processed cheese—the kind that comes in rectangular blocks. The Texas-born-and-bred grocery chain H-E-B markets a good one under the name Easy Melt—The Party Cheese.

Dip

1 pound pasteurized processed cheese
1 medium onion, chopped
1 large garlic clove, minced
2 teaspoons chili powder
1 can Ro-tel Diced Tomatoes with Chilies

Combine all ingredients in the top of a double boiler over simmering water. Cook, stirring often, until cheese has melted and mixture is creamy. Continue to cook for 20 more minutes. Serve hot with Homemade Tortilla Chips.

Homemade Tortilla Chips

White corn tortillas, cut into 4 wedges
Canola oil for deep-drying, heated to 350 degrees

Cut as many tortilla wedges as desired, but make enough for all of your guests to eat up that Chili Con Queso. Fry the chips in batches, taking care not to crowd the oil. Cook just until they are crisp and light golden in color. Drain on brown grocery bags or absorbent paper towels. Lightly salt the chips and serve them warm. The chips are best eaten the same day they are fried.

CHILLED SHRIMP WITH SPICY AND COOL DIPPING SAUCE

I love this dish. It meets all my requirements for successful party food—it's visually pleasing, it's made from ingredients that folks are familiar with, and it's mighty tasty. The serious heat of the chipotle chili is balanced by the cool taste of the cucumber and set in motion by fresh and zesty lime juice. Another reason I really like this dish is that it can be transformed into a first course simply by arranging the shrimp on a bed of greens and drizzling the sauce over them.

Texas Hills Vineyard recently released a new wine named Due Bianco, a blend of Pinot Grigio and Chardonnay. It's a highly drinkable white party wine, and I am fond of serving it with spicy foods such as this dish. It not only stands up to the heat, but the flavor undergoes a really interesting metamorphosis when paired with spice!

3 canned chipotle chilies in adobo sauce
1 tablespoon adobo sauce from the chilies
½ of a medium cucumber (about 5 ounces), peeled, pulp and seeds removed
1½ cups sour cream
¼ cup minced fresh cilantro
3 tablespoons fresh lime juice
1½ teaspoons salt
2 pounds chilled, boiled shrimp, peeled and deveined with tail section left intact

Combine all ingredients except shrimp in work bowl of food processor fitted with steel blade and process until smooth. Refrigerate, covered, until ready to serve.

Transfer the dip to a serving bowl and arrange the boiled shrimp around the bowl.

ca **Makes 2 cups.**

SERRANO CHILI GUACAMOLE

*N*obody in Texas would dare have a major get-together without serving guacamole. I mean, whether you call it guacamole or "avocado dip" is a moot point, but I'm sure we can all agree that to exclude it would be, why, downright un-Texan! This recipe is the way they make it in Mexico, without all the gringo stuff like mayonnaise, chili powder, and other adulterous ingredients some people insist on putting in their guacamole. It contains only the real nitty-gritty ingredients and the taste is as clean and straightforward as a summer breeze on the upwind side of the corral. Serve with your favorite store-bought corn chips, or make your own (see recipe for Chili Con Queso Dip with Homemade Tortilla Chips).

3 serrano chilies, seeds and veins removed, coarsely chopped

4 large cilantro sprigs (stems and leaves), coarsely chopped

1 small white onion, peeled and coarsely chopped

4 very ripe Haas avocados, peeled, seeds removed, and cut into chunks

Salt to taste

Shredded lettuce and tomato wedges as garnish

Place serrano chilies, cilantro sprigs, and onion in work bowl of food processor fitted with steel blade. Process until the vegetables are pureed and smooth. Add the avocado chunks and process to desired consistency. Some people like it real smooth, or you can leave some small chunks of the avocado if you prefer. Turn the mixture out into a bowl and stir in the salt to taste. Don't be stingy with the salt, or your guacamole will have a flat, boring taste.

An old trick for storing guacamole before serving is to place the seeds from the avocados on the surface of the mixture and push them in slightly. Cover tightly with plastic wrap and refrigerate until ready to serve. The seeds will prevent drastic color change for about 4 hours.

To serve, arrange the shredded lettuce in the center of a serving platter and turn the guacamole out onto the lettuce. Place tomato wedges around the edge of the guacamole.

❧ **Makes about 4 cups.**

BLUE HERON INN'S HOT CRABMEAT DIP

*T*he Blue Heron Inn in Rockport is one of the most delightful bed and breakfast inns in the state. The two-story Federal-style brick home overlooking Rockport's Little Bay was built in 1890 by an Oklahoma attorney and developer and later purchased by one of the town's mayors. One of the few nineteenth-century homes remaining in the area, it was restored and refurbished in 1993 and opened as a bed and breakfast inn. Meeting the two sisters who own the Blue Heron, Vera Archer and JoAnn MacCurdy, is one of the highlights of a stay at the inn. Vera and JoAnn always have great munchies on hand. Vera is in charge of the cooking, and this great and easy dip is one of her favorites. Serve it with melba toasts or crisp-fried flour tortillas broken into chips. Perfect for Texas party grazing.

8 ounces regular lump crabmeat

1 8-ounce package cream cheese, softened

3 tablespoons mayonnaise

1 tablespoon prepared horseradish

2 teaspoons Worcestershire sauce

6 ounces toasted, sliced almonds (skin on)

Carefully pick through the crabmeat to remove any bits of shell or cartilage. Set aside. Melt the cream cheese in a heavy 2-quart saucepan over medium-low heat. Stir in mayonnaise, horseradish, and Worcestershire sauce, blending well. Fold in the crabmeat. When ready to serve, transfer the dip to a chafing dish to keep warm. Scatter the toasted almonds over the top.

❧ **Makes about 3 cups.**

CHORIZO-STUFFED NEW POTATOES

*C*horizo sausage is a Mexican import to Texas, and I'm sure glad it made the trip with the folks who came north across the border. It has a flavor that is unique in the sausage world and has become an integral part of modern Tejano cooking. In Texas we fry the fat, spicy links up for breakfast and serve 'em with scrambled eggs topped with salsa and some softened corn tortillas. I created these potato munchies as one element on a first-course plate of assorted finger foods, and they became a favorite with customers. The topping features Manchego cheese, Spain's most popular cheese. Made from sheep's milk, it is available at specialty markets as a young, mild cheese aged for about two months, or semi-aged and slightly piquant, or wheels aged indefinitely. At any age, the flavor of Manchego cheese is mild, with a slight briny nuttiness, and rather dry on the palate.

10 small, unpeeled red new potatoes, about
    2 ounces each
12 ounces chorizo sausage
½ teaspoon salt
5 green onions, chopped, including green tops
2 tablespoons minced cilantro
10 tablespoons Mexican crema fresca (see "Basics")
Salt and freshly ground black pepper
5 ounces (1¼ cups) shredded Manchego cheese

Scrub the potatoes well with a vegetable brush. Place them in a heavy, 3-quart saucepan and add cold water to cover. Bring to a rolling boil and cook for 20 minutes, or until potatoes are soft when pierced with a metal skewer. Drain potatoes and set them aside to cool.

Squeeze the chorizo out of its casings and break up the lumps. Sauté the chorizo and salt (no oil is necessary) in a heavy skillet until evenly browned. Add the green onions and blend well. Remove pan from heat and drain off all fat. Stir in the cilantro and set aside to keep warm.

When potatoes are cool enough to handle, slice them in half. Cut a very thin slice from the bottom of each half so that they will sit flat without tipping over. Using a melon-baller, scoop out all the potato pulp, leaving a thin shell. Take care not to break the edges or bottom of the shell. Salt and pepper the inside of the shells.

Spoon 1 teaspoon of the crema fresca into each potato shell. Add a portion of the chorizo mixture and top with some of the shredded cheese. Place the stuffed potatoes on a baking sheet.

Preheat oven to 350 degrees. Bake the potatoes just long enough to heat the shells and melt the cheese, about 6 minutes. Serve warm.

ଔ **Makes 20 pieces.**

SALT

SALT IS ONE OF NATURE'S BEST FLAVOR ENHANCERS. UNFORTUNATELY, IT'S BECOME A VERY MUCH MALIGNED INGREDIENT IN THE PAST 20 YEARS. WHILE THERE ARE SOME HEALTH CONSIDERATIONS CONNECTED TO EATING TOO MUCH SALT, THE BODY MUST HAVE SOME SALT TO FUNCTION PROPERLY. AT HOME AND IN MY PROFESSIONAL KITCHEN, SEA SALT AND KOSHER SALT ARE THE ONLY SALTS I USE. THESE SALTS ARE PURE SALTS AND CONTAIN NO ADDITIVES. LOOK AT THE INGREDIENTS LABEL ON YOUR CONTAINER OF TABLE SALT—YOU'LL BE AMAZED TO SEE WHAT'S IN IT, INCLUDING DEXTROSE, A SUGAR! YOU'LL FIND YOU USE LESS SALT IF YOU USE SEA SALT. WHEN TASTING A DISH FOR CORRECT SEASONING DURING COOKING, ALWAYS TRY A LITTLE MORE SALT FIRST IF THE TASTE IS FLAT AND BORING. YOU'LL USUALLY BE SURPRISED AT HOW THE FLAVOR PERKS UP.

CRAWFISH BOULETTES WITH ORANGE-TEQUILA SAUCE

For years, crawfish have been traveling over the border from our neighbor state of Louisiana as fast as the Cajuns can boil them up. I think Texans love them every bit as much as the Cajuns do. This is one of my favorite crawfish concoctions. Boulette is a Cajun-French word that simply means "meatball." A boulette can be made from any combination of meats, vegetables, and grains. The spicy little devils are more addictive than the best potato chip. Eat one and it just says "More." They make great party munchies, or tuck a couple on the side of the plate with a seafood entrée. I developed the recipe after eating a similar dish made with real Cajun boudin at a tiny little authentic Cajun restaurant by the name of Etie's (pronounced A-tee-A's) in San Leon, right on Galveston Bay.

BOULETTES

2 pounds boiled crawfish tails, ground in food processor

1 cup bacon drippings or lard

2 medium onions, finely chopped

1 large green bell pepper, finely chopped

2 celery stalks, finely chopped

3 large garlic cloves, minced

3 cups chicken stock

1 teaspoon freshly ground black pepper

1 teaspoon red (cayenne) pepper, or to taste

½ teaspoon salt

¼ cup minced flat-leaf parsley

6 green onions, minced, including green tops

4 cups cooked white rice, overcooked until slightly sticky (see "Basics")

6 cups Seasoned Flour for Frying (see "Basics")

Egg wash made by thoroughly whisking 5 eggs into 1 quart milk

Japanese (panko) breadcrumbs, seasoned with salt and Cajun seafood seasoning

Canola oil for deep-frying, heated to 350 degrees

ORANGE-TEQUILA SAUCE

1 18-ounce jar good-quality orange marmalade

1½ cups rich chicken stock

½ cup medium-hot picante sauce

1 canned chipotle chili in adobo sauce, minced

2 tablespoons cornstarch whisked into ¼ cup fresh lime juice

⅓ cup Jose Cuervo Gold tequila

Prepare the Orange-Tequila Sauce. Combine the marmalade, chicken stock, picante sauce, and minced chipotle chili. Bring to a rolling boil and cook, stirring often, until the marmalade has melted and mixture is somewhat reduced, about 8 minutes. Quickly whisk in the cornstarch/lime juice mixture and boil over high heat until thickened, about 2 minutes. Remove from heat and whisk in the tequila. Set aside.

To make the boulettes, heat the bacon drippings or lard in a heavy, deep skillet over medium-high heat. Add the ground crawfish tails, onions, bell pepper, celery, and garlic. Cook until the vegetables are wilted and transparent, about 10 minutes. Add the chicken stock, black pepper, red (cayenne) pepper, and salt, scraping bottom of pan to release any browned bits. Reduce heat to low and cook, stirring occasionally, until thickened, about 45 minutes. Stir in the parsley, green onions, and rice, blending evenly. Cook until mixture is thick and rice is sticky, about 15 minutes. Remove from heat and transfer to a shallow baking dish. Refrigerate until well chilled.

Roll the chilled rice mixture into balls about the size of golf balls. Dip each ball first in the seasoned flour, shaking to remove all excess flour, then in the egg wash and the seasoned Japanese breadcrumbs, coating well. Press the breadcrumbs into the balls and shake off all excess crumbs. Deep-fry the balls in the hot oil until crisp and golden brown, about 4 minutes. Drain on a wire cooling rack set over a baking sheet. Serve hot with a bowl of the warmed Orange-Tequila Sauce.

❧ **Makes about 40 boulettes.**

CRABMEAT QUESADILLAS WITH PICO DE GALLO

*T*ex-Mex, or Tejano cuisine, as it is now being called, is an exciting new cuisine born in Texas in the last two decades. It combines the Hispanic cuisine of the state's many Mexican immigrants, itself a blending of Spanish and native Indian foods, with the newly evolving Texas Cuisine. Many popular elements of this new cuisine are finding their way around the country, with the likes of quesadillas, burritos, and chimichangas appearing as far away as Manhattan.

12 ounces lump crabmeat

3 cups (12 ounces) shredded Monterey Jack cheese

4 green onions, chopped, including green tops

1 4-ounce can diced green chilies, well drained

⅓ cup sliced ripe olives

⅓ cup chopped pickled jalapeños

1 tablespoon minced cilantro

9 9-inch flour tortillas

Peanut oil

PICO DE GALLO

4 large Roma tomatoes, cut into ¼-inch dice

1 small onion, finely chopped

4 serrano chilies, seeds and veins removed, minced

1 heaping tablespoon minced cilantro

2 tablespoons fresh lime juice

1 tablespoon olive oil

Salt to taste

Make the Pico de Gallo by combining all ingredients in a non-aluminum bowl and stirring to blend. Refrigerate until ready to serve.

To make the quesadillas, carefully pick through the crabmeat to remove any bits of shell or cartilage. Place in bowl and add all remaining ingredients except tortillas and peanut oil. Stir to blend well, taking care not to break up the lumps of crabmeat. Divide the crabmeat mixture among the tortillas, spreading it on half of each tortilla. Fold the tortillas over, pressing down around the edges to seal.

Heat about 1 tablespoon of the peanut oil in a heavy 12-inch skillet over medium heat. Fry 2 of the folded tortillas at a time over medium heat, turning once. Cook just until the cheese is melted and bubbly, about 5 minutes. While the quesadillas are cooking, press down on them frequently with a flat spatula to make sure the halves stick together. Place on baking sheets in a warm oven while cooking the remaining quesadillas. To serve, cut each folded tortilla in half, forming two wedges, or into fourths, depending on size desired. Serve with a bowl of the Pico de Gallo.

☙ **Makes 18 pieces.**

LITTLE SMOKIES IN WHISKEY SAUCE

I really can't remember how long ago I first tasted these soused little sausages. A friend of mine served them at a party he hosted. I loved them and stole his recipe on the spot. There are certain individuals among my friends who would get really cantankerous if I had a party without serving Little Smokies. They're the easiest party munchies you can imagine.

1 cup Jack Daniel's whiskey

1 cup Heinz chili sauce

1½ teaspoons Tabasco sauce

1 cup firmly packed light brown sugar

2 pounds cocktail sausages

Combine the whiskey, chili sauce, Tabasco sauce, and brown sugar in a 4-quart saucepan over medium heat. Stir to blend, then simmer for 15 minutes. Add the sausages and cook until they are heated through, about 10 minutes. When ready to serve, transfer to a chafing dish. Place wooden picks nearby for spearing the sausages.

☙ **Serves 25 to 30.**

TEXAS GULF SHRIMP TOASTS

*S*hrimp is one of the most versatile ingredients to work with. Good, fresh shrimp has a nice taste of its own if you want to serve it just plain boiled; its taste also marries well with just about any herb. It stars well in spicy, down-home dishes, in bold gumbos, or in upscale presentations. It even has an excellent history in those really frilly dishes with cream and sherry. In this simple but really tasty finger food, the honest taste of the boiled shrimp is paired with the assertive twang of Gruyère, a fine, bold-flavored Swiss cheese. The result is mighty tasty. The topping for the toasts can be made in advance of your shindig and it even freezes well, but don't put the topping on the toasts until you're ready to bake and serve them.

50 ¼-inch-thick French-style baguette slices

12 tablespoons unsalted butter, melted

 1 teaspoon salt

 1 tablespoon minced fresh thyme

 8 ounces peeled, boiled shrimp, minced

 ¼ cup Italian-seasoned breadcrumbs

 6 ounces shredded Emmenthal or Gruyère cheese

 ½ cup mayonnaise

 ½ teaspoon red (cayenne) pepper

 ¼ teaspoon additional salt, or to taste

Radish slices

Preheat oven to 350 degrees. Arrange the bread slices on baking sheet and set aside. Combine the melted butter, 1 teaspoon salt, and thyme. Using a pastry brush, brush each toast with some of the butter mixture, making sure that each toast gets some of the herb. Bake the toasts in preheated oven until lightly browned, about 5 minutes. Cool on wire racks.

Combine the remaining ingredients, except radish slices, blending well. Spread a portion of the mixture on each baked toast. Arrange toasts on baking sheet and bake in preheated oven for 7 minutes, or until mixture is slightly bubbly. Do not overcook. Garnish each toast with a radish slice. Serve warm or at room temperature.

∝ **Makes 50 toasts.**

Fayette County prairie near LaGrange

MUSHROOMS STUFFED WITH CRABMEAT, ROASTED GARLIC, AND SPINACH

I love stuffed mushrooms. Mushrooms stuffed with just about anything can reduce me to a whimpering state, unless, of course, they have been overcooked. When a stuffed mushroom is overcooked, the mushroom becomes a mushy, sponge-like disk that has bled out its entire flavor and completely lost its starch. The poor mushrooms flatten out and spill out their delicious stuffing onto the plate, or your floor, or the bodice of someone attempting to eat them. In this recipe the mushrooms are dipped in a bold butter sauce that pairs Dijon-style mustard with two of my favorite spicy ingredients—Oriental chili paste with garlic and Japanese wasabi paste, the really, really hot stuff.

MUSHROOMS

24 stuffing-size mushrooms (about 2 inches in diameter)

1 pound unsalted butter

½ cup Dijon-style mustard

1 tablespoon wasabi paste

¼ cup fresh lime juice

1 tablespoon chili paste with garlic

STUFFING

1 pound lump crabmeat

¼ pound (1 stick) unsalted butter

2 tablespoons Dijon-style mustard

12 ounces fresh spinach leaves, washed, tough stems removed, and torn into bite-size pieces

12 large garlic cloves, roasted and minced (see "Basics")

¼ cup minced fresh basil

1 cup grated Parmesan cheese

Salt and freshly ground black pepper to taste

Prepare the mushrooms. Remove stems and wipe the caps clean with paper towels; set aside. Melt the butter and add the remaining ingredients. Whisk rapidly over medium-high heat until the buttery dip is smooth and well blended. Remove from heat and allow to cool slightly. When the butter glaze has cooled enough that you won't burn your fingers, dip the mushroom caps in the dip, coating them liberally, inside and out. Arrange the caps on a shallow baking sheet.

Prepare the stuffing. Pick through the crabmeat to remove any bits of shell or cartilage. Melt the butter in a heavy 14-inch skillet over medium heat. Whisk in the mustard to blend well. Add the spinach all at once and toss with chef's tongs just until the leaves begin to wilt. Remove pan from heat and stir in the roasted garlic, basil, ½ cup of the Parmesan cheese, and crabmeat. Add salt and pepper to taste. Preheat oven to 350 degrees.

Stuff each mushroom with a portion of the crab mixture. Scatter the remaining Parmesan cheese over the mushrooms. Bake for 15 minutes in preheated oven. Serve hot.

ଔ Makes 24 stuffed mushrooms.

OYSTER PATTIES

*T*he rule in Texas is that if you're a real true-blue native Texan, you have to love oysters. My father was not a born Texan, but he lived here for so long and he loved the state so much that he passed himself off as one. When really pressed, he would adopt the attitude of "Well, I may not be a native Texan, but I got here as soon as I could." The one problem he always had with credibility, though, was that he hated oysters in any shape or form.

I created these great little finger foods many years ago and once served them at a party in my parents' home. My mother put one to his mouth with the admonition "Here, eat this." He complied and went back for more. Later in the evening we told him what he had been eating, pronouncing him an Official Texan. The moral of this story is that even oyster-haters love these munchies.

PATTY SHELLS

½ cup unsalted butter, melted
24 soft white sandwich bread slices

OYSTER FILLING

¼ cup unsalted butter
4 green onions, finely minced
1 small celery stalk, minced
½ of a small green bell pepper, minced
1 small onion, minced
¼ cup all-purpose flour
1 pint shucked oysters and their liquor, finely chopped and liquor reserved
1 bay leaf, minced
¼ cup minced flat-leaf parsley
1 teaspoon minced fresh sage
½ teaspoon red (cayenne) pepper
¼ teaspoon freshly ground black pepper
Salt to taste
½ cup dried breadcrumbs tossed with 1 tablespoon melted butter

Prepare Patty Shells (they can be made in advance and frozen). Preheat oven to 350 degrees. Using a pastry brush, coat inside of 24 miniature (2-inch-diameter) muffin tins with the melted butter. Set aside. Using a 2½-inch round cutter, cut a round from each slice of bread. Save the scraps from the bread slices to dry for breadcrumbs. Push each round gently into the buttered muffin cups, pressing snugly against bottom and sides. If bread tears, make a "patch" with a small piece of bread from the scraps. Pat any patches firmly in place. Bake the shells in preheated oven until lightly browned, about 10 minutes. Remove patty shells from muffin tins; cool on wire racks.

Prepare Oyster Filling. Melt the butter in a heavy 12-inch skillet over medium heat. Add green onions, celery, bell pepper, and minced onion. Sauté until vegetables wilt, about 5 minutes. Stir in the flour and cook, stirring, for 2 to 3 minutes. Stir in the chopped oysters, their liquor, and remaining ingredients, except breadcrumbs, blending well. Bring the mixture to a boil, stirring. Reduce heat and simmer until thickened, about 4 minutes. The amount of liquor with the oysters will vary; if the filling is too thick, add a small amount of whipping cream to achieve desired consistency. Preheat oven to 350 degrees. Fill each patty shell with some of the filling and set the filled shells on an ungreased baking sheet. Scatter the buttered breadcrumbs on the filled shells. Bake in preheated oven until filling bubbles, about 10 minutes. Serve warm.

ଔ **Makes 24 bite-size patties.**

Tomato Salsa with Garlic Toasts

*O*ne of the best things about summer is fresh tomatoes. Nothing beats the taste of a homegrown tomato. Even to pick one up and smell the skin is a great sensory treat. When I was little, I used to imagine that a tomato fresh from the garden was given its special taste by the sunshine. We use tons of tomatoes in Texas to produce the many Mexican-style salsas. Every Mexican restaurant has its own unique salsa. Some are very hot, with the major taste element being chilies. Others are milder and depend on the tomato for the bulk of their taste. This one, which was adapted from a salsa served at Lynette Madola's La Mora restaurant in Houston, falls in the latter category and has more of an Italian flavor. It's a really good summer snack—one of those goodies I like to whip out of the refrigerator when unexpected guests drop by the house. If you don't have homegrown tomatoes, be sure that you buy Roma tomatoes for this recipe. Commercially grown Romas seem to have been spared some of the horrors that have been inflicted on regular tomatoes. Most other tomatoes have been bred into tasteless, mealy-textured, cardboard-skinned ghosts of tomatoes past.

Tomato Salsa

¼ cup extra-virgin olive oil

¼ cup minced garlic

3 anchovy fillets, minced

2 cups finely diced Roma tomatoes

½ teaspoon crushed red pepper flakes

3 tablespoons chopped fresh basil

3 tablespoons minced flat-leaf parsley

1 tablespoon plus 1 teaspoon balsamic vinegar

1 tablespoon freshly squeezed lemon juice

Kosher or sea salt and freshly ground black pepper to taste

Garlic Toasts

2 French bread baguettes, sliced into ¼-inch-thick rounds

4 garlic cloves, minced

1 cup extra-virgin olive oil

2 teaspoons salt

Prepare the Tomato Salsa. Heat the olive oil in a 12-inch skillet over medium heat. When the oil is moderately hot, add the garlic and anchovies. Cook, stirring often, until garlic is soft but not browned. Remove the pan from the heat and allow the oil to cool. In a medium bowl combine the tomatoes, crushed red pepper, basil, parsley, vinegar, and lemon juice. Pour the cooled garlic mixture over the tomatoes and stir to blend well. Season to taste with salt and black pepper. Chill before serving.

To make the Garlic Toasts, preheat oven to 375 degrees. Combine the olive oil, garlic, and salt in a small saucepan and simmer for 5 minutes. Remove from heat and pour through a fine strainer; discard garlic. Using a pastry brush, coat each bread slice with the flavored oil and place on baking sheets. Toast until light golden in color, about 10 minutes. Do not allow the toasts to brown, or they will have a somewhat bitter taste. Cool on wire racks before serving.

To serve, place the salsa in an attractive serving bowl and place a basket of the Garlic Toasts alongside.

❧ **Makes about 3 cups of salsa.**

Tomato and Basil Crostini
with Paula Lambert's Texas-Made Mozzarella

Paula Lambert is a Texas girl who went to live in Italy for a while several years ago. When she came home to Dallas, the thing she missed most was fresh, handmade mozzarella. Nobody in Texas at the time even knew what it was! So she built a cheese factory in the Deep Ellum section of Dallas and began making soft, fresh mozzarella cheese—about 100 pounds of cheese per week. Her little factory is now the Mozzarella Company, selling hand-crafted, award-winning specialty cheeses throughout the United States to restaurants, hotels, and gourmet shops as well as to cheese lovers around the country. In 1999 the company produced over a quarter of a million pounds of handmade cheeses from cow's milk and goat's milk. Crostini are very traditional Italian canapés. They are made from hearty, country-style breads with their crusts left on, and they may be topped with anything the imagination can conjure up. This really yummy version is one of my favorite ways to showcase Paula's mozzarella.

2 French-style baguettes, sliced ¼ inch thick

2 pounds Mozzarella Company fresh mozzarella, shredded (see "The Texas Cook's Pantry")

4 cups minced, oil-packed sun-dried tomatoes, drained

⅔ cup julienne strips of fresh basil

Preheat oven to 350 degrees. Arrange bread slices on baking sheets. Scatter a portion of the sun-dried tomatoes on each slice and top with a portion of the basil strips. Top each crostini with a generous portion of the shredded cheese. Bake in preheated oven just until the cheese has begun to melt, about 5 to 7 minutes. Serve warm or at room temperature.

(Unbaked crostini can be covered with plastic wrap and stored in the refrigerator until you're ready to serve them.)

❧ **Makes about 75 to 80 crostini.**

Texas Tornados

These peppery little nibbles are one of my favorite grazing goodies. They've become the center of attention at many parties. They're spicy, they're different, and they're addictive, so be sure to make plenty. Even mushroom-haters love 'em. If you get hooked, scatter a few on top of your next grilled steak for another noteworthy taste experience.

2 pounds tiny button mushrooms or larger mushrooms cut into quarters

1 cup (2 sticks) unsalted butter

1 5-ounce bottle Worcestershire sauce

¼ cup finely ground black pepper

¼ teaspoon salt

1 teaspoon Tabasco sauce

Wipe the mushrooms clean and trim away any tough, woody stems. Melt the butter in a heavy 3-quart saucepan over medium heat. Add the mushrooms and toss to coat with butter. Stir in the remaining ingredients, again coating the mushrooms completely. Increase heat to medium-high and cover the pan. Cook the mushrooms, stirring frequently to prevent sticking, until the butter separates from the Worcestershire sauce, about 15 minutes. (The mushrooms will be glazed with a sticky, dark, caramel-colored syrup that will start to stick to the bottom of the pan.) Do not lower the heat during the cooking process. Remove pan from burner and spoon out the mushrooms using a slotted spoon. Discard sticky residue in bottom of pan. Serve hot or at room temperature with toothpicks.

❧ **Makes about 6 cups.**

GRILLED PIZZA

I've often heard it said that in Texas "if it's edible, we'll put it on the grill." I reckon that's probably pretty close to the truth, too, because I have become addicted to pizza cooked on the gas grill. The dough takes on a wonderful, slightly smoky taste and if you're a fan of thin and crispy, well, it's the crispiest! Serve Grilled Pizza at your next get-together and listen to the oohs and aahs. It's really easy to do—just be sure to spray the grill racks well with non-stick vegetable spray and be liberal with the olive oil "bath" for your dough. Don't try to put too many toppings on a grilled pizza. Keep it down to a couple of your favorites, or try the combinations suggested below.

I have fond memories of pizza outings when I was a teenager in Houston. There was an Italian restaurant on South Main, across from the old Shamrock Hotel. The name of the restaurant was Valian's and it had wonderful pizza. It was always crowded and the proprietors must have been saints to accommodate the hordes of hell-raising teenyboppers who invaded the place on Friday and Saturday nights. Both the Shamrock and Valian's are gone now, but they sure left Houston with some memories.

BASIC PIZZA DOUGH

1½ cups warm water (105–115 degrees)

 1 tablespoon sugar

1½ tablespoons instant-rise dry yeast

3½ cups bread flour

⅓ cup powdered milk

1½ teaspoons salt

 3 tablespoons additional sugar

 3 tablespoons canola oil

 1 egg

Olive oil for coating dough

SUGGESTED TOPPINGS

∞ *Thin-sliced onions, thin julienne strips of red bell pepper, thin julienne strips of sun-dried tomatoes, julienne strips of fresh basil, and shredded fresh mozzarella cheese*

∞ *Crumbled, pre-cooked Italian sausage, paper-thin slices of proscuitto, julienne strips of fresh basil, thin-sliced mushrooms, and shredded Asiago cheese*

∞ *Tiny (gumbo-size) whole boiled shrimp, thin slices of onion, sliced ripe olives, and Gorgonzola cheese*

∞ *Sliced fresh Roma tomatoes seasoned with salt and black pepper, julienne strips of fresh basil, and shredded Fontina cheese*

Combine water, 1 tablespoon sugar, and yeast in a 2-cup glass measuring cup. Stir to blend well and set aside to proof the yeast, about 4 minutes. Combine the remaining ingredients in work bowl of food processor fitted with steel blade. Pulse 3 or 4 times to blend. Add the yeast mixture to work bowl, scraping cup with a rubber spatula to include all yeast. Process dough for about 15 seconds. Stop and check consistency of the dough. It should be medium-stiff and not sticky. Add additional water or bread flour as necessary, about 1 tablespoon at a time, to correct the dough. Process dough after each addition. When proper consistency has been reached, process for 20 seconds to knead the dough. Turn dough out onto work surface and knead for a couple of minutes by hand to form a smooth dough ball.

Pour about ½ cup of the olive oil in a large bowl and place the dough ball in the bowl, turning to coat all sides. Cover bowl with plastic wrap and set aside to rise until doubled in bulk, about 45 minutes. Preheat the grill and spray the grill rack liberally with non-stick vegetable spray. Punch dough down and divide in half. Stretch and pat the dough balls into thin, free-form shapes. Coat both sides of the dough with some of the olive oil from the bowl. When grill is good and hot, lay the dough directly on the grill rack. It will start to stiffen quickly. The trick is to keep it moving around, either with your fingertips or a pair of chef's tongs. As soon as the crust is barely stiff, add one of the topping combinations, or create you own. Keep the dough moving around. When toppings are hot and cheese is melted, slide the pizza onto a baking sheet and slice. Serve hot.

∞ **Makes 2 14-inch pizzas.**

Mexican Pizzas with Serrano Chili Guacamole

One of the hottest trends of the decade on the Texas party circuit is tapas. Tapas are a Spanish tradition that has spread not only to other Spanish-speaking countries but to the United States in the form of tapas bars. Tapas are tidbits of food eaten with drinks at a bar prior to a meal. Dallas, Houston, Austin, and San Antonio have become meccas for tapas bars, serving great wines, drinks, and fancy munchies. Adapting the tapas concept to home parties is easy. Invite a manageable number of guests and prepare seven or eight really good small finger foods. Tapas can range from something as simple as three kinds of olives and a cocktail onion on a wooden skewer, to meats or vegetables on toasted bread rounds, to more substantial items like this attractive and gratifying "pizza."

Pizzas

  3 tablespoons canola oil

  4 ounces lean ground beef

  4 ounces lean ground pork

  1 medium onion, chopped

  2 medium garlic cloves, minced

  2 Roma tomatoes, blistered, peeled, seeded, and chopped

½ cup prepared picante sauce, heat level to taste

  2 teaspoons ground cumin

  1 teaspoon ground chili powder

½ teaspoon salt

½ teaspoon freshly ground black pepper

1½ tablespoons minced cilantro

  4 8-inch flour tortillas

  2 cups (8 ounces) shredded Monterey Jack cheese

Shredded lettuce

Serrano Chili Guacamole (see separate recipe)

Preheat oven to 350 degrees. Heat canola oil in a heavy 12-inch skillet over medium heat. Add ground beef and pork, onion, and garlic. Sauté until meats are evenly browned, about 7 minutes. Drain off all fat from pan and return to heat. Add the tomatoes, picante sauce, cumin, chili powder, salt, and pepper. Stir to blend well and cook, stirring frequently, until liquid has evaporated and mixture is thickened, about 15 minutes. Remove pan from heat and stir in the cilantro. Place two of the flour tortillas on a large baking sheet. Divide the meat mixture between the tortillas, spreading evenly all the way to the edge. Scatter the shredded cheese over the meat. Press the remaining tortillas on top of the cheese.

Bake the pizzas in preheated oven for 10 to 15 minutes, or until cheese has melted and the top tortilla is firmly attached. Cut the pizzas into 4 or 8 wedges. Scatter some of the shredded lettuce in the center of two 12-inch round platters and spoon a portion of the Serrano Chili Guacamole on top. Arrange the pizza wedges around the guacamole and serve.

&ca; **Makes 2 8-inch pizzas.**

El Mercado vendor, San Antonio

GRILLED PORTABELLO PIZZAS

*T*he portabello is the giant of the mushroom world, with the dark tan caps sometimes measuring 6 inches in diameter. In Texas we like things Big, so I figure that's one of the reasons why they've become so popular around the state. Another reason is that when you grill a portabello mushroom, it tastes a whole lot like a great cut of beef and everybody knows how we feel about beef. I serve a grilled portabello "steak" on my non-meat menu at the lodge. These pizzas make excellent party food. If you're serving things on plates, then simply cut the pizzas into four wedges and plate 'em up. If it's strictly finger food, then arrange the wedges on an attractive serving platter.

MUSHROOMS AND MARINADE

6 portabello mushrooms, stems removed

½ cup extra-virgin olive oil

1 tablespoon balsamic vinegar

3 large garlic cloves, minced

1 heaping teaspoon crushed red pepper flakes

2 teaspoons minced flat-leaf parsley

2 teaspoons minced fresh cilantro

½ teaspoon salt

¼ teaspoon freshly ground black pepper

1 teaspoon sugar

PIZZA SAUCE

¼ cup mascarpone cheese

2 tablespoons half-and-half

¼ cup prepared spaghetti sauce

½ teaspoon crushed red pepper flakes

Salt to taste

PIZZA TOPPING

2 links (8 ounces) mild or hot Italian sausage

1 small green bell pepper, cut into thin julienne strips 2 inches long

1 small red bell pepper, blistered, peeled, and cut into thin julienne strips 2 inches long (see "Basics")

½ of a small onion, halved lengthwise, then sliced thin

⅓ cup sliced ripe olives

1 ounce thin-sliced pepperoni

½ cup shredded Asiago cheese

½ cup shredded fresh mozzarella cheese

¼ cup grated Parmesan cheese

Begin by marinating the mushrooms. Combine all marinade ingredients; whisk to blend well. Wipe the outside of the caps gently with a damp paper towel. Place mushrooms in a large baking dish and spread the marinade on both sides of the caps, coating well. Set aside at room temperature for 1 hour. Heat gas grill and quickly grill the mushrooms, turning once, until slightly soft, about 3 minutes per side. Remove from grill and set aside.

Prepare the Pizza Sauce by combining all ingredients and blending well. Arrange the mushrooms, gill sides up, on a baking sheet. Spoon a portion of the sauce over the inside of each mushroom. Preheat oven to 375 degrees.

Prepare the Pizza Topping. Bake the Italian sausage until done. Cut the links into chunks and process in food processor fitted with steel blade until ground. Scatter a portion of the sausage over each mushroom, and then arrange the vegetables and pepperoni on the pizzas. Combine the three cheeses and scatter over the pizzas. Place baking sheet in preheated oven and bake the pizzas for about 8 to 10 minutes, or just until the cheese has melted and is barely browned on top. Remove from oven and slice each mushroom into four wedges. Serve warm.

℘ **Makes 6 pizzas or 24 wedges.**

GRILLED EGGPLANT ROLLUPS

*E*ggplant is an old vegetable, long favored by southern cooks. With the recent influx of Asian peoples to America, new exotic varieties of eggplant have appeared in our markets. They differ in color, shape, and even taste from our familiar, fat, pear-shaped favorite with its deep purple skin. I love them all, but for this finger food I prefer the old tried-and-true. When buying eggplant, select ones that are relatively heavy for their size. This means they're ripe, but not overly ripe, and full of meat, not pithy. The skin should be shiny, smooth, and taut, with no wrinkles. Once they show flabby, bronzed, dented, or pitted areas, they are past their prime and will be bitter in taste. They should be firm when pressed. The fuzzy green caps and stems should be vibrant green and tightly intact, free of anything resembling mold. Eggplants are highly perishable vegetables, so never purchase them more than two days in advance of using them.

2 large eggplants, about 24–28 ounces each

MARINADE

⅓ cup balsamic vinegar

1 tablespoon Dijon-style mustard

4 large garlic cloves, minced

2 teaspoons crushed red pepper flakes

1 tablespoon minced flat-leaf parsley

1 tablespoon minced fresh cilantro

½ teaspoon salt

¼ teaspoon freshly ground black pepper

1 cup extra-virgin olive oil

FILLING

8 ounces imported hard ricotta cheese, crumbled

3 ounces shredded provolone cheese

¼ cup grated Parmesan cheese

1 tablespoon minced fresh basil

1 tablespoon minced flat-leaf parsley

½ cup minced sun-dried tomatoes (oil-packed)

¼ cup toasted pine nuts, coarsely chopped

Salt and freshly ground black pepper to taste

Begin by preparing the filling. Combine all ingredients in a medium bowl and stir to blend well. Refrigerate until ready to use.

Next blend all marinade ingredients together and whisk vigorously. Slice each eggplant lengthwise into 5 or 6 slices, each slightly less than ½-inch thick. Lay the eggplant slices on shallow baking sheets and coat with the marinade, covering both sides well.

Grill the eggplant slices on a gas grill until they are well marked and slightly limp. Baste with remaining marinade while grilling. Set the slices aside to cool slightly. Preheat oven to 350 degrees.

When the grilled eggplant slices are cool enough to handle, place a portion of the filling about ⅔ of the way down the eggplant from the narrow top edge. Roll the eggplant over the filling and place rollup, seam side down, on baking sheet. Bake rollups in preheated oven until cheese filling is melted and bubbly, about 10 to 15 minutes. Cut each rollup in half to make them bite-size. Serve on a decorative platter.

Hay rake, Washington County

Texas Goat Cheese with Sun-Dried Tomato Pesto and Cayenne Pepper Toasts

*T*exans love party foods that they can spread on crackers. We find that they provide a great way to meet everybody at the party—you know, while you're standing there at the food table waiting for everybody in front of you to get through with the little spreading knife, you've got nothing better to do but make conversation with the other people standing in line for the goodies. This one is worth waiting for, too. The pesto can be made in advance and stored up to a week in the refrigerator. In fact, it tastes better when made at least a day ahead of time, which allows time for the flavors to blend together well. The Cayenne Pepper Toasts can also be made in advance and stored in zip-sealing bags or frozen. If you freeze them, crisp them in a 350-degree oven for about 5 minutes before serving. A warning: they're addictive.

Sun-Dried Tomato Pesto

- 1 8-ounce jar oil-packed sun-dried tomatoes and their oil
- ¼ cup extra-virgin olive oil
- ½ cup (loosely packed) fresh basil leaves
- ½ cup sliced ripe olives
- ¼ cup (loosely packed) flat-leaf parsley
- 2 large garlic cloves, peeled
- ½ teaspoon salt
- ½ teaspoon sugar
- 2 green onions, coarsely chopped, including green tops

Several blocks of Texas goat cheese or other goat cheese

Combine all ingredients except goat cheese in work bowl of food processor fitted with steel blade and process until all ingredients are minced. You'll get the best results by using the pulse feature on the processor, pulsing until you get the right consistency. Refrigerate until ready to serve. Serve at room temperature, poured over the goat cheese. Accompany with a basket of Cayenne Pepper Toasts.

Cayenne Pepper Toasts

- 2 French-style baguette loaves, sliced ⅛ inch to ¼ inch thick
- 1½ cups extra-virgin olive oil
- 2 teaspoons red (cayenne) pepper
- 1½ teaspoons salt
- 2 teaspoons sugar
- 1½ teaspoons finely ground black pepper
- 1½ teaspoons paprika
- 1½ teaspoons granulated garlic
- 1½ teaspoons onion powder
- 1 teaspoon dried leaf oregano

Preheat oven to 250 degrees. Lay the bread slices on baking sheets; set aside. Combine remaining ingredients in small bowl and whisk to blend well. Using a pastry brush, paint each toast lightly with the oil mixture. Re-whisk often, as the seasonings have a tendency to settle to the bottom. Place baking sheets in preheated oven and cook for about 45 minutes or until toasts are dry and crisp. Cool on wire racks. When toasts are completely cool, store in zip-sealing plastic bags if not serving right away.

ᙅ **Serves 15 to 20 (about 120 toasts).**

Susan's Spicy Olive Spread

*S*usan Slimko is a member of our kitchen team at the Maner Lake Lodge. She is almost as much of an olive lover as I am. Neither of us can resist the lure of an olive—any olive. We keep green pimento-stuffed olives, green olives stuffed with jalapeños, Kalamata olives, Niçoise olives, Moroccan oil-cured olives, and ripe olives in our cooler for use in various recipes. Whenever one of those giant jars comes out of the cooler, she snatches a few for the two of us to nibble on. Susan put this spread together one day during an olive-mania moment and we loved it. It is really decadent when served with Cumin and Garlic Flatbread (see "Soups, Salads, and Great Breads").

6 ounces cream cheese, softened
½ cup mayonnaise
⅛ teaspoon freshly ground black pepper
1 teaspoon Tabasco sauce
½ cup toasted, chopped pecans
2 tablespoons chopped jalapeño-stuffed olives
1 cup chopped pimento-stuffed olives

Combine cream cheese, mayonnaise, black pepper, and Tabasco sauce in work bowl of food processor fitted with steel blade. Process until smooth. Add the remaining ingredients and use the pulse feature to blend them into the cream cheese mixture. Do not overprocess. The olives and pecans should still have some identity. Refrigerate until ready to serve.

☙ **Makes about 2¼ cups.**

Vegetable stand on the courthouse square, Bastrop

Wild Mushroom Nachos

*W*ild, *or woodland, mushrooms have become a very* de rigueur *ingredient in upscale cooking today. The scrumptious little guys are readily available in dried form at gourmet markets or from specialty food catalogs. (The portabello mushroom, the giant of the mushroom world, is actually not wild but rather a cultivated species.) This dish elevates the quintessential nacho of Texas Cuisine to a whole new level! These "nachos" would be equally at home on the ranch or in a city place like Highland Park or River Oaks! The topping can be prepared ahead of time and reheated, as can the fried tortillas, but cook the polenta right before serving.*

5 white corn tortillas, quartered

Canola oil for frying

2 cups chicken stock

½ teaspoon salt

½ cup medium-grain polenta

1¼ cups (5 ounces) shredded Asiago cheese

Minced flat-leaf parsley as garnish

Wild Mushroom Topping

1 ounce dried morel mushrooms

1 ounce dried chanterelle mushrooms

1 large portabello mushroom, stem removed, chopped

¼ cup extra-virgin olive oil

6 medium garlic cloves, minced

3 French shallots, minced

2 teaspoons minced fresh thyme

½ teaspoon freshly ground black pepper

⅔ cup dry vermouth

1 16-ounce can Italian-seasoned tomatoes, chopped, and their liquid

⅔ cup beef broth

Prepare the Wild Mushroom Topping. Combine the morels and chanterelles in a bowl and add warm water to cover. Set aside for 30 minutes, or until mushrooms are fully softened. Squeeze all moisture from mushrooms and slice thin. Combine with the chopped portabello mushroom; set aside. Heat the olive oil in a heavy 12-inch skillet over medium heat. When oil is hot, add mushrooms, garlic, shallots, thyme, and black pepper. Cook, stirring often, until mushrooms are slightly wilted, about 5 minutes. Add the vermouth. Cook until liquid is reduced almost to a glaze. Add the tomatoes and their liquid and the beef broth. Cook, stirring often, until a thick sauce has formed, about 15 minutes. Set aside and keep warm.

To assemble the nachos, heat the canola oil in a deep skillet. When oil is hot, add the tortilla wedges and fry until crisp, about 2 minutes. Drain on absorbent paper towels; set aside and keep warm.

Combine the chicken stock and salt in a heavy 2-quart saucepan over medium heat. Bring to a full boil, then whisk in the polenta. Continue to whisk vigorously until polenta is thickened and smooth, about 3 minutes. Be sure that no lumps remain. Remove pan from heat and quickly whisk in the shredded cheese. Whisk until cheese is melted and polenta has a silky, loose texture.

Spoon a portion of the hot polenta on each tortilla wedge. Next spoon some of the Wild Mushroom Topping on each. Garnish with minced parsley and arrange on a colorful serving platter.

ର **Makes 20 nachos.**

SOUPS, SALADS, AND GREAT BREADS

*T*he old adage "Man cannot live by bread alone" is a real true statement. But add a great bowl of soup and a cold, crisp salad and you've got yourself a delicious, life-sustaining meal.

Texans love soup and salad meals. They fit our laid-back lifestyle. They also fit our climates, of which there are several, depending on which part of the state you're discussing. In the arid regions of West Texas, the summers are dry and very hot, the winters bitterly cold. In the marshy regions of Southeast Texas, the winters are mild and the summers are very humid and very hot, sort of like a perpetual steambath. In the Rio Grande Valley, it's warm during the winter months and blazing hot in the summer.

Salads can cool us down. Texans make salads from the bounty of greens grown in the state, combined with fresh fish or shellfish from our coastal and inland waterways, the plentiful citrus fruits grown in our Rio Grande Valley, or fresh handmade cheeses from our artisan cheesemakers.

Soups can be cooling, soothing brews, or hearty thick concoctions like chili that warm us up. Soups in

Farmer's market, San Antonio; Live oak savannah, Uvalde County (pages 48–49).

Texas are often created around the fiery heat of chilies, moderated to personal taste by roasting the chilies and diluting their spice in rich broths and cream. It may seem counterproductive to eat hot soups made from spicy hot chilies in hot weather, but here's how that works: as you eat hot chilies, your pores sweat. A fine mist of sweat forms on the skin. When air drifts over the sweat-moistened skin, a cooling barrier forms! Chilies have historically been grown and eaten in the regions of the world where it gets really hot.

In Texas we take our breads seriously, using the wealth of common and exotic grains grown in our High Plains region to bake up hearty loaves. Nothing is more satisfying than the aroma and taste of a freshly baked loaf of bread. Even if you're not an avid bread baker, anybody can make cornbread—and boy, do we grow great corn in Texas!

So get out the soup bowls, pile the salad on a plate, and slice the bread. Let's have a great meal—whatever the temperature outside.

Cabbage harvesting, Lower Rio Grande Valley; Lower Rio Grande River, Cameron County (pages 52–53).

Rattlesnake Roundup Chili with Roasted Red Bell Pepper Pico de Gallo

Rattlesnake meat has a delicate taste with an exciting hint of earthiness—just enough to remind you where it came from. Now, I don't recommend that you go scouting for rattlesnakes if you want to try this recipe. Leave that to the pros, like the daredevils who participate in the annual Rattlesnake Roundups out in Sweetwater or down in Freer. I first developed this recipe for a dinner that my staff and I prepared for a regional meeting of Texas game wardens. It was a big hit. For a source of rattlesnake meat, see "The Texas Cook's Pantry."

Chili

8 ounces bulk-style spicy Mexican chorizo sausage

2 pounds skinned and cleaned rattlesnake meat

1½ teaspoons whole cumin seeds

1½ teaspoons whole coriander seeds

½ cup canola oil

2 medium yellow onions, chopped

5 large garlic cloves, chopped

1½ pounds tomatillos, husked, washed, and chopped

2 jalapeño chilies, seeds and veins removed, minced

½ teaspoon ground cinnamon

¼ teaspoon allspice

½ teaspoon ground cloves

3 fresh bay leaves, minced

1 cup Cabernet Sauvignon or other dry red wine

1 quart chicken stock (see "Basics")

1 quart beef stock (see "Basics")

2 16-ounce cans kidney beans, drained

1 cup shredded mustard greens

½ cup minced fresh cilantro

Roasted Red Bell Pepper Pico de Gallo

2 large red bell peppers, blistered, peeled, and seeded (see "Basics")

1 canned chipotle chili in adobo sauce

3 Roma tomatoes, finely diced

⅓ cup finely diced red onion

3 green onions, chopped, including green tops

3 serrano chilies, seeds and veins removed, minced

2 small ripe avocados, cut into small dice

2 tablespoons minced fresh cilantro

2 tablespoons fresh lime juice

Salt to taste

Prepare the Roasted Red Bell Pepper Pico de Gallo. Chop the roasted red bell pepper into coarse chunks and place in work bowl of blender with the chipotle chili. Puree until smooth. Remove puree from blender bowl and set aside. Combine the remaining ingredients in medium bowl and stir in the bell pepper puree. Blend well, adding salt to taste. Refrigerate until ready to use.

To prepare the chili, sauté the chorizo sausage in a heavy 12-inch skillet over medium heat. Stir to prevent clumps from forming. Cook until meat has evenly browned and fat has been rendered. Strain the sausage to remove all grease; set sausage aside. Wash the rattlesnake meat well under running water. Pat dry using absorbent paper towels. Cut the meat into ½-inch dice; season liberally with salt and freshly ground black pepper. Set aside. Place the cumin seeds and coriander seeds in a small dry skillet and toast over high heat until they begin to give off a strong aroma. (Do not burn them!) Grind the spices in a mortar and pestle or electric spice grinder; set aside.

Heat the canola oil in a heavy 8-quart soup pot over medium heat. When the oil is hot, add the onions, garlic, and rattlesnake meat. Cook, stirring often, until vegetables are very wilted and meat is lightly browned, about 10 minutes.

Stir in the chopped tomatillos, jalapeños, reserved ground seeds, cinnamon, allspice, cloves, and minced bay leaves, blending well. Cook, stirring often, until tomatillos are very wilted, about 8 minutes. Add the red wine and cook until wine is reduced by half. Add the combined chicken and beef stocks and kidney beans, blending well. Stir in the reserved chorizo. Cover pot and simmer the chili for 45 minutes. Add the mustard greens and cilantro and cook an additional 15 minutes. Add salt to taste and freshly ground black pepper. To serve, ladle into individual bowls and spoon a portion of the Roasted Red Bell Pepper Pico de Gallo into each bowl.

ↀ **Serves 8 to 10.**

CHUCKWAGON CHILI WITH BEANS

*T*he very word chili *brings to mind images of campfires and cowboys. Now every cowboy in Texas, whether real or of the urban variety, claims to make the best chili you've ever tasted. So don't even bother bragging about yours. Then there is the controversy over whether real, he-man chili has beans or not. Well, I love beans and beans are an essential element of Texas cookery. So it's my personal theory that chili, which is real Texan stuff, and beans, which are real Texan stuff, should just go together. Now that's my opinion and if, after you taste my chili, you don't agree, then make yours without beans! I always like to make chili the day before I'm going to serve it. The flavors undergo a melding process that always makes it taste better the second day.*

⅓ cup lard or solid shortening

1 pound beef chuck, trimmed and chopped into ½-inch dice

1 pound pork butt, trimmed and chopped into ½-inch dice

2 medium onions, chopped

2 celery stalks, chopped

1 green bell pepper, chopped

1 red bell pepper, chopped

3 large garlic cloves, minced

3 fresh jalapeño chilies, seeds and veins removed, minced

2 serrano chilies, seeds and veins removed, minced

½ teaspoon freshly ground black pepper

1 5-ounce can tomato paste

1 28-ounce can Italian plum tomatoes, chopped, and their juice

1½ cups tomato sauce

1 10-ounce can Ro-tel Diced Tomatoes and Chilies

2 cups chicken stock (see "Basics")

2 cups beef stock (see "Basics")

1 12-ounce can of beer

⅔ cup dry red wine, such as Cabernet Sauvignon

1 tablespoon dried Mexican oregano

2 teaspoons whole cumin seeds

1 tablespoon ground cumin

1 tablespoon ground coriander

¼ cup dark chili powder, or to taste

1 16-ounce can red kidney beans and their juice

1 16-ounce can pinto beans and their juice

1 16-ounce can navy beans and their juice

1 16-ounce can black beans and their juice

Shredded Colby cheese

Chopped onions as garnish

Melt the shortening in a heavy 10-quart soup pot over medium-high heat. When the fat is hot, add the diced meats and cook until their pink color is gone and the juices from the meat have evaporated, about 25 minutes. The meat should be starting to brown. Add all vegetables and the black pepper, stirring to blend well. Cook, stirring often to prevent sticking, until vegetables are very wilted, about 20 minutes. Add the tomato paste and stir to blend well. Cook until the paste is thick and dark red in color. Add the chopped tomatoes and their juice, tomato sauce, Ro-Tel tomatoes, stocks, beer, and red wine. Stir in all seasonings, blending well. Bring to a gentle boil, then lower heat and simmer for 1½ hours, stirring occasionally. Taste for seasoning and adjust as needed, keeping in mind that chili is supposed to be on the spicy side. Add salt as needed. *Skim all fat from surface.* Stir in the four kinds of beans, blending well. Cook an additional 30 minutes. Serve hot, garnished with shredded Colby cheese and chopped onions.

ભ **Serves 8 to 10.**

GOLDEN TRIANGLE SEAFOOD AND OKRA GUMBO

*G*ood gumbo is the perfect meal, "Just what the doctor ordered," on a blustery winter day. Give me a steaming bowl of gumbo, a slice of good French bread, a cold Shiner Bock, and I'm a contented woman.

Gumbo, that dark, spicy brew from the mysterious swamp and bayou country, has become very popular in Texas. Its prominent spread into Texas correlates with the advent of the oil industry in this state. The first oil-producing region in Texas was close to the Louisiana border, around the Beaumont–Port Arthur–Orange area, now known as "The Golden Triangle." The oil boom brought many Cajun oil-field workers to settle in the area. With them came their gumbos, concocted from a roux and whatever bits of meat or seafood they had on hand. Okra is added for both its flavor and thickening power. Filé powder is also used as a thickener and flavoring ingredient. There is some controversy over whether both okra and filé should be used in the same gumbo, but I like thick gumbo, so I use them both.

3 cups Gumbo Roux (see "Basics")

2 medium onions, chopped

3 celery stalks, chopped

1 large green bell pepper, chopped

1 large red bell pepper, chopped

3 large garlic cloves, minced

2 tablespoons minced flat-leaf parsley

2 teaspoons minced fresh thyme

2 teaspoons minced fresh basil

1 heaping tablespoon filé powder

½ teaspoon freshly ground black pepper

½ teaspoon dried Mexican oregano

2 fresh bay leaves, minced

4 quarts Seafood Stock (see "Basics")

2 pounds peeled and deveined small (70 to 90 count) shrimp

1 pound claw crabmeat

1 teaspoon red (cayenne) pepper, or to taste

Salt to taste

2 cups fresh or frozen sliced okra

Cooked white rice (see "Basics")

Sliced green onions as garnish

Tabasco sauce, as desired

Prepare roux as directed. When roux has reached the proper color, add the vegetables and all seasonings except cayenne pepper and salt. If you have frozen the roux, thaw it first, then melt it in a heavy, deep, 14-inch pan over medium heat. Cook the vegetables, stirring frequently, until they are quite limp, about 15 minutes. While vegetables are cooking in the roux, bring the stock to a rolling boil in a 10-quart soup pot. Add the roux-vegetable mixture to the boiling stock all at once. Continue to boil for 10 minutes, stirring often. Add the shrimp and crabmeat, stirring to blend. Continue to boil for another 10 minutes.

Reduce heat to a simmer and season to taste with cayenne pepper and salt. Cover the pot and simmer for 45 minutes.

Stir in the okra and cook an additional 20 minutes.

To serve the gumbo, spoon about ⅔ cup of cooked white rice into each serving bowl; ladle the gumbo over the rice. Top with a scattering of the green onions. Serve hot, passing the bottle of Tabasco sauce for those who want to kick up the fire.

ᶜ⁊ **Serves 8 to 10.**

EAGLE LAKE DUCK AND SAUSAGE GUMBO "YA-YA"

Gumbo "Ya-Ya" has its roots deep in New Orleans. "Ya-ya" is a term used by the Cajuns that means "Everybody talk at once." I speculate that the term was applied to this type of gumbo because of the many tastes contained at once in a single dish—sort of a cacophony in the mouth! It is traditionally made with andouille sausage and chicken. I've taken some Texas liberty with it, though, because I love the rich, musky taste of duck meat, which marries well with the dark, "smoldering" taste of the roux. Eagle Lake, prime wetlands country, is known to be one of the greatest duck and goose hunting spots in the country. The vermouth and artichoke hearts in the gumbo are my touches that elevate its social standing. Socially elite or not, keep in mind that good gumbo should be spicy. There's an art to finding that balance between bland and so spicy that the taste experience is unpleasant and the palate is rendered unable to taste any other component. What you're striving for is what I refer to as a "back-of-the-throat" spiciness. After you've savored a few bites, you should get a nice, warm glow in the back of the throat. It should stay right at that nice, interestingly exciting stage of heat. Kind of a Mardi Gras for your mouth!

3 cups Gumbo Roux (see "Basics")

1 medium onion, chopped

6 French shallots, chopped

2 large green bell peppers, chopped

3 large celery stalks, chopped

2 tablespoons minced flat-leaf parsley

2 teaspoons minced fresh thyme

½ teaspoon freshly ground black pepper

3 fresh bay leaves, minced

1 teaspoon minced fresh marjoram

2 heaping tablespoons filé powder

1 pound andouille sausage, cut into bite-size slices

4 quarts chicken stock (see "Basics")

1 cup dry vermouth

2 pounds duck meat, cut into bite-size pieces

2 cups chopped artichoke hearts (not marinated)

1 teaspoon red (cayenne) pepper, or to taste

Salt to taste

Cooked white rice (see "Basics")

Sliced green onions as garnish

Preheat oven to 350 degrees. Prepare roux as directed. When roux has reached a deep mahogany color, add the vegetables and all seasonings except cayenne pepper and salt. If you have frozen the roux, thaw it first. Or if you have simply prepared it ahead of time, melt it in a heavy, deep, 14-inch pan over medium heat. Cook the vegetables, stirring often, until they are very wilted and onions are translucent, about 15 minutes. Remove pan from heat and set aside. While vegetables are cooking, arrange the sliced andouille sausage on a baking sheet and bake in preheated oven for about 20 minutes, or until fat has been rendered. Drain and pat the sausage with absorbent paper towels to remove all traces of fat. Bring the chicken stock and vermouth to a full boil in a 10-quart soup pot. When the vegetables are cooked, add the roux mixture to the boiling stock; boil hard for 10 minutes, stirring frequently. Stir in the duck meat and the cooked andouille. Continue to boil for another 10 minutes. Lower heat to a simmer and stir in the artichoke hearts. Season to taste with cayenne pepper and salt. Cover the pot and simmer for 45 minutes.

To serve the gumbo, spoon about ⅔ cup of cooked white rice into each serving bowl; ladle the gumbo over the rice. Top with a scattering of the green onions. Serve hot.

ॐ **Serves 8 to 10.**

Barton Springs, Austin

FILÉ POWDER

FILÉ POWDER, ALSO CALLED GUMBO FILÉ, IS MADE FROM THE LEAVES OF THE SASSAFRAS TREE. THE NATIVE CHOCTAW INDIANS INTRODUCED THE EARLY CAJUN AND CREOLE SETTLERS IN THE LOUISIANA TERRITORY TO THE HERB. THE INDIANS DRIED THE LEAVES AND GROUND THEM TO A POWDER. IT WAS USED AS BOTH A FLAVORING AND THICKENING INGREDIENT IN THE GUMBO CREATED BY THE FRENCH CAJUNS. THESE CAJUNS NAMED THE HERB FILÉ, FROM THE FRENCH VERB <u>FILER</u>, "TO SPIN THREADS." WHEN FILÉ IS ADDED TO HOT LIQUIDS, IT PRODUCES THREAD-LIKE, GELATINOUS STRANDS THAT THICKEN THE LIQUID. WHEN PURCHASING FILÉ POWDER, BE SURE YOU ARE BUYING THE PURE KIND. SOME ARE BLENDED WITH THYME, WHICH CAN UPSET THE FLAVOR BALANCE IN YOUR GUMBO. SEE "THE TEXAS COOK'S PANTRY" FOR A GOOD SOURCE FOR FILÉ AND OTHER SPICES.

CRABMEAT GAZPACHO

*R*umor has it that gazpacho is a "sissified" kind of soup and that no real buckaroo would eat cold soup anyhow. Just try this version on for size! When you bite into that sweet lump crabmeat all tangled up in that sinfully delicious creamy mascarpone cheese, try to tell yourself it's a sissy food you have in your mouth. Make the soup about 4 hours before serving to allow the flavors of the fresh ingredients time to meld, but don't add the club soda until you're ready to serve the soup.

4 ounces lump crabmeat

10 firm tomatillos, husked, washed, and coarsely chopped

3 ripe Roma tomatoes, seeded and coarsely chopped

1 small red onion, coarsely chopped

2 medium garlic cloves, minced

2 medium cucumbers, peeled and seeded, then coarsely chopped

2 serrano chilies, seeds and veins removed, minced

10 cilantro sprigs, leaves and tender top sprigs only

½ cup freshly squeezed lime juice

1 tablespoon sugar, or to taste

Salt to taste

1 cup club soda

½ cup mascarpone cheese

Your favorite picante sauce or salsa

Using your fingers, pick through the crabmeat to remove any bits of shell or cartilage, taking care not to break up the lumps of the meat. Set aside. Combine the tomatillos, tomatoes, onion, garlic, cucumber, chilies, cilantro, lime juice, and sugar in work bowl of food processor fitted with steel blade. Process until smooth. Add salt to taste (but don't be stingy, or the flavors won't be right!) and process to blend in the salt. Refrigerate until ready to serve.

To serve, stir the club soda into the soup. Divide soup among 4 soup plates. Divide the crabmeat between the bowls, scattering it on top of the soup. Spoon 2 tablespoons of the mascarpone cheese into each bowl and top with a little picante sauce or salsa. Serve at once.

Serves 4.

Baptistry of Mission Espíritu Santo, Goliad

TERLINGUA TORTILLA SOUP

Terlingua is an abandoned cinnabar-mining town in Brewster County, out by Big Bend. But this particular ghost town has a colorful modern-day history, too. Terlingua was the site of the first chili cookoff in Texas. It happened on an October weekend in 1967, which was described later as 1967's only month-long weekend. The original contest pitted Wick Fowler, founder of the Dallas Chili Appreciation Society, against newspaper columnist and humorist H. Allen Smith from New York. Now, of course, you automatically know whom the Texans were rooting for. It was a weekend that changed the status of chili forevermore. H. Allen Smith lost the cookoff and never got over it. In fact, he later moved to Alpine, became a Texan, and wrote a wonderfully funny book about the event by the name of The Great Chili Confrontation.*

Tortilla soup is one of my favorite Mexican imports. It is now very popular in Texas, found on the menus of many upscale, non-Mexican restaurants. There are probably as many renditions of tortilla soup as there are of chili. Who knows? Maybe some day we'll have the Great Tortilla Soup Showdown out there in Terlingua.*

6 white corn tortillas

Oil for deep-frying, heated to 350 degrees

2 tablespoons plus 2 teaspoons solid shortening, divided

1 large onion, halved lengthwise, then sliced thin

4 large garlic cloves, minced

4 Roma tomatoes, blistered, peeled, and seeded (see "Basics")

2 quarts chicken stock (see "Basics")

1 heaping teaspoon dark chili powder

1 heaping teaspoon ground coriander

Salt to taste

1½ cups whole kernel corn

5 dried pasilla chilies, seeded and deveined, snipped into very thin julienne strips

Lime wedges, one for each bowl of soup

3 cups (12 ounces) shredded Monterey Jack cheese

2 avocados, peeled, seeded, and cut into ¼-inch dice

Begin by frying the tortillas. If they are very fresh or very moist, then dry them out for a few minutes in a single layer. Cut the tortillas in half, then slice the halves into ¼-inch-wide strips. Fry in the hot oil until they are crisp but not brown. Drain well on absorbent paper towels or brown grocery bags. Store in a tightly covered container until ready to use.

To make the soup, heat 1 tablespoon plus 1 teaspoon of the shortening in a 6-quart soup pot over medium heat. Add the onion, garlic, and tomatoes. Fry until onion is deep golden brown, about 20 minutes, stirring often. Transfer vegetables to work bowl of food processor fitted with steel blade and process until smooth.

Heat the remaining half of the shortening in the same pot over medium-high heat. When oil is very hot, add the pureed vegetables and stir constantly until thick and darkened in color, about 5 minutes. Stir in the chicken stock, chili powder, coriander, and corn. Cover and simmer for 30 minutes on medium-low heat. Taste for seasoning, adding salt if needed.

While soup is simmering, place the pasilla chili strips in any empty skillet and toast over high heat until they begin to give off an aroma. Shake pan and toss chilies constantly. Do not burn the chilies. Set aside.

When ready to serve, divide the fried tortilla strips equally among the serving bowls. Top each with a portion of the cheese and toasted chili strips. Squeeze a lime wedge into each bowl. Ladle the hot broth over the top and garnish with a scattering of the diced avocado. Serve hot.

੒ **Serves 6 to 8.**

RABBIT AND WILD MUSHROOM SOUP WITH FRIED LEEKS

*R*abbit *has been prized as a game animal and table delicacy in many countries for centuries, Texas being no exception. If you're not a hunter or don't have the heart to cause the demise of the little cottontails, then try the farm-raised rabbit that is becoming readily available in specialty markets.*

This recipe has an interesting history. Before being elected vice-president, Richard Cheney was the CEO of the Halliburton Corporation. Halliburton owns Maner Lake Lodge, the hunting and fishing lodge where I am executive chef. Mr. Cheney made reservations to come to the lodge for a quiet meeting and a little fishing with two other corporate officers. They wanted a relaxed, low-key evening meal. Knowing that he was an avid hunter and lover of game, I developed this recipe for the first course of the meal. We served it with the wonderfully dry and crisp Becker Vineyards Chardonnay.

½ ounce dried shiitake mushrooms

½ ounce dried morel mushrooms

6 tablespoons unsalted butter

¼ cup canola oil

¾ cup all-purpose flour

4 slices uncooked applewood-smoked bacon, minced

⅓ cup chopped French shallots

2 medium garlic cloves, minced

1 teaspoon minced fresh thyme

1 teaspoon minced fresh sage

¼ teaspoon freshly ground black pepper

1 pound rabbit meat, cut into ½-inch dice

1 quart hot beef stock (see "Basics")

1 quart hot chicken stock (see "Basics")

½ cup dry Madeira

Salt to taste

2 teaspoons Tabasco sauce

3 large leeks, well washed and trimmed, discarding green tops

Canola oil for deep-frying, heated to 350 degrees

Combine the dried mushrooms in a medium bowl and cover with hot water. Set aside until mushrooms are completely soft and pliable, about 30 minutes. Drain, squeeze out water, and finely chop the mushrooms; set aside.

Melt the butter in a heavy 6-quart soup pot over medium heat. Stir in the canola oil to blend well. Add the flour all at once. Cook, stirring constantly, until a light, peanut butter–colored roux is formed, about 15 minutes.

Add the minced bacon, shallots, garlic, thyme, sage, reserved mushrooms, black pepper, and rabbit meat. Cook, stirring often, until shallots are wilted and transparent and meat has lost all traces of pink color, about 10 minutes. Stir in the combined stocks and the Madeira. Add salt to taste. Bring the soup to a rapid boil to thicken slightly, then reduce heat and simmer, covered, for 1 hour.

When ready to serve the soup, slice the leeks into thin, matchstick-size julienne strips. Quickly fry the leeks in batches in the preheated oil until light golden brown and crisp, about 30 to 45 seconds per batch. Drain well on absorbent paper towels. Set aside.

Stir the Tabasco sauce into the soup and cook for 10 minutes. To serve, ladle soup into bowls and place a portion of the crisp leeks on top of each serving.

ભ **Serves 8 to 10.**

LIL'S TWO-STEPPIN' TEXAS CHEESE AND CHILI SOUP

*L*il Sheldon is one of my best friends. Our friendship goes way back over twenty years. We have traveled together and had some really crazy times during those years, but the one thing we have done most often is cook and eat together. Lil is a marvelous cook and she never tires of cooking—whatever size the crowd. In 1993 she opened Sheldon's Touch of Hospitality, one of the best cooking schools in the Houston area, due in part to Lil's plucky temperament and her wonderful wisdom.

½ cup (1 stick) unsalted butter

1 cup frozen whole-kernel corn, thawed

1 cup finely chopped carrots (about 3 medium carrots)

1 medium onion, chopped

3 celery stalks, chopped

2 large garlic cloves, minced

1 4-ounce can diced green chilies, drained

½ cup all-purpose flour

½ teaspoon Hungarian paprika

½ teaspoon freshly ground black pepper

½ teaspoon red (cayenne) pepper

2 teaspoons ground cumin

1 tablespoon dark chili powder

1½ quarts chicken stock (see "Basics")

2 cups half-and-half

2½ cups (12 ounces) shredded sharp cheddar cheese

5 medium (about 1¾ pounds) Yukon Gold potatoes, diced fine and boiled until soft, about 20 minutes

Melt the butter in a heavy 6-quart soup pot over medium heat. Sauté the corn, carrots, onion, celery, garlic, and green chilies until onion is wilted and transparent, about 15 minutes. Add the flour and all seasonings; stir to blend well. Stir in the chicken stock slowly; bring to a boil, stirring constantly. Boil for one minute. Reduce heat and stir in the half-and-half, cheese, and potatoes. Heat just until the cheese is melted. Do not allow the soup to boil again. Serve hot.

❧ **Serves 6 to 8.**

POBLANO CHILI BISQUE

*T*he poblano chili is used often in Texas cooking. It's the one that looks something like a green bell pepper, only it's darker and tapers to a point at the blossom end. On Mark Miller's Chili Heat Scale of 1 to 10, the poblano rates a 3, so it's usually not a real tongue-scorcher. Poblanos are never eaten raw but rather roasted until the skin blisters, then peeled. This process gives them a rich, slightly smoky taste, which provides a great flavor dimension to this soup.

¼ cup extra-virgin olive oil

3 large poblano chilies, blistered, peeled, seeded, and diced (see "Basics")

3 large red bell peppers, blistered, peeled, seeded, and diced (see "Basics")

3 ripe Roma tomatoes, blistered, peeled, seeded, and diced (see "Basics")

1 medium onion, chopped

1 medium carrot, peeled and chopped fine

¼ cup all-purpose flour

1 quart plus ½ cup chicken stock (see "Basics")

½ teaspoon freshly ground black pepper

½ cup half-and-half

½ cup whipping cream

Salt to taste

4 white corn tortillas, cut in half, then cut into ¼-inch-wide julienne strips, fried just until crisp, then drained on absorbent paper towels

6 ounces quesadilla or Monterey Jack cheese, shredded

3 tablespoons minced fresh cilantro as garnish

Heat the olive oil in a heavy 4-quart saucepan over medium heat. When oil is hot, add the poblano chilies, red bell pepper, tomatoes, onion, and carrot. Cook, stirring occasionally, until vegetables are wilted, about 15 minutes. Stir in the flour all at once, blending well. Cook, stirring constantly, for 3 to 4 minutes. Add the stock slowly, stirring to blend well. Add pepper. Bring soup to a full boil to thicken, then lower heat and simmer, covered, for 30 minutes. Remove from heat and puree in batches in a blender. Be sure that all vegetables are pureed and that the soup is completely smooth. Return soup to heat and add the half-and-half and whipping cream. Season to taste with salt. Cook just to heat the cream through, about 10 minutes.

To serve, divide the fried tortilla strips and cheese among serving bowls. Ladle the soup over them and garnish with a scattering of the minced cilantro.

ভ **Serves 6 to 8.**

ROASTED RED BELL PEPPER BISQUE

*T*his ever-so-slightly-spicy and smoky bisque is one of my favorites. It calls for two ingredients that are somewhat uncommon—tomatillos and ancho chilies. Although tomatillo means "little tomato" and is sometimes called a green tomato, it is not in the tomato family. The ripe tomatillo, which rarely exceeds 2 inches in diameter, is bright green and grows inside a papery brown husk. The plant abounds in Mexico and Guatemala where it was a staple in the Aztec and Mayan cuisines. The Marinated Ancho Chilies, a concoction of my sous-chef, Cecilio Solis, are made from the pleasantly spicy dried ancho chili. We keep them on hand for use in seasoning various dishes, one of those chef's "secret ingredients."

¼ cup canola oil

1 medium onion, coarsely chopped

2 medium tomatillos, husks removed, washed and coarsely chopped

3 large Roma tomatoes, coarsely chopped

6 large red bell peppers, blistered, peeled, seeded, and coarsely chopped (see "Basics")

4 large garlic cloves, minced

1 quart plus 1 cup chicken stock (see "Basics")

½ cup chopped Marinated Ancho Chilies (recipe follows)

½ teaspoon freshly ground black pepper

Salt to taste

1 cup whipping cream

1½ tablespoons minced fresh cilantro

Heat canola oil in a heavy 6-quart soup pot over medium-high heat. When oil is hot, stir in the onions, tomatillos, tomatoes, red bell peppers, and garlic cloves. Cook, stirring occasionally,

until vegetables are very wilted, about 20 minutes. Add the chicken stock and stir to blend well. Simmer, covered, for about 30 minutes. Stir in the Marinated Ancho Chilies and puree the soup in batches in the food processor or blender. Be sure that the soup is completely smooth. Return soup to clean pan over medium heat. Season with black pepper and salt to taste. Stir in the whipping cream; cook just until the soup is heated through. Stir in the cilantro and remove from heat. Serve hot.

ভ **Serves 6 to 8.**

MARINATED ANCHO CHILIES

7 large dried ancho chilies

3 cups orange juice

2 tablespoons balsamic vinegar

2 tablespoons good-quality real maple syrup

Split the dried chilies open and remove all seeds, veins, and stems. Soak the chilies in hot water for 30 minutes, or until they are very soft and pliable. Drain the chilies and place in medium bowl. Stir in the orange juice, balsamic vinegar, and maple syrup. Cover and refrigerate until ready to use.

Vaquero near La Gloria

OYSTER AND ARTICHOKE BISQUE

I am an inveterate oyster lover. I will eat oysters any way they come—raw on the half shell, baked on the half shell, broiled en brochette, in stews and soups like this one, or fried. Eating oysters is a very sensuous affair, I must warn you. One of my most vivid oyster recollections is of a brisk, cool day when my husband and I were wade-fishing in Matagorda Bay. We came upon an oyster reef. Roger pried several oysters loose and opened them. We stood right there in the chilly water and ate them from the shells. They were wonderful—tasted like the very essence of the sea itself.

1 quart shucked oysters and their liquor

5 bacon slices, cut into small dice

½ cup (1 stick) unsalted butter

4 green onions, chopped, including green tops

1 medium onion, chopped

3 large garlic cloves, minced

2 medium celery stalks and their leafy tops, chopped

1 14-ounce can artichoke hearts (not marinated), drained

2 fresh bay leaves, minced

1½ teaspoons minced fresh thyme

1½ teaspoons minced fresh sage

1 tablespoon minced flat-leaf parsley

½ cup all-purpose flour

2 cups hot seafood stock (see "Basics")

2 cups hot chicken stock (see "Basics")

Reserved oyster liquor

Salt to taste

½ teaspoon red (cayenne) pepper, or to taste

¼ teaspoon freshly ground black pepper

2 cups whipping cream

½ cup sour cream

Thinly sliced green onions as garnish

Drain the oysters, reserving the liquor in a separate container; set aside. Cook the bacon in a heavy 6-quart soup pot over medium heat until crisp. Remove bacon with a slotted spoon, leaving the bacon drippings in the pot; reserve bacon. Add the butter to bacon drippings; stir until melted. Add the green onions, onion, garlic, celery, artichoke hearts, bay leaves, thyme, sage, and parsley. Stir to blend well. Sauté, stirring often, for 10 minutes, or until onions are wilted and transparent. Add the flour all at once and stir until completely blended. Cook, stirring constantly, for 3 to 4 minutes. Slowly add the combined hot stocks, stirring to incorporate the flour roux. Stir in the reserved oyster liquor and reserved cooked bacon. Lower heat to a simmer and cook the soup, covered, for 30 minutes. Add the oysters and cook for an additional 20 minutes. Puree the soup in batches in a blender until smooth, then return to soup pot over medium heat. Add the salt to taste, red (cayenne) pepper, and black pepper. Whisk in the whipping cream and sour cream, blending well. Taste for seasoning and adjust, if desired. Cook just to heat through, about 10 minutes. Serve hot, garnished with sliced green onions.

ଔ Serves 6 to 8.

Town square, Gonzales (facing page).

CRAB AND CORN BISQUE

*W*henever *I place this soup on a menu, it becomes a hands-down favorite. The taste is so delicate that those sweet, juicy little morsels of lump crabmeat will make you glad you're alive.*

  1 pound regular lump crabmeat
½ cup (1 stick) unsalted butter
  1 medium onion, chopped
  2 large garlic cloves, minced
⅓ cup plus 2 tablespoons all-purpose flour
  3 cups seafood stock (see "Basics")
  3 cups chicken stock (see "Basics")
  2 cups frozen whole-kernel corn, thawed
  1 heaping teaspoon minced fresh thyme
½ teaspoon freshly ground black pepper
¼ teaspoon red (cayenne) pepper, or to taste
2½ cups whipping cream
Salt to taste
  3 green onions, chopped, including green tops

Carefully pick through the crabmeat to remove any bits of shell or cartilage; set aside. Melt the butter in a heavy 4-quart pan over medium heat. Add onion and garlic. Sauté until onion is wilted and transparent, about 5 minutes. Add flour all at once; stir until blended. Cook, stirring constantly, for 3 to 4 minutes. Slowly stir in the stocks and bring to a full boil to thicken. Stir in the corn, thyme, black pepper, cayenne pepper, and crabmeat. Reduce heat to a simmer and cook for 25 minutes. Stir in the whipping cream, salt, and green onions; cook for 15 minutes. Serve hot.

☙ **Serves 6 to 8.**

CITRUS SALAD WITH GREEN CHILI AND HONEY DRESSING

The Texas Rio Grande Valley, on the border with Mexico, is a major citrus-producing region. The industry is located in Hidalgo, Cameron, and Willacy counties. Two varieties of grapefruit were developed by Texas A&M University for production in this semi-tropical region with fertile soil and sunny weather. The Ruby-Sweet and Rio-Star are incredibly sweet, red-meat grapefruit varieties.

The grapefruit got its name from the way it grows in grape-like clusters on the trees. It is notoriously good for you, loaded with Vitamins C and A. It also contains a phytochemical called lycopene, which has been shown to reduce the risk of certain cancers. To gild the lily, it is also an excellent source of dietary fiber and contains no fat, sodium, or cholesterol! When it's in season during the dreary winter months, I eat it ravenously. The grapefruit's luscious taste conjures up images of warm, balmy days. I created this salad, which is a palate-stimulating combination of citrus and chili, in the fruit's honor.

DRESSING

℺ Makes about 2½ cups.

1 cup sour cream

¼ cup honey

2 tablespoons Dijon-style mustard

2 tablespoons balsamic vinegar

Zest and juice of 1 large lemon

¼ cup minced flat-leaf parsley

6 fresh jalapeño chilies, seeds and veins removed, minced

3 fresh serrano chilies, seeds and veins removed, minced

¼ cup finely chopped onion

1 teaspoon salt

½ teaspoon freshly ground black pepper

SALAD

½ head romaine lettuce, washed, dried, and torn into bite-size pieces

½ head escarole, torn into bite-size pieces

¼ cup mint leaves

¼ cup cilantro leaves

1 large Ruby-Sweet or Rio-Star grapefruit

2 medium navel oranges

1 large ripe Haas avocado, peeled, pitted, and sliced

Slivered red onion

Prepare the dressing at least 8 hours before serving to allow time for the flavors to meld together. Combine all ingredients in work bowl of food processor fitted with steel blade. Process until smooth. Refrigerate.

When you're ready to put the salad together, segment the grapefruit by slicing off the rind and all the white pith. Then cut out the segments of fruit from between the membranes. Peel the oranges and remove the white pith. Slice them in half lengthwise, and then slice into thin half rounds. Or the oranges may be segmented like the grapefruit.

Toss the torn romaine and escarole with the mint and cilantro leaves. Arrange a bed of the lettuce mix on individual serving plates. Arrange some of the grapefruit segments and orange and avocado slices on the greens. Scatter a few slivers of red onion over the top. Drizzle desired portion of the dressing over the top and serve.

℺ Serves 4 to 6.

MIXED GREEN SALAD
WITH CILANTRO DRESSING

*T*his salad features our "house dressing" at the lodge where I am chef. We get rave reviews and many requests for the recipe. It's a refreshingly different salad dressing, with a real zesty, in-your-face taste. The dressing will keep, refrigerated, for about a week.

Lots of cooks get confused about the term "zest." The zest is the very thin, colored outer portion of the citrus rind. Use a grater or a special kitchen tool called, appropriately enough, a "zester" to remove only the colored portion, never cutting into the white pith, which will impart a bitter taste. Be sure to use fresh jalapeños in this recipe. The pickled ones would change the taste structure of the dressing.

SALAD

Mixed greens, including field greens, if available
Very thinly sliced red onion
Cherry tomatoes, sliced in half
Cucumber rounds
Avocado slices

CILANTRO DRESSING

℞ **Makes about 2 cups.**

2 cups lightly packed cilantro sprigs, leaves and stems
1 tablespoon minced garlic
1 tablespoon minced fresh jalapeño chili, seeds and veins removed
2 tablespoons Champagne vinegar
¼ teaspoon salt, or to taste
1 teaspoon real maple syrup
1 tablespoon freshly squeezed lime juice
¾ teaspoon minced lime zest
1 cup mayonnaise

Make the Cilantro Dressing. Combine all ingredients in work bowl of food processor fitted with steel blade. Process until smooth. Refrigerate, covered, for about 4 hours before using to allow time for the flavors to meld.

Arrange the mixed greens on individual salad plates and

pour desired amount of dressing over the top. Garnish the salad with slivered red onions, cherry tomato halves, cucumber rounds, and avocado slices.

℞ **Serves 4 to 6.**

GREEN SALAD WITH ORANGES AND
ALMOND PRALINES

I love serving this salad with a light summer meal. It is visually attractive, with the dark green of the spinach and the lighter green of the romaine, garnished with the bright orange slices and the golden pralines. That's PRAY-leens to those who don't speak Texan. The pralines can be made in advance and stored in an airtight container. You might want to make extra pralines, too, because it's mighty tempting to nibble them away once they're done.

SALAD

8 cups torn fresh spinach leaves and romaine lettuce
1 cup thinly sliced celery
½ of a small red onion sliced lengthwise, then sliced into thin slices
4 navel oranges (peel and white pith sliced off), cut into thin rounds

ALMOND PRALINES

8 tablespoons sugar
1¼ cups sliced almonds (skin on)

DRESSING

¼ cup apple cider vinegar
½ teaspoon salt
Pinch of freshly ground black pepper
2 tablespoons minced flat-leaf parsley
¼ cup sugar
1 teaspoon Tabasco sauce
½ cup extra-virgin olive oil

Begin by making the dressing. Combine all ingredients except olive oil in work bowl of food processor fitted with steel blade.

Process until smooth. With the processor running, add the olive oil in a thin, steady stream through the feed tube until all has been added. Process for a few seconds to form a strong emulsion. Refrigerate dressing until ready to serve.

To make the Almond Pralines, place the sugar in a heavy 12-inch skillet over medium heat. Shake the pan to spread the sugar out in a thin layer. Melt the sugar without stirring. When the sugar has melted and is a light caramel color, stir in the almonds quickly to coat them with the caramel. Turn the mixture out onto a heavy baking sheet, quickly spreading it in a thin layer with no clumps of almonds. Let the pralines set until hard. Using a thin metal spatula, remove the pralines and break them up into small pieces. Set aside or store in a container with a tight-fitting lid.

To serve the salad, toss the greens with the celery. Arrange a portion of the greens on each salad plate. Top with a few slices of the red onion and orange; drizzle the desired portion of dressing on each salad. Garnish with pieces of the pralines.

℞ **Serves 4 to 6.**

Travertine spring with maidenhair fern, Travis County

It's Not a Barbecue without Coleslaw

*N*ow that's a real true statement. Anytime you go to a barbecue, there's gonna be coleslaw somewhere on the table. But you know, all those coleslaws at all those barbecues always seemed to have the same ho-hum taste. I always figured, "Why bother eating it, when it doesn't have any taste and it just fills up space that could hold more sausage or brisket?" So I set about to create a coleslaw that would stand up and be noticed. Here it is.

COLESLAW

1 package prepared coleslaw mix
1 medium green bell pepper, finely chopped
1 medium red bell pepper, finely chopped
1 medium tomato, finely diced
4 tablespoons finely chopped onion
½ cup finely chopped celery
2 tablespoons minced flat-leaf parsley

DRESSING

⅔ cup mayonnaise
¼ cup sugar
1 tablespoon whole-grain mustard
1 tablespoon prepared horseradish
1½ teaspoons red wine vinegar
1½ teaspoons white wine vinegar
¼ teaspoon celery seeds
¼ teaspoon granulated garlic
1 teaspoon Tabasco sauce
¾ teaspoon freshly ground black pepper
1 tablespoon dried dill weed
Salt to taste

Make the dressing by combining all ingredients in a medium bowl. Whisk until smooth and well blended. In a large bowl, combine all slaw ingredients, tossing well. Pour the dressing over the slaw and toss to blend well. Chill until ready to serve.

℞ **Serves 6 to 8.**

Caprock Curried Coleslaw

When the occasion calls for an informal salad like coleslaw but you really want a dish with some pizzazz, try this decidedly different version of the traditional coleslaw. Its exotic taste gives a hint of the Far East, although the recipe originated in the fascinating Caprock region of the state. Serve with grilled red meats or fish.

3 cups shredded cabbage

½ cup golden raisins

4 green onions, chopped, including green tops

8 applewood-smoked bacon slices, cooked, drained, and crumbled

½ cup salted peanuts

½ cup mayonnaise

1 tablespoon white wine vinegar

1 teaspoon sugar

1½ teaspoons good-quality curry powder

Freshly ground black pepper to taste

Salt to taste

Combine the cabbage, raisins, and chopped green onions. In a separate bowl combine the mayonnaise, vinegar, sugar, curry powder, and salt and pepper to taste. When ready to serve, add the peanuts and chopped bacon to cabbage mix. Add the dressing and toss to coat the cabbage. Taste for salt and pepper; adjust as needed.

d **Serve 6 to 8.**

Spanish Skirts sediments of the Llano Estacado, Caprock Canyons State Park

FRIED OYSTER SALAD WITH ROSEMARY DRESSING AND GOAT CHEESE

*S*eafood salads make great first courses for evening meals or, paired with a cup of soup and a tasty bread, a perfect luncheon entrée. I especially like this salad with oysters fried just long enough to form a crust, paired with an aromatic dressing using fresh rosemary, an often overlooked herb. Seek out colorful mixed greens—"Spring Mix"—to make a very attractive salad.

ROSEMARY DRESSING

1 egg yolk
1 tablespoon Dijon-style mustard
3 tablespoons balsamic vinegar
1 teaspoon sugar
1½ teaspoons Worcestershire sauce
1½ teaspoons minced fresh rosemary
1 medium French shallot, minced
½ teaspoon freshly ground black pepper
Dash Tabasco sauce
⅔ cup extra-virgin olive oil
Salt to taste

SALAD

Spring Mix salad greens, washed and dried
6 large mushrooms, sliced
4 ounces Texas goat cheese, crumbled
Tomato wedges
5 bacon strips, cooked crisp and crumbled
3 green onions, thinly sliced, including green tops
2 cups olive oil
16 raw oysters, patted very dry on absorbent paper towels
5 egg whites, beaten until frothy
2 cups dry breadcrumbs, seasoned with 1½ teaspoons each of minced fresh sage, minced fresh rosemary, minced flat-leaf parsley, salt, and freshly ground black pepper

Prepare the Rosemary Dressing. Combine all ingredients except olive oil and salt in work bowl of food processor fitted with steel blade. Process until smooth and thickened, about 2 minutes. With processor running, add the olive oil in a steady stream through the feed tube. When all has been added, add salt to taste and process for an additional 15 seconds to form a strong emulsion. Refrigerate until ready to serve.

To prepare the salad, heat the 2 cups of olive oil in a large, deep skillet until hot. Arrange the greens on chilled plates. Scatter the sliced mushrooms and crumbled goat cheese over each salad and garnish with tomato wedges.

Dip the oysters in the beaten egg whites, then dredge them in the seasoned breadcrumbs, coating well. Sauté the oysters quickly in the hot oil. Cook just long enough to form a golden crust on both sides, turning once. Drain oysters on a wire rack set over a baking sheet. Drizzle the dressing over each salad and arrange 4 oysters on each. Scatter the crumbled bacon and green onion slices over the top and serve.

ᙍ **Serves 4 to 6.**

SHRIMP AND PASTA SALAD WITH BASIL AND GARLIC DRESSING

*P*asta salads are one of those dishes that never seem to go completely out of vogue. Of course, since they've become so common that even the supermarket delis have four varieties every day, I've tasted some pasta salads that were really lame. The measure of a good one, as in any culinary creation, lies in the quality and innovative use of its ingredients. This is a good one—zesty, exciting taste and just the right amount of spicy zing to make it really interesting.

BASIL AND GARLIC DRESSING

ᙍ **Makes about ⅔ cup.**

2 tablespoons red wine vinegar
1 tablespoon Dijon-style mustard
3 large garlic cloves, minced
½ teaspoon salt
Pinch of freshly ground black pepper
½ teaspoon Tabasco sauce
1 heaping teaspoon minced fresh basil
½ cup extra-virgin olive oil

SALAD

1 4-ounce jar marinated artichoke hearts, drained and chopped

½ cup sliced ripe olives

6 oil-packed sun-dried tomatoes, chopped

1 teaspoon crushed red pepper flakes

½ teaspoon salt

1 pound small (70 to 90 count) shrimp, boiled, peeled, deveined, and chilled

½ pound Penne Rigate or other tubular pasta, cooked al dente and drained

½ cup grated Parmesan cheese

Red-tipped leaf lettuce leaves, washed and dried

Prepare the dressing by combining all ingredients except olive oil in work bowl of food processor fitted with steel blade. Process until smooth. With processor running, add the olive oil in a slow, steady stream through the feed tube until all is added. Process an additional 15 seconds to form a strong emulsion. Refrigerate until needed.

To prepare the salad, combine all ingredients except lettuce leaves in a large bowl. Toss to blend well. Add the dressing and stir to incorporate. Refrigerate until ready to serve.

To serve, place lettuce leaves on individual serving plates and spoon a portion of the salad on each.

🥄 Serves 4 to 6.

CRABMEAT SALAD
WITH CURRY-CUMIN DRESSING

*T*he meat of the blue crab is one of the sweetest, most succulent tastes to come out of the Gulf waters. I could eat crabmeat every day and never tire of it. During the summer, when Roger and I retreat to Rockport as often as we can, we always set out crab traps. On those occasions we do eat crabmeat every day. If you boil and pick your own crabs, you get the meat at its best—fresh! Picking those crabs is a tedious process, though, and the yield is small—about ½ to ⅔ cup of meat per medium crab. The choicest meat is the backfin lump—only two per crab. These two huge lumps of pure white meat are located adjacent to the "swimmer" fins at the bottom of the crab. The backfin lump meat is the most expensive in seafood markets, of course, because it takes a lot of crabs to make a pound of it! But don't discount the meat of the claws. It actually has the best depth of flavor, although it is not as delicate in taste as the other meat. I prefer to use the claw meat in gumbo for this reason. The stronger taste stands up to the bold seasonings of gumbo.

SALAD

1½ pounds regular lump crabmeat

Bibb or green leaf lettuce leaves

1 cup sliced ripe olives

Cucumber slices

Avocado slices

Julienne strips of red bell pepper

Minced cilantro as garnish

DRESSING

🥄 **Makes about 3 cups.**

1½ cups mayonnaise

¾ cup sour cream

1 tablespoon sugar

Salt to taste

1 tablespoon good-quality curry powder

1 tablespoon plus ¼ teaspoon ground cumin

¾ teaspoon red (cayenne) pepper, or to taste

1 to 1½ cups whipping cream

Make the dressing 8 hours before serving. Combine all ingredients except whipping cream and whisk to blend. Add 1 cup of whipping cream and whisk. Add additional cream as needed to make a medium-thick dressing. Refrigerate.

To assemble the salad, carefully pick through the crabmeat to remove any bits of shell or cartilage, taking care not to break up the lumps. Arrange the lettuce leaves on individual serving plates. Mound a portion of the crabmeat in the center of each lettuce-lined plate. Spoon a portion of the dressing over the crabmeat. Garnish the plate with the ripe olives, cucumber slices, avocado slices, and red bell pepper strips. Scatter minced cilantro over the plate.

🥄 Serves 4 to 6.

Sky Terrace Shrimp Salad with Remoulade Sauce

*R*emoulade sauce, the culinary historians tell us, has been around since the seventeenth century. The sauce is believed to have originated in France as a mayonnaise-based concoction with mustard. Perhaps it came to America with the Cajuns, as did many other great French foods. The Cajuns and Creoles, however, made some serious changes to the original concept, spicing it up considerably. I love the spicy, tomato-ey version with Creole Mustard served in New Orleans restaurants, but my favorite version was born in Houston. The late, great Sakowitz store, located in downtown Houston before the downtown renaissance, had a marvelous restaurant called the Sky Terrace. To go there was a special treat as a child—a reward for spending the day shopping with Mother. When I was older, I was given a bridal luncheon there. But I always ordered the same thing—Shrimp Salad Remoulade. There were two sizes, the large, which was served nested in the outer ten or so leaves of a head of iceberg lettuce, and the small, which was piled on an avocado half arranged on a bed of lettuce.

2 pounds small (70 to 90 count) shrimp, boiled, peeled, and deveined

½ cup finely chopped celery

⅓ cup mayonnaise

2 tablespoons freshly squeezed lemon juice

2 hard-cooked eggs, chopped

Salt to taste

Green leaf lettuce leaves

4 to 6 avocado halves, peeled, seeds removed

Tomato wedges

Minced flat-leaf parsley as garnish

Remoulade Sauce

2 green onions, finely chopped, including green tops

2 medium garlic cloves, minced

3 tablespoons chopped, cooked spinach

¾ cup mayonnaise

1½ teaspoons each of Worcestershire sauce, whole-grain mustard, and freshly squeezed lemon juice

¾ teaspoon anchovy paste

1 canned chipotle chili in adobo sauce, minced

¾ teaspoon adobo sauce from chipotle chilies

¼ teaspoon Tabasco sauce

2 teaspoons prepared horseradish

Prepare the Remoulade Sauce the day before serving to allow the flavors time to meld together. Combine all ingredients in work bowl of food processor fitted with steel blade and process until smooth. Refrigerate until ready to use.

To prepare the salad, combine shrimp, celery, mayonnaise, eggs, lemon juice, and salt in a medium bowl. Stir in the Remoulade Sauce. Chill until ready to serve.

To serve, place lettuce leaves on individual serving plates and nest an avocado half in the center. Using an ice cream scoop, scoop a portion of the salad over the top of the avocado. Garnish plate with tomato wedges and scatter minced parsley over the salad.

ℭ **Serves 4 to 6.**

Mid-19th-century home, Victoria

SHRIMP AND CRAWFISH SALAD ON FRIED EGGPLANT STEAKS

*I*t was love at first bite when I developed this recipe combining shrimp and mudbugs, as crawfish are often called. The dressing is one of my favorites—it's actually homemade ketchup based on red bell peppers and canned chipotle chilies. Feel free to use it anywhere you'd use plain old ketchup. It'll add zing to your day. I wanted to serve this salad for an evening meal once, but the occasion demanded something a bit more substantial than just a salad, so I added the eggplant steaks. It was an instant hit. The taste contrasts in this dish make it a very exciting meal.

SHRIMP AND CRAWFISH SALAD

  1 pound small (70 to 90 count) shrimp, boiled, peeled, deveined, and chilled

  1 pound boiled and chilled crawfish tails

  1 tablespoon minced cilantro

  ¼ cup finely chopped red onion

Chipotle Chili Dressing (see recipe below)

Green leaf lettuce leaves

CHIPOTLE CHILI DRESSING

ᑐ **Makes approximately 2 cups.**

  2 tablespoons canola oil

  1 large red bell pepper, seeded and diced

  1 small white onion, chopped

  2 large garlic cloves, minced

  2 Roma tomatoes, chopped

  2 tablespoons Champagne vinegar

  2 tablespoons sugar

2½ tablespoons minced canned chipotle chilies in adobo sauce, chilies and sauce included

FRIED EGGPLANT STEAKS

  6 ½-inch-thick slices of large eggplant, unpeeled

Seasoned Flour for Frying (see "Basics")

Egg wash made from 4 eggs beaten into 4 cups milk

Dried breadcrumbs, seasoned with granulated garlic and salt

Canola oil for deep-frying, heated to 350 degrees

Prepare the Chipotle Chili Dressing. Heat canola oil in a heavy 2-quart saucepan over medium-high heat. When oil is hot, add the red bell pepper, onions, garlic, and tomatoes. Cook, stirring often, until vegetables are very wilted, about 25 minutes. Add the vinegar and sugar and cook, stirring often, until sugar has dissolved, about 5 minutes. Transfer the mixture to blender. Add the chipotle chilies and adobo sauce; blend until very smooth. Return to clean saucepan over medium heat. Simmer gently for about 15 minutes. Remove from heat and stir through a fine strainer. Refrigerate until well chilled before using.

To prepare the Fried Eggplant Steaks, dredge the eggplant slices first in the seasoned flour, shaking off all excess flour. Next dip them in the egg wash, coating both sides. Finally dredge them in the breadcrumbs, pressing the crumbs to coat both sides.

Deep-fry the slices until golden brown on both sides. Drain on wire racks. Keep hot.

To assemble the salad, toss the boiled shrimp and crawfish tails with the cilantro and red onion. Add desired amount of Chipotle Chili Dressing, using enough to make a creamy mixture, and stir to blend well. Arrange a couple of green leaf lettuce leaves on each serving plate and set a Fried Eggplant Steak in the center. Spoon a portion of the salad in the center of the eggplant and serve.

ᑐ **Serves 4 to 6.**

FANTINE'S FOCACCIA BREAD

*D*on't be afraid to make your own yeast breads. It's easy, once you know a few basics—even easier if you own a food processor, which every kitchen should have. Have on hand the right basic ingredients to start yourself off right. Use active dry, instant-rise yeast and specially milled bread flour, which is readily available at the supermarket. A few simple pointers: (1) don't combine the yeast with a liquid hotter than 115 degrees, or you'll kill it; (2) knead the dough long enough to make it really springy and elastic—15 minutes by hand, 10 minutes with a mixer and dough hook, 20 seconds with a food processor; (3) don't add too much flour, or you'll make a cannonball loaf (if the dough is slightly sticky, leave it that way). Now, try your hand at this yummy bread created by the great baker on my staff, Fantine Dean-Wilson. Focaccia, or "fougasse," as it is also known, is an Italian flatbread that has become very much in vogue as Texans wholeheartedly embrace Italian foods. Focaccia is traditionally served with a seasoned olive oil dipping sauce. I like to serve focaccia bread with seafood salads and, of course, with Italian foods.

1¼ cups milk

1 cup warm water (105–115 degrees)

2 tablespoons active dry, instant-rise yeast

1½ tablespoons sugar

1½ teaspoons salt

¼ cup plus 2 tablespoons olive oil

6 cups sifted bread flour

OLIVE OIL DIPPING SAUCE

1 tablespoon crushed red pepper flakes

1 tablespoon freshly ground black pepper

1 tablespoon dried leaf oregano

2 tablespoons minced fresh basil

2 tablespoons minced flat-leaf parsley

1 tablespoon granulated garlic

1 tablespoon minced garlic cloves

2 teaspoons salt

Extra-virgin olive oil

To make dipping sauce, combine all seasonings, tossing with a fork to blend well. Put about 2 teaspoons of the seasoning mixture in each small dipping bowl. Add extra-virgin olive oil and set aside.

Place milk in a 1-quart saucepan and heat to the scalding point. (Tiny bubbles will begin to appear around the edges of the pan.) Remove from heat and set aside to cool. Combine the water, yeast, and sugar in a 2-cup glass measuring cup, stirring gently to blend. Set aside to proof until yeast has dissolved and mixture is foamy and bubbly. Combine 3 cups of the flour with the cooled milk, salt, ¼ cup olive oil, and the proofed yeast. Process just to blend well, about 25 seconds. Add an additional 2½ cups of flour and process for another 25 seconds, or until dough is smooth and cohesive. Turn dough out onto work surface and knead in the remaining ½ cup of flour by hand. The dough should be smooth, springy, and elastic. Place in a large bowl, cover with plastic wrap, and set aside to rise for 20 minutes.

Preheat oven to 350 degrees. Lightly grease 2 12-inch-diameter pizza pans; set aside. Punch the dough down and work out air bubbles. Divide into two portions. Flatten each portion onto the prepared pans. Using your index finger, press several indentations in the dough. Brush the breads with the remaining 2 tablespoons of olive oil. Set aside to rise for 20 minutes.

Place the pans in preheated oven and bake for 30 to 40 minutes, or until dough is light golden brown. Transfer to wire racks and cool. Slice as desired and serve with small bowls of the Olive Oil Dipping Sauce.

Makes 2 round loaves.

Texas Baguettes

*T*here just aren't many meals that a great loaf of crusty French bread won't make just a little bit better. If you thought you could never make it at home, well, you were wrong. Follow this quick and easy recipe and get out the butter 'cause just the smell of this bread cooking will have the whole neighborhood in your kitchen. Don't be tempted to leave out the vinegar because it sounds like a strange ingredient in bread. It works some real magic in there, giving the bread a hint of the taste of sourdough. This is a very wet and sticky dough. Don't add more flour and be sure you have the double-trough French bread pans.

1 tablespoon active dry, instant-rise yeast

1 tablespoon sugar

1½ cups warm water (105–115 degrees)

3½ cups bread flour

1 teaspoon apple cider vinegar

1½ teaspoons salt

½ cup canola oil

Glaze

4 tablespoons unsalted butter

2 large garlic cloves, minced

1 teaspoon salt

In a 2-cup liquid measuring cup, combine the yeast, sugar, and warm water. Stir gently to blend well. Set aside for about 3 minutes, or until yeast begins to bubble.

In work bowl of food processor fitted with steel blade, combine the bread flour, vinegar, and salt. Pulse 3 or 4 times to blend ingredients. Add the yeast mixture, scraping out cup with rubber spatula. Process to blend in the yeast, about 10 seconds. Stop the processor and check the consistency of the dough. It should be very wet and sticky with just a bit of body. If it is

really runny, add a couple of extra tablespoons of bread flour, but no more! Process for 25 seconds to knead the dough. Pour the canola oil into a large ceramic or stainless steel bowl and swirl to coat the sides with the oil. Grease your hands with some of the oil. Turn dough out into the bowl and use your hands to scrape it off the blade and the sides of the processor bowl; add to main dough. Turn the dough over in the oil to coat all sides. Cover bowl tightly with plastic wrap and set aside to rise in a draft-free spot for 45 minutes, or until doubled in bulk.

While the dough is rising, melt the butter for the glaze in a small saucepan. Add the minced garlic and salt. Cook over medium heat for 2 to 3 minutes. Remove from heat and set aside.

When dough has risen, preheat oven to 400 degrees and place oven rack in center position. Line a double-trough French bread pan with parchment paper and spray the parchment with non-stick vegetable spray; set aside. Grease your hands again with some of the canola oil in the dough bowl, and then flatten the dough, punching out all of the air. Pinch the dough mass in half. Lift each half of the dough and stretch it into a long piece almost as long as the pan. Place one piece of dough in each half of the pan. Don't worry about bumps or wrinkles in the dough. They'll iron out as the dough rises.

Strain the garlic out of the butter and discard it. Brush both loaves liberally with the butter using a pastry brush. Place the bread pan on a long, shallow cookie sheet and cover the dough loosely with plastic wrap. Set aside to rise until dough has risen about a half inch above the sides of the pan, about 30 to 40 minutes. Place bread in preheated oven and bake for 20 minutes, or until golden brown and crisp on top. Carefully turn the loaves over in the pan to brown the bottoms, then cook an additional 5 to 8 minutes. Place loaves on wire rack and cool slightly before slicing.

❧ Makes 2 baguette-shaped loaves.

ALMOND HEARTH LOAVES

*T*his light, airy, free-form bread pairs well with just about any meal. My daughter always loved it toasted for breakfast! The bread owes a large part of its taste to toasted almonds. Be sure to use the sliced, skin-on variety. Toasting any nuts briefly in a 350-degree oven will bring their full flavor potential to life.

1¼ cups warm water (105–115 degrees)

1 tablespoon sugar

1½ tablespoons active dry, instant-rise yeast

4 cups bread flour

½ cup sliced almonds (skin on), toasted

⅓ cup powdered milk

1½ teaspoons salt

2 tablespoons additional sugar

2 tablespoons canola oil

1 egg

Melted butter as glaze (optional)

Combine the water, 1 tablespoon sugar, and yeast in a 2-cup glass measuring cup. Stir to blend and set aside until yeast is foamy and bubbly. Combine remaining ingredients in work bowl of food processor fitted with steel blade. Pulse 3 or 4 times to blend ingredients. Add the yeast mixture to work bowl, scraping cup with a rubber spatula to include all yeast. Process dough for about 15 seconds. Stop and check consistency of the dough, adding additional flour or water as necessary to produce a medium-stiff, cohesive dough. Process briefly after each addition of flour or water. When proper consistency has been reached, process for 20 seconds to knead the dough. Turn dough out onto floured work surface and knead for 2 to 3 minutes by hand to form a smooth, elastic dough ball.

Place the dough in a lightly oiled large bowl, cover with plastic wrap, and set aside to rise until doubled in bulk, about 45 minutes. Punch dough down and form into two oval hearth loaves. Place loaves on baking sheets lined with parchment paper and make three parallel diagonal slits in the top of each loaf, using a serrated bread knife. Apply melted butter with pastry brush, if desired. Cover loaves loosely with plastic wrap and set aside to rise until doubled in bulk, about 20 to 30 minutes. Preheat oven to 350 degrees.

When loaves have doubled in size, bake in preheated oven for 45 minutes, or until golden brown. Loaves should sound hollow when tapped lightly on the bottom. Cool on wire racks before slicing.

ଔ **Makes 2 loaves.**

Artisan baker, Bastrop

Onion-Parmesan-Olive Loaves

*W*hat a taste these hearty, rolled and filled loaves have. Even the aroma while they're baking will make you giddy from anticipation. If you have trouble rolling the dough out because it's too elastic and springy, simply cover it with plastic wrap and let it "relax" for 10 minutes. Then it should behave better.

Dough

1 cup warmed milk (105–115 degrees)

¼ cup warm water (105–115 degrees)

1 tablespoon sugar

1 tablespoon active dry, instant-rise yeast

3¾ cups bread flour

1½ teaspoons salt

1 egg

2 tablespoons softened unsalted butter

Filling

4 tablespoons unsalted butter

1 large onion, finely chopped

4 large garlic cloves, minced

½ cup chopped, pitted Kalamata olives

½ cup grated Parmesan cheese

½ teaspoon salt

1 teaspoon poppy seeds

In a 2-cup glass measuring cup, combine the milk and water with sugar. Stir in the yeast and set aside to proof. Yeast should be dissolved and bubbly.

In work bowl of food processor fitted with steel blade, combine flour, salt, egg, and butter. Pulse 3 or 4 times. Add the yeast mixture to the work bowl and process a few seconds to blend the ingredients. Adjust consistency of dough as needed with additional bread flour or water to form a smooth, elastic dough. Process for 20 seconds to knead the dough.

Turn dough out onto lightly floured work surface and knead for 2 or 3 minutes by hand. Place dough in lightly oiled large bowl, turning to coat all surfaces. Cover bowl tightly with plastic wrap and set aside to rise until doubled in bulk, about 45 minutes.

While dough is rising, prepare the filling. Melt butter in a heavy 12-inch skillet over medium heat. Sauté the onion, garlic, and olives just until onion is wilted and transparent. Do not brown. Remove from heat; set aside to cool. In a separate bowl, combine Parmesan cheese, salt, and poppy seeds; set aside.

When dough has doubled, punch down and divide in half. Lightly flour work surface and roll each portion of the dough out into a 12-by-15-inch rectangle. Spoon half of the fillings on each dough portion, leaving a border of 1 inch on all sides. Roll the dough from the long sides, pinwheel-style. Pinch the seams together well and place the loaves, seam sides down, on baking sheets lined with parchment paper. Cover loosely with plastic wrap and set aside to rise until doubled in size. Preheat oven to 350 degrees.

When loaves have risen, bake in preheated oven for about 30 to 35 minutes, or until golden brown and hollow-sounding when tapped on the bottom. Cool on wire racks.

❧ Makes 2 loaves.

ROSEMARY AND GARLIC COUNTRY BREAD

*R*oasted garlic is one of my favorite chef's "secret ingredients." The delicate, nutty taste of the roasted cloves adds a wonderful flavor dimension to sauces, batters, soups, and even breads. This robust-flavored bread doesn't even need a meal. It's so good you could eat it all by itself.

1¼ cups warm water (105–115 degrees)
  1 tablespoon sugar
1½ tablespoons active dry, instant-rise yeast
  4 cups bread flour
  ½ cup toasted pine nuts
  ⅓ cup powdered milk
  1 tablespoon minced fresh rosemary
10 cloves roasted garlic (see "Basics")
  2 tablespoons additional sugar
  2 tablespoons olive oil
  1 egg

Combine the water, 1 tablespoon sugar, and yeast in a 2-cup glass measuring cup. Stir to blend and set aside to proof until yeast is foamy and bubbly. Combine remaining ingredients in work bowl of food processor fitted with steel blade. Pulse 3 or 4 times to blend ingredients. Add the yeast mixture to work bowl, scraping cup with a rubber spatula to include all yeast. Process dough for about 15 seconds. Stop and check consistency of the dough, adding additional flour or water as needed to produce a medium-stiff, cohesive dough. Process briefly after each addition. When proper consistency has been reached, process for 20 seconds to knead the dough. Turn dough out onto floured work surface and knead 2 to 3 minutes by hand to form a smooth dough ball.

Place dough in lightly oiled large bowl, cover with plastic wrap, and set aside to rise until doubled in bulk, about 45 minutes. Punch dough down and form into two round loaves. Place loaves on baking sheets lined with parchment paper. Make three parallel diagonal slits in center of each loaf using a serrated bread knife. Cover loaves loosely with plastic wrap and set aside to rise until doubled in size, about 30 to 45 minutes. Preheat oven to 350 degrees.

When loaves have doubled, bake in preheated oven for 45 minutes, or until golden brown. Loaves should sound hollow when lightly tapped on the bottom. Cool on wire racks before slicing.

☙ **Makes 2 round loaves.**

TEXAS TOAST

*N*obody seems to know how Texas Toast got started in Texas. One thing is for sure, though: it's a Texas favorite. The yummy, butter-basted, thick-cut slices of rich white bread are a required accompaniment to chicken-fried steak. Unless you bake your own white bread in the big Pullman-loaf pans, you'll have to get the bread at your favorite bakery. You can substitute good-quality, rounded-top white bread—it just won't look the same as the square Texas Toast at your favorite steakhouse.

Unsliced white bread loaves
Melted unsalted butter

Slice the bread into thick slices, about 1 inch thick, using a serrated bread knife. Heat a flat griddle or a large skillet until medium-hot. Using a pastry brush, baste both sides of the bread slices with melted butter. Be sure to brush all the way to the edges.

Lay the buttered slices on the hot griddle or in the skillet and cook until golden brown on both sides, turning once. Don't allow the bread to actually brown. It should be light golden in color and slightly crisp. Cut the slices in half diagonally and serve hot.

TERRY'S TENDER, FLAKY, LIGHTER-THAN-AIR BISCUITS

For a real cowboy breakfast, you gotta have biscuits and gravy. You can have other stuff too, but the biscuits and gravy had better be there. I'm always amazed at the number of people who are terrified of making biscuits. If there's any secret to making great biscuits, it's probably to handle the dough quickly and gently. Overwork it, and the biscuits will be really tough and dense, kind of like hockey pucks.

   3 cups all-purpose flour
   ¼ cup powdered milk
   2 tablespoons baking powder
   2 tablespoons sugar
   1 teaspoon salt
   1 teaspoon cream of tartar
   ½ cup solid shortening
   ½ cup (1 stick) softened unsalted butter, cut into chunks
   ¾ cup plus 2 tablespoons buttermilk
Melted unsalted butter for brushing tops

Preheat oven to 400 degrees. Spray a 12-by-9-inch baking pan with non-stick vegetable spray; set aside. In a large bowl, combine all ingredients except shortening, butter, and buttermilk. Toss to blend well. Add the shortening and butter. Using your hands or a pastry blender, work the fat into the dry mixture until it resembles coarse oatmeal. Make a well in the center of the mixture and pour in the buttermilk. Using a spoon, quickly and lightly combine the ingredients, making sure all dry ingredients are well blended.

Turn the dough out onto a well-floured work surface and, with floured hands, knead it 8 or 10 times to form a smooth and cohesive dough. Roll the dough out gently to a ¾-inch thickness. Using a 2½-inch biscuit cutter, cut the dough into biscuits. Be sure to use a straight, forceful, downward motion with the cutter and do not twist it. Place biscuits in the baking pan with their sides touching. Gently gather any dough scraps together and pat again to ¾-inch thickness. Cut remaining dough into biscuits.

Bake in preheated oven for 15 to 18 minutes, or until light golden brown and cooked through. Remove pan from oven and brush the tops of the biscuits with the melted butter.

ભ **Makes 12 biscuits.**

EMILY STONE'S PERSIMMON BREAD

The persimmon is a plum-shaped fruit that has a delicate, understated taste with nuances of plum, honey, and pumpkin. Select only ripe, soft fruits with deep flame-orange coloring. Persimmons have long been seasonal favorites with home cooks who create everything from beer to sauces to breads, like this favorite of mine from Emily Stone. I love to cut a slice, toast it, and slather it with softened cream cheese. Great with morning coffee.

   2 cups sifted all-purpose flour
   ¾ cup sugar
   1 teaspoon baking soda
   1 teaspoon baking powder
   ½ teaspoon salt
   2 eggs, beaten
   ½ cup canola oil
   1 cup pureed pulp from peeled persimmons
   ½ cup golden raisins
   ½ cup chopped pecans

Preheat oven to 325 degrees. Lightly butter a 9-by-5-by-3-inch loaf pan. Combine all dry ingredients in a bowl; toss with a fork to distribute ingredients well. Combine remaining ingredients in bowl of electric mixer. Beat at medium speed until well blended. Add dry ingredients in thirds, scraping down side of bowl after each addition. Beat just to blend; do not overbeat.

Turn batter out into prepared loaf pan and bake in preheated oven for 1 hour and 15 minutes, or until a metal skewer inserted in the center comes out clean. Turn loaf out onto wire rack and cool before slicing.

ભ **Makes 1 loaf.**

CUMIN AND GARLIC FLATBREAD

Cumin is the dried seedlike fruit of a small annual herb in the same botanical family as parsley. The spice was used in ancient Rome and spread across the Mediterranean region to the Middle East, China, Japan, Indonesia, and India, where it is used as an ingredient in garam masala and other curry powders. It is also used extensively in Latin American and Mexican cooking, hence its popularity in Texas Cuisine. Cumin, next to ground chilies, is the most important ingredient in chili con carne seasonings. Cumin can be purchased either in whole-seed form or ground. For the most flavor "bang for your buck" with cumin, buy the whole seeds, then toast them lightly in a dry skillet right before using and grind them in a spice mill or coffee bean grinder.

2 teaspoons dried cumin seeds

8 oil-packed sun-dried tomatoes, minced

1 cup whole wheat flour

1 cup all-purpose flour

2 tablespoons sugar

½ teaspoon salt

1 teaspoon baking powder

½ teaspoon red (cayenne) pepper

2 teaspoons minced fresh thyme

2 tablespoons minced garlic

2 teaspoons Mexican oregano

1 cup finely chopped walnuts

4 eggs, beaten

Preheat oven to 350 degrees. Spray 2 12-inch pizza pans with non-stick vegetable spray and set aside. Place the cumin seeds in a dry skillet over medium-high heat. Cook the seeds, shaking the pan, until they begin to give off a strong aroma. Remove from heat and set the toasted seeds aside.

Combine cumin seeds and all other ingredients except eggs. Toss to blend well. Add the eggs and stir to form a cohesive dough. The dough will be very stiff. Divide the dough into 2 equal portions. Lightly flour work surface and roll one portion of the dough out into a 10-inch round. Using a pizza cutter, cut the dough into 8 wedges. Place the wedges slightly apart on prepared pizza pan. Repeat with the remaining portion of dough. Bake the flatbreads in preheated oven for about 18 to 20 minutes, or until crisp on the outside but slightly soft when pressed. Cool on wire racks before serving.

൙ **Makes 2 rounds or 16 wedges.**

BLUE CORNMEAL CORNBREAD

Blue cornmeal is ground from Native American blue corn. It has a taste that is best described as slightly more corn-like than white or yellow cornmeal. It makes a bread with a pleasing, light bluish gray color—definitely a conversation piece at the table.

2 fresh jalapeño chilies, veins and seeds removed, minced

1 14-ounce can cream-style corn

2 teaspoons baking soda

1½ teaspoons salt

1 tablespoon sugar

2 eggs, beaten

¾ cup buttermilk

⅓ cup bacon drippings

1 cup (4 ounces) shredded cheddar cheese

1 cup blue cornmeal

1 cup all-purpose flour

Additional bacon drippings for greasing pans

Preheat oven to 425 degrees. Thoroughly grease 2 8-inch cast iron skillets with bacon grease and place them in the hot oven. In a large bowl, combine the minced jalapeños with the creamed corn. Beat in the baking soda, salt, and sugar. Add the eggs, buttermilk, and bacon drippings; beat well. Stir in the cheese, cornmeal, and all-purpose flour. Beat just to blend; do not overbeat. Carefully remove the hot skillets from the oven and divide the batter between them. Place skillets in oven and cook for 20 minutes, or until a metal skewer inserted in the center of the cornbread comes out clean. Turn out onto cutting board and slice as desired. Serve hot with plenty of butter!

൙ **Makes 2 breads.**

If It Swims

Texas has been richly blessed with water. Within our boundaries we have some of the best rivers and lakes for fishing in the country. Our waters are brimming with catfish, perch, crappie, bluegills, and a host of other delicious freshwater fish.

Our southern border lies on the Gulf of Mexico, with its bounty of saltwater fish and shellfish. Even if you're not an angler, the state boasts excellent seafood markets where all types of fish and shellfish are available. For tips on selecting fish and seafood, see "Basics."

Fish is very good for us. It's low in calories and low in fat. What little fat or oil it does contain is either unsaturated or polyunsaturated, unlike the saturated fats found in red meats. Polyunsaturated fats such as fish oils have been found to keep cholesterol levels in check. Replacing saturated-fat meats with fish may even lower cholesterol levels. Fish is also very high in protein, the body's building blocks—an average of 25 percent higher than beef! It's also very high in vitamins, especially A and D, high in minerals, and very low in sodium. Also, because it has so little connective tissue, fish is very easy on the digestive system.

And it's quick and easy to cook, once you learn a few basics. When cooking fish, the most important thing to avoid is overcooking it. If you come across a recipe in your grandmother's cookbook that tells you

Retired shrimper, Port Bolivar; Shore below the Mansfield Cut, South Padre Island (pages 88–89).

to cook fish until it "flakes easily when pierced with a fork," ignore this advice. Fish that falls apart has been overcooked. Overcooking will break down the delicate connective fat tissue in fish, and it will lose its moisture and most of its good taste in the process. Fish should be cooked for 10 minutes per inch of thickness, measured at the thickest part of the fish—never longer. So, whether you are baking, broiling, grilling, or frying a fish fillet that is half an inch thick, it will cook for only 5 minutes! A perfectly cooked piece of fish is a work of culinary art, with a taste that can't be beaten.

When cooking fish and shellfish, experiment with the different varieties available—see what you like. If you've done any serious fishing in Gulf Coast waters, more than likely you've hooked something that you didn't want—such as a shark or stingray. You probably said a few cuss words in the process of getting it off your hook. Maybe you took the easy way out and just cut the line. But next time you hook one, keep it. This chapter will show you some delicious ways of preparing these species.

Combine shellfish with fish, as in many of the recipes in this chapter. Try different sauces and herbs as well as different cooking methods. Don't get in a rut of always frying fish! Just remember—buy fresh and cook briefly!

Sorting crabs, Port O'Connor; Shrimp fleet, Port Lavaca (pages 92–93).

BROILED RED SNAPPER WITH LEMON AND CAPER BUTTER SAUCE

*T*rue red snapper is one of the most popular and delicious of all the Gulf fish. I say "true" red snapper because a similarly colored fish called rockfish is often passed off as snapper under the name Pacific snapper. Don't be fooled. Real red snapper is completely red in color. Even the eyes are bright red. If you get your hands on some fresh whole red snapper, be sure to fry the cheeks and throat—they're incredibly sweet and tasty. This dish is quick and easy, one of my very favorites when I'm in the mood for good fish in a simple sauce.

RED SNAPPER

4 6- to 8-ounce red snapper fillets, skinned

4 tablespoons melted unsalted butter

Salt and light dusting of Chef Paul's Seafood Magic or other spicy seafood seasoning

LEMON AND CAPER BUTTER SAUCE

3 egg yolks

1 teaspoon Dijon-style mustard

¼ teaspoon salt, or to taste

¼ teaspoon red (cayenne) pepper

2 tablespoons freshly squeezed lemon juice

½ teaspoon minced lemon zest

3 tablespoons seafood stock (see "Basics")

2 teaspoons capers, drained

12 tablespoons (1½ sticks) unsalted butter, melted

Preheat broiler and place oven rack 4 to 6 inches below heat source.

Make the Lemon and Caper Butter Sauce. In work bowl of food processor fitted with steel blade, combine all ingredients except melted butter. Process until egg yolks are thick and light in color, about 2 to 3 minutes. With processor running, add the hot melted butter in a slow, steady stream through the feed tube. Process an additional minute to form a strong emulsion. Transfer sauce to a bowl, cover with plastic wrap to keep warm, and set aside while broiling the fish. The sauce, a derivative of hollandaise sauce, cannot be reheated.

To prepare the fish, pat the fillets very dry using absorbent paper towels. Place fish on a baking sheet and brush with the melted butter. Season lightly with salt and seafood seasoning. Place the tray under preheated broiler and cook just until fish are opaque and lightly browned, about 4 to 5 minutes. Do not overcook the fish.

To serve, place one fillet on each serving plate and top with a portion of the sauce. Serve at once.

ᏣᎨ **Serves 4.**

SUGGESTED WINES

BECKER VINEYARDS FUMÉ BLANC ESTATE BOTTLED

CAP*ROCK WINERY CHARDONNAY

COMFORT CELLARS CHENIN BLANC

HAAK VINEYARDS AND WINERY BARREL-FERMENTED CHARDONNAY

TEXAS HILLS VINEYARD CHARDONNAY

Seashells on McFadden Beach, High Island

POTATO-CRUSTED RED SNAPPER WITH CRAWFISH ÉTOUFFÉE TOPPING

É touffée is one of many dishes that have crossed over the border from Louisiana and entered the mainstream of Texas food. The dish is especially popular in the Beaumont–Port Arthur–Orange area, which is made up of mostly Texanized, transplanted Cajuns.

Putting crawfish étouffée on top of fried fish is a very typical Cajun presentation, but a new dimension added here is in breading the fish fillets with instant mashed potato flakes. What a marvelous crisp and tasty crust it makes. Any fish suitable for frying can be substituted.

6 6- to 8-ounce red snapper fillets

Seasoned Flour for Frying (see "Basics")

Egg wash made from 4 eggs beaten into 5 cups milk

4 cups instant mashed potato flakes, seasoned with 1½ teaspoons salt, 1½ teaspoons black pepper, and 1½ teaspoons granulated garlic

Canola oil for deep-frying, heated to 350 degrees

CRAWFISH ÉTOUFFÉE

1½ cups solid shortening or lard

1½ cups all-purpose flour

1 large yellow onion, chopped

1 large green bell pepper, chopped

1 large red bell pepper, chopped

3 large garlic cloves, minced

2 medium celery stalks, chopped

¼ cup minced fresh basil

2 teaspoons minced fresh thyme

½ cup tomato paste

1½ pounds peeled crawfish tails

3 cups seafood stock, or more as needed (see "Basics")

¼ teaspoon red (cayenne) pepper, or to taste

¼ teaspoon freshly ground black pepper

Salt to taste

3 green onions, chopped as garnish

Minced flat-leaf parsley, as garnish

Prepare the Crawfish Étouffée. Make a roux by melting shortening or lard in a heavy, deep, 12-inch skillet over medium heat. When the fat is hot, whisk in the flour all at once, blending quickly. Cook the roux over medium heat, whisking constantly until it is a deep mahogany color, about 30 to 45 minutes.

When the roux is the desired color, stir in the onion, garlic, bell peppers, celery, basil, and thyme. Cook, stirring constantly, until vegetables are wilted, about 10 minutes. Stir in the tomato paste, blending well. Cook, stirring, for about 3 minutes to brown the tomato paste. Add crawfish tails, stock, and seasonings. Reduce heat and simmer for about 30 minutes. Taste for seasonings and adjust as needed. Add additional stock as needed during cooking to make a medium-thick gravy. Keep the étouffée warm while frying the snapper.

To prepare the Red Snapper, pat the fillets very dry on absorbent paper towels. Dredge the fillets first in the seasoned flour, shaking off all excess. Next dip them into the egg wash, turning to coat well. Finally coat fillets with the instant mashed potato flakes, pressing the flakes into the fish, then shaking off all loose flakes.

Deep-fry the fish just until the crust is golden brown. Do not overcook and do not crowd the oil. Transfer cooked fish to wire rack set over baking sheet to drain. Serve hot, topped with a portion of the Crawfish Étouffée. Garnish with chopped green onions and minced parsley.

ଓ **Serves 4 to 6.**

SUGGESTED WINES

ALAMOSA WINE CELLARS ROSATO DI SANGIOVESE

FALL CREEK VINEYARDS SAUVIGNON BLANC

MESSINA HOF GEWÜRZTRAMINER

SISTER CREEK VINEYARDS PINOT NOIR

SPICEWOOD VINEYARDS SAUVIGNON BLANC

MIKE WICKER'S REDFISH ON THE HALF SHELL

Mike Wicker, the manager of Halliburton's Maner Lake Lodge, is an extraordinary fisherman who knows the bays, inlets, and saltwater lakes and bayous of the Gulf Coast like most of us know the road home. When Mike goes out fishing, other fishermen like to follow him so they can find out where the fish are. He always seems to know where to catch the big reds. Of course, most great fishermen also know a trick or two about cooking fish, and Mike is no exception. His method of grilling unscaled redfish is very unique and makes for great conversation when you fix them for guests. The method of cooking produces a moist and most yummy piece of fish.

4 12- to 13-ounce redfish fillets, unscaled

1 cup Worcestershire sauce

6 tablespoons unsalted butter

Juice of 2 large lemons

Lemon-pepper seasoning

Tony's Creole Seasoning

Heat gas grill to medium heat. Combine Worcestershire sauce, butter, and lemon juice in a small saucepan over medium heat. Cook until butter has melted, stirring often. Place the fish fillets, skin side down, in a large baking dish. Baste liberally with the butter mixture. Save remaining butter for basting while grilling. Season the fillets to taste with lemon-pepper seasoning and Tony's Creole Seasoning.

Grill the redfish, skin side down, for 15 to 20 minutes, or until meat turns opaque throughout. Baste often with the remaining butter mixture. Do not turn the fish while grilling. Do not overcook. Remove to serving plates and serve hot.

ભ **Serves 4 to 6.**

SUGGESTED WINES

ALAMOSA WINE CELLARS FUMÉ BLANC

HAAK VINEYARDS AND WINERY
BARREL-FERMENTED CHARDONNAY

HIDDEN SPRINGS WINERY CHARDONNAY

SISTER CREEK VINEYARDS CHARDONNAY

TEXAS HILLS VINEYARDS MOSCATO

BROILED STINGRAY WINGS WITH BROWN BUTTER SAUCE

Stingray, believe it or not, is very tasty. The flavor has been compared to scallops. The flesh is low in oil content and very delicate. Fillet the "wings" on either side of the skeletal structure down the middle of the stingray. (It's easy to feel.) If the stingray is large, you can also remove the two wing fillets from the bottom side, much like the bottom fillet of a flounder, only there are two. Skin them just like you would a fish fillet. The skin is very tough and leathery, so you'll need a sharp filleting knife.

4 filleted and skinned stingray wings, about 6 to 8
   ounces each

1 cup (2 sticks) unsalted butter

2 tablespoons freshly squeezed lemon juice

1 teaspoon minced lemon zest

1 teaspoon minced fresh thyme

1 large garlic clove, minced

½ teaspoon freshly ground black pepper

1 teaspoon salt

Place the stingray wings on a heavy baking sheet; set aside. Preheat broiler and place oven rack 6 inches below the heat source. Melt the butter in a small saucepan and add remaining ingredients. Stir to blend and cook over medium heat for about 5 minutes. Brush a small amount of the butter over the wings. Place the baking sheet under preheated broiler and cook until meat is opaque throughout and well browned, about 5 to 7 minutes. While the fish is broiling, continue to cook the butter sauce until it is browned to a hazelnut color. To serve, place the fish on individual serving plates and spoon a portion of the browned butter sauce over each. Serve hot.

ભ **Serves 4.**

GRILLED SPECKLED TROUT WITH MANGO ESSENCE

Speckled trout is one of the most highly prized fish by saltwater anglers. Its meat is pure white and firm, and the taste is one of the most delicate of any saltwater fish. Pairing saltwater fish with sauces made from exotic fruits has become a favorite menu item with Gulf Coast chefs. The two seem to have a natural affinity for one another. This sauce, with mangoes and melons, is one of my favorites.

4 6- to 8-ounce speckled trout fillets, skinned
Extra-virgin olive oil
Salt and freshly ground black pepper

MANGO ESSENCE

¼ cup extra-virgin olive oil
3 large mangoes, peeled and diced
¾ cup diced cantaloupe
¾ cup diced honeydew melon
1 large red bell pepper, blistered, peeled, and diced (see "Basics")
2 serrano chilies, seeds and veins removed, minced
⅓ cup firmly packed light brown sugar
⅓ cup apple cider vinegar
1 tablespoon minced cilantro
Lemon slices as garnish

Begin by preparing the Mango Essence. Heat olive oil in a heavy 10-inch skillet over medium heat. When oil is hot, add the diced mango, cantaloupe, honeydew, red bell pepper, and serrano chilies. Cook, stirring often, until the mixture is very wilted and pulpy, about 15 minutes. Add the brown sugar and vinegar. Cook, stirring often, until thickened. Stir in the cilantro. Remove from heat and puree the sauce in food processor fitted with steel blade or in blender. Set aside and keep warm while grilling the trout.

To grill the trout, preheat a gas grill to medium-high heat. Brush both sides of the fillets with olive oil and salt and pepper to taste. Grill the fish, turning once, just until the flesh has lost its translucence and is opaque throughout, about 5 to 6 minutes. Do not overcook the fish. To serve, spoon a bed of the Mango Essence in center of each plate and place a grilled fish in the middle of the sauce. Garnish fillets with lemon slices and serve hot.

ᕱ **Serves 4.**

MANGOS

MANGOS ARE VERY FRAGRANT FRUITS, NATIVE TO SOUTHEAST ASIA, WHERE THEY HAVE BEEN CULTIVATED FOR AS LONG AS 6,000 YEARS. THE EXOTIC FRUIT IS NOW GROWN IN FLORIDA, WHICH ACCOUNTS FOR ABOUT 15 PERCENT OF THE U.S. MARKET. MOST MANGOS SOLD IN TEXAS ARE GROWN IN MEXICO. SELECT FULL, PARTLY RIPE FRUIT THAT SHOWS SOME YELLOW OR RED. THE SKIN SHOULD BE TAUT AND SOMEWHAT FIRM, NOT WRINKLED. AVOID MANGOS WITH SOFT SPOTS. SNIFF THE STEM END. THERE SHOULD BE A PLEASANT SCENT. NO PERFUME MEANS NO FLAVOR. IF THE SMELL IS SOUR OR ALCOHOL-LIKE, PASS THAT ONE UP—IT HAS BEGUN TO FERMENT.

SUGGESTED WINES

ALAMOSA WINE CELLARS VIOGNIER
FALL CREEK VINEYARDS CASCADE SEMILLON/SAUVIGNON BLANC
HIDDEN SPRINGS WINERY MUSCAT CANELLI
MESSINA HOF MUSCAT CANELLI
TEXAS HILLS VINEYARD PINOT GRIGIO

BLACKENED AHI TUNA

Blackening is a cooking method that has been misunderstood and abused since Paul Prudhomme made the term a household word. The Creoles were blackening fish before the turn of the twentieth century in their wood-fired and brick ovens. The temperatures were never consistent and if the fire was "new," it was very hot, so over the years they became used to the taste of the charred fish. Paul created the method of blackening fish in a red-hot cast-iron skillet and it took off. When done properly, blackening produces a succulent and moist serving of fish or meat with a crisp crust and great taste. Blackening a fish does not mean that it should be so spicy you can't eat it or so charred that it tastes bitter and burned. Season the fish to your taste, but be sure to use dried thyme in the blackening butter (the oils in fresh thyme will result in a bitter taste). Also, you really can't properly blacken any fish or meat that is over half an inch thick, or it will not be cooked in the middle. (You can sear thicker meats or fish in the skillet, then finish cooking them in the oven.) Tuna loin is the perfect meat for blackening. Cut the steaks about 1 inch thick and blacken them quickly on both sides. They will be medium-rare in the middle, which is the only way to serve tuna.

4 pounds ahi tuna loin

BLACKENING BUTTER

2½ cups unsalted butter

½ cup freshly squeezed lemon juice

1½ teaspoons red (cayenne) pepper, or to taste

1 teaspoon salt

2 teaspoons freshly ground black pepper

2 teaspoons dried leaf thyme

Begin by preparing the Blackening Butter. Combine all ingredients in a heavy 3-quart saucepan over medium heat. Cook, stirring often, for about 5 minutes. Remove from heat and cool to lukewarm.

Skin the tuna loin and remove the small tenderloin piece, if still attached. (Freeze for a stir-fry later.) Remove the dark "blood vein" and discard. Cut the trimmed loin into 6 1-inch steaks and set aside.

Turn on vent fan over stove. Place an empty 10-inch cast-iron skillet over the highest heat and allow the pan to heat until the inside bottom has a white haze on the surface.

Pat the tuna steaks very dry on absorbent paper towels. Using chef's tongs, dip the steaks, one at a time, in the blackening butter, coating well.

Carefully lay the steak in the hot skillet using the tongs. The first piece will spit and sputter and usually flame, but don't worry—it will extinguish itself. Cook the first side for 30 seconds, then turn quickly and blacken the other side, about 45 seconds to 1 minute. Remove to a platter and keep warm while blackening the remaining steaks. Do not overcook. They should be medium-rare.

When all steaks have been blackened, turn off the heat and carefully wipe any charred bits from the skillet. Pour the remaining blackening butter into the skillet and, using heavy potholders, carefully swirl the skillet to blacken the butter sauce. Quickly transfer sauce to a bowl to stop the cooking.

To serve, place a blackened steak on each plate and drizzle a liberal portion of the Blackening Butter over the top.

๛ **Serves 6.**

SUGGESTED WINES

CAP*ROCK WINERY RESERVE CHARDONNAY
COMFORT CELLARS COMFORT BLUSH
LA BUENA VIDA SPRINGTOWN MERLOT
LLANO ESTACADO SAUVIGNON BLANC
MESSINA HOF GEWÜRZTRAMINER

Shark Steaks Grilled in Hoja Santa with Sun-Dried Tomato and Walnut Pesto

Shark meat is very tasty and nutritious. It is low in calories and sodium, and very high in protein (about 22.7 percent). The fat content is 0.5 percent, and 80 percent of that is polyunsaturated. It's also high in minerals and Vitamins A and B. Because it is so lean, it must be cooked by moist-heat methods—like "wrapping"—or it will be dry and cottony. All varieties of shark produce varying levels of urea to maintain their salt balance. When the fish dies and decomposition begins, the urea turns to ammonia. Although it is harmless, some varieties of shark contain unpalatable levels of the substance. These varieties have a very intense ammonia odor and would have a strong, pungent taste. If you don't know one shark from another, smell the meat up close. If it has an unbearable smell of ammonia, toss it. If you catch a shark that you wish to cook, cut the tail off and let the shark bleed for about 30 minutes before cleaning and skinning it. Mako and thresher sharks are the varieties most prized for cooking. They both have textures similar to that of swordfish and a great taste. Before cooking any shark meat, soak it for an hour in milk to neutralize any ammonia present.

2 shark steaks, 12 to 14 ounces each

About 12 large hoja santa leaves (see "The Texas Cook's Pantry")

Several toothpicks, soaked in water

Sun-Dried Tomato and Walnut Pesto

1 cup oil-packed sun-dried tomatoes and their oil

¼ cup extra-virgin olive oil

½ cup loosely packed fresh basil leaves

½ cup sliced ripe olives

¼ cup walnuts

¼ cup loosely packed flat-leaf parsley leaves

2 large garlic cloves, peeled

½ teaspoon salt

½ teaspoon sugar

2 green onions, coarsely chopped, including green tops

Make the Sun-Dried Tomato and Walnut Pesto. Combine all ingredients in work bowl of food processor fitted with steel blade and process until all ingredients are minced. You'll get the best consistency by using the pulse feature. Remove pesto from work bowl and set aside.

To prepare the shark steaks, cut each shark steak in half. Using scissors, cut the thick stems from the hoja santa leaves. Arrange 3 of the leaves, overlapping, on work surface. Place a heaping tablespoon of the Sun-Dried Tomato and Walnut Pesto in the center of the leaves. Place a piece of the shark on top of the pesto. Top with another heaping tablespoon of the pesto. Fold the edges of the leaves over the shark, enclosing it completely. Secure the leaves in place with a few of the wet toothpicks. Repeat with remaining pieces of fish.

Preheat gas grill to medium heat. Place the grilling grate about 6 inches over the coals. Grill the fish for 5 minutes per side, turning once. The hoja santa leaves will be moderately charred. Remove all toothpicks from the leaves and place the bundles on individual serving plates. Serve hot.

ભ Serves 4.

SUGGESTED WINES

Cap*Rock Winery Sparkling Wine, Blanc de Noir

Comfort Cellars Chenin Blanc

Llano Estacado Winery Sauvignon Blanc

Texas Hills Vineyard Pinot Grigio

Four-Cheese and Spinach-Stuffed Flounder Roulades with Basil and Tomato Sauce

Flounder are really great fish. If you're an angler, you know that they are great sport to land with a rod and reel. They really fight and when you finally get your catch in the boat, you have earned your prize. You will be rewarded for your hard work when you cook the flounder and sink your teeth into the firm but delicate white flesh with its sublime mild taste. If you're not a fisherman, you can purchase flounder from the seafood market. It'll be almost as good! The flounder, which is in the same family as sole and halibut, is a bottom dweller and has evolved with both eyes on its top side to watch for the enemy. Flounders can burrow into the bottom when alarmed, their dull brownish gray coloring making them hard to spot down there. Flounders have two fillets—a top one, which is thicker, and a bottom one under the bones, which is easily removed once the top fillet is cut away. Flounder is one of the few fish that is adaptable to every cooking method with great results. Fry it, grill it, broil it, stuff it, smoke it, or bake it—any way you cook it, it's a winner.

Flounder and Stuffing

4 large flounder top fillets, about 8 ounces each

2 ounces shredded Mozzarella Company Scamorza cheese or other smoked mozzarella cheese

2 ounces shredded Fontina cheese

2 ounces grated Parmesan cheese

2 ounces crumbled feta cheese

1 10-ounce package frozen chopped spinach, thawed, all traces of moisture pressed out

⅓ cup Italian-seasoned breadcrumbs

2 French shallots, chopped

2 large garlic cloves, minced

½ teaspoon dried Mexican oregano

Salt and freshly ground black pepper to taste

Melted unsalted butter

Minced flat-leaf parsley as garnish

Basil and Tomato Sauce

8 large Roma tomatoes, blistered, peeled, and seeded (see "Basics")

3 tablespoons extra-virgin olive oil

2 tablespoons minced fresh basil

4 medium garlic cloves, minced

¼ teaspoon freshly ground black pepper

½ cup dry vermouth

2 cups whipping cream

Salt to taste

Preheat oven to 375 degrees. Cut the flounder fillets in half lengthwise; set aside. Combine the stuffing ingredients, except melted butter and parsley, tossing to blend well. Add salt and pepper to taste. Divide the stuffing between the flounder fillets, placing a portion on the widest part of the fillet, about 1 inch from the front edge. Roll the fillet over the filling, pinwheel-style. Place the roulades in a shallow baking dish with the loose tail end of the fillet underneath. Brush each roulade lightly with the melted butter. Salt and pepper each roulade. Refrigerate until ready to bake.

Make the Basil and Tomato Sauce. Place the roasted tomatoes in work bowl of food processor fitted with steel blade and process until smooth.

Heat olive oil in a heavy 10-inch skillet over medium heat. Add the pureed tomatoes, basil, garlic, and black pepper. Cook, stirring often, until tomato puree has thickened, about 8 minutes. Stir in the vermouth and cook until liquor is reduced by about half. Add whipping cream and cook for 10 minutes. Season with salt to taste. Keep warm.

Bake the roulades in preheated oven for 15 to 20 minutes, or until lightly browned and cheeses have melted. To serve, place 2 roulades on each serving plate and spoon a portion of the Basil and Tomato Sauce over them. Garnish with minced parsley. Serve hot.

❧ Serves 4.

SUGGESTED WINES

Delaney Vineyards and Winery Texas Champagne Brut

La Buena Vida Vineyards Springtown Red

Llano Estacado Winery Cellar Select Chardonnay

Messina Hof Wine Cellars Private Reserve Chardonnay

Brazos Catfish with Crawfish Cream

Catfish is one of the most readily available species of fish. You can catch them in lakes and rivers, and there are even some that thrive in the brackish river water on the Gulf Coast. There are many species of catfish that are excellent. Among them are spotted bullhead, blue catfish, channel catfish, flathead catfish (one of the best), and, the best of all, yellow bullhead catfish. Many people discard the gafftop catfish because of the slimy covering on its skin, but they are excellent, too. (Remove the lateral bloodline from the gafftop before cooking.) One species to avoid is the "hardhead" sea catfish. The quality of the meat is very poor, and the taste is unappealing at best. Always skin any catfish before cooking. If you catch your own catfish, be sure to put it on ice at once or the flesh tends to become mushy.

8 3- to 5-ounce catfish fillets

4 cups all-purpose flour, seasoned with 2 teaspoons each of salt, freshly ground black pepper, and red (cayenne) pepper

3 eggs beaten into 4 cups milk

4 cups yellow cornmeal, seasoned with 2 teaspoons each of salt, freshly ground black pepper, red (cayenne) pepper, and granulated garlic

Canola oil for deep-frying, heated to 350 degrees

Minced flat-leaf parsley as garnish

Crawfish Cream

4 tablespoons unsalted butter

1 pound boiled crawfish tails

1 pound tiny button mushrooms, or cut larger ones into four quarters

2 French shallots, minced

1 large red bell pepper, blistered, peeled, seeded, and cut into ½-inch dice (see "Basics")

1 tablespoon minced flat-leaf parsley

1 teaspoon minced fresh thyme

¼ teaspoon red (cayenne) pepper

1 cup seafood stock (see "Basics")

1 cup chicken stock (see "Basics")

2 cups whipping cream

Salt and freshly ground black pepper to taste

2 tablespoons Beurre Manié (see "Basics")

Prepare the Crawfish Cream first. Melt the butter in a heavy 12-inch skillet over medium heat. Add the crawfish tails, mushrooms, shallots, red pepper, parsley, thyme, and red (cayenne) pepper. Sauté, stirring often, until mushroom liquid has evaporated, about 10 minutes. Add the seafood stock and chicken stock; stir to scrape up any browned bits from bottom of skillet. Cook to reduce the liquid by about half. Stir in the whipping cream and season to taste with salt and black pepper. Bring the liquid to a boil and add the Beurre Manié. Stir rapidly until the sauce has thickened. Lower heat and keep warm while frying the fish.

To prepare the catfish fillets, pat dry on absorbent paper towels and dredge first in the seasoned flour, shaking off all excess flour. Next dip them in the egg mixture, coating well. Finally coat them well with the seasoned cornmeal, again shaking off any excess. Lower the fillets into the preheated oil and fry just until a golden crust forms, about 5 minutes. Do not crowd the pan. Do not overcook the fish. Drain on wire racks.

To serve, place 2 pieces of fish in the center of each serving plate and spoon a portion of the Crawfish Cream across the center of the fish toward the edges of the plate. Garnish with the minced parsley

❧ Serves 4.

SUGGESTED WINES

Alamosa Wine Cellars Viognier

Hidden Springs Winery Muscat Canelli

Messina Hof Gewürztraminer

Texas Hills Vineyard Pinot Grigio

FRIED CRAPPIE, BREAM, OR RED-EARED PERCH WITH HOMEMADE TARTAR SAUCE

*W*hen we're talking about these particular fish, we're talking about the epitome of fried fish. You really have to either be a fisherman or know a fisherman who will share to get any of these wonderful little critters, though. They are rarely sold in fish markets. They start to "run" in late winter and early spring in freshwater lakes. You can catch hundreds of them, and they're great little fighters even though they rarely weigh over a pound. The best way to cook them is whole. Just scale and gut them and cut off the heads. Pile the fried fish up on platters and serve with a big bowl of *Homemade Tartar Sauce*, which will keep in the refrigerator for up to a month. Oh, and don't forget lots of ice-cold Shiner Bock from the Spoetzle Brewery in Shiner.

24 crappie, bream, or red-eared perch, scaled, gutted, and heads removed

8 cups Seasoned Flour for Frying (see "Basics")

½ gallon buttermilk

8 cups yellow cornmeal, seasoned with the same seasonings as the flour

Canola oil for deep-drying, heated to 350 degrees

HOMEMADE TARTAR SAUCE

& **Makes 2 quarts.**

1 quart plus 1 cup mayonnaise

1⅓ cups dill relish

3 tablespoons sweet relish

1 cup finely chopped, pimento-stuffed green olives

1 medium onion, minced

¼ cup freshly squeezed lemon juice

2 teaspoons minced lemon zest

2 teaspoons salt

2 teaspoons freshly ground black pepper

2 teaspoons sugar

1 teaspoon red (cayenne) pepper, or to taste

Make the Homemade Tartar Sauce first. Combine all ingredients in a large bowl and whisk to blend well. Refrigerate until ready to use. The tartar sauce will taste best if made at least 8 hours before use.

To fry the fish, line baking sheets with parchment paper; set aside. Pat fish dry using absorbent paper towels. Dredge them first in the seasoned flour, coating well and shaking off all excess flour. Next dip them in the buttermilk, turning to coat well. Finally, roll them in the seasoned cornmeal, coating well and shaking off all excess. After breading each fish, lay it on a prepared baking sheet. When all are breaded, lower the fish into the preheated oil, a few at a time, and fry just until they turn golden brown, about 7 to 8 minutes. Drain on wire racks and keep warm while frying the remaining fish. Serve hot with plenty of Homemade Tartar Sauce.

& **Serves 6 to 8.**

MUSTARD-FRIED CATFISH FINGERS

*I*f you want a really good, fun dish for a summer patio party, then fire up the deep-fryer and give this one a try. The secret to the dish is to use fairly thin catfish fillets and to avoid overcooking them. As is true when deep-frying anything in large quantities, don't crowd the fryer. If too many pieces are added to the oil at one time, the temperature will drop and the fish will not fry quickly enough to form a good crust before the essential fluids of the fish seep out and the oil seeps in. The result is soggy, greasy fish. Always drain fried fish as soon as they come out of the oil. I like to use a wire cake or bread cooling rack set over a baking sheet. If you lay the fish on paper towels on a non-porous surface, the bottoms tend to steam and the crust will become soggy. Don't get fancy with the mustard here, either. Use just plain old hot-dog mustard. Shiner Bock Beer from the Spoetzle Brewery in Shiner is a good beverage with fried catfish if you prefer beer instead of wine.

4 pounds skinned catfish fillets

3 cups prepared yellow mustard

5 eggs, well beaten

4 large garlic cloves, minced

2¼ teaspoons Tabasco sauce

2 cups yellow cornmeal

2 cups corn flour (sold as Unseasoned Fish Fry)

2 cups Italian-seasoned breadcrumbs

2 teaspoons salt

2 teaspoons freshly ground black pepper

2 teaspoons Hungarian paprika

2 teaspoons granulated garlic

Canola oil for deep-frying, preheated to 350 degrees

Homemade Tartar Sauce (see recipe for Fried Crappie, Bream, or Red-Eared Perch with Homemade Tartar Sauce)

Pat the catfish fillets dry on absorbent paper towels. Using a sharp knife, cut the fillets into 1-inch-wide strips across the width of the fillet; set aside.

In a large bowl, combine mustard, eggs, garlic, and Tabasco sauce. Whisk to blend well. In another bowl, combine the cornmeal and remaining ingredients except canola oil and Homemade Tartar Sauce. Toss with a fork to blend well. Dredge the fish pieces in the mustard mixture, turning to coat well. Next dip them in the cornmeal mixture, coating well. Shake off all excess breading. Lower the breaded pieces into the preheated oil. Do not overcrowd the oil. Fry just until golden brown and crisp, about 3 to 4 minutes. Drain on wire racks. Repeat until all fish pieces have been cooked. Serve hot with Homemade Tartar Sauce.

ର Serves 6 to 8.

SUGGESTED WINES

Becker Vineyards Estate Bottled Fumé Blanc

Comfort Cellars Winery Comfort Blush

Delaney Vineyards and Winery Texas Champagne Brut

Texas Hills Vineyard Chardonnay

Tabasco Brine for Smoked Fish

Smoking is one of the best methods for cooking oily fish. Wahoo and Spanish mackerel are excellent choices, but you can also smoke small fish such as croakers or bream. My personal favorite is mullet. They're easy to catch with a cast net and are very tasty when smoked. In the Deep South smoked mullet are called "Biloxi Bacon," and they're great for a leisurely weekend breakfast or brunch with scrambled eggs. To properly smoke fish you need to have a smoker unit that is capable of cooking at low temperatures, around 115 degrees,

so that the fish is actually "cold-smoked." Cooking at higher temperatures on a barbecue grill will cook the fish too fast, and it will not have the taste and texture of a truly smoked fish. If you have a serious barbecue rig with a separate slow-cooking chamber on the opposite end of the firebox and a temperature gauge, it will make a great slow smoker. The fish should be smoked whole with the head and skin on. Just scale and gut them. The salt brine is a necessary step in slow-smoking fish because it draws the blood and excess fluids out of the fish, inhibiting the growth of bacteria during the low-temperature smoking process.

ର Makes 1 gallon.

1 gallon water

1½ cups sea salt or kosher salt

¾ cup firmly packed light brown sugar

2 tablespoons finely ground black pepper

3 tablespoons minced fresh tarragon or Mexican mint marigold leaves

5 fresh bay leaves, minced, or 4 dried bay leaves, crumbled

¼ cup Tabasco sauce

Combine all ingredients in a large, non-aluminum bowl and whisk to blend well and dissolve sugar and salt. Place the fish in a single layer in a pan large enough to hold them. Pour the brine over the fish to completely cover. Cover with plastic wrap and refrigerate for 5 hours.

Prepare fire in large barbecue pit or electric smoker. You may use whatever "flavor" of wood or wood chips you choose. My favorites are oak, apple, and pecan. If you use wood chips, be sure to soak them in water for an hour before using. Before you begin smoking the fish, make sure the temperature in the smoking chamber is between 100 and 115 degrees. Smoke the fish for about 4 hours, then increase the temperature of the fire to about 165 to 185 degrees and smoke for 2 more hours. Smoked fish can be served hot or cold.

SUGGESTED WINES

Alamosa Wine Cellars Rosato di Sangiovese

Cap*Rock Winery Topaz Royale

Comfort Cellars Winery Raisin Wine

Delaney Vineyards and Winery Merlot

Fall Creek Vineyards Granite Reserve Cabernet Sauvignon

CRISP ANGELS ON HORSEBACK

*T*hroughout culinary history we find records of oysters being served as a first course to meals—either raw on the half shell or cooked in various dishes. The succulent little bivalves are believed to enhance the appetite without filling the stomach. Perfect specifications for a first course!

16 oysters, drained

1 cup dry white wine, such as Chardonnay

1 teaspoon freshly ground black pepper

2 large garlic cloves, minced

8 applewood-smoked bacon slices, cut in half and pre-cooked just until the edges begin to curl and bacon is still flexible

Lemon and Caper Butter Sauce (see recipe for Broiled Red Snapper with Lemon and Caper Butter Sauce)

Seasoned Flour for Frying (see "Basics")

Canola oil for deep-frying, heated to 350 degrees

BATTER

2 cups all-purpose flour

2 eggs, beaten

½ teaspoon salt

¼ teaspoon red (cayenne) pepper

2 cups ice water

To marinate the oysters, pat them dry and place in a single layer in a non-aluminum baking dish. Combine the wine, black pepper, and garlic and pour over the oysters. Cover with plastic wrap and marinate, refrigerated, for 2 hours.

Remove oysters from marinade and pat dry on absorbent paper towels. Discard marinade. Wrap half a bacon slice around each oyster and secure with a toothpick; set aside.

Prepare the Lemon and Caper Butter Sauce.

Prepare the batter. Combine all ingredients except ice water and whisk until very smooth and well blended. Whisk in the ice water only when you are ready to fry the oysters. Dip the bacon-wrapped oysters in the seasoned flour, coating well and shaking off any excess flour. Dredge them in the batter, coating well, and immediately drop them in the preheated oil. Fry just until the batter is light golden brown, about 2 to 3 minutes. Drain on wire racks. Carefully remove the toothpicks and arrange four oysters on each serving plate. Spoon a portion of the Lemon and Caper Butter Sauce over each serving. Serve hot.

℘ **Serves 4 as a first course.**

SUGGESTED WINES

ALAMOSA WINE CELLARS ROSATO DI SANGIOVESE

COMFORT CELLARS WINERY CHENIN BLANC

DELANEY VINEYARDS AND WINERY
BARREL-FERMENTED CHARDONNAY

LA BUENA VIDA VINEYARDS SPRINGTOWN CHARDONNAY

East End Historic District, Galveston; Christmastime at Mission Espíritu Santo, Goliad (pages 104–105).

FLASH-FRIED OYSTERS ON SPINACH WITH ROASTED PEPPER SAUCE

I have a very serious relationship with oysters and am constantly creating new ways to enjoy them. I had a divine dish similar to this at The Nest, a wonderful restaurant in Fredericksburg in the Texas Hill Country. This is the perfect first course for a nice evening meal. The secret to its success is to avoid overcooking the oysters—"flash" them in the hot oil just until a crust forms. The sauce can be made in advance and reheated just before serving.

1 pint oysters, liquor reserved

5 egg whites, beaten until frothy

2 cups dry breadcrumbs, seasoned with 2 teaspoons minced cilantro, 1 teaspoon ground cumin, 1 teaspoon granulated garlic, 1 teaspoon salt, and ½ teaspoon freshly ground black pepper

3 bunches fresh spinach leaves, washed and patted dry

8 green onions, trimmed and sliced into thin matchstick strips 2 inches long

Canola oil for deep-frying, heated to 350 degrees

ROASTED PEPPER SAUCE

4 red bell peppers, roasted, peeled, and seeded (see "Basics")

3½ cups chicken stock (see "Basics")

½ cup liquor from oysters

1 teaspoon Tabasco sauce

1 cup whipping cream

1 tablespoon minced cilantro

2 teaspoons cornstarch

1 tablespoon cold water

Prepare the Roasted Pepper Sauce. Roughly chop the roasted peppers and puree them in blender with the chicken stock. Transfer puree to a 3-quart saucepan and add oyster liquor. Simmer for about 30 minutes to reduce and concentrate. Stir in the Tabasco sauce, whipping cream, and cilantro. Bring to a rapid boil. Combine the cornstarch and cold water, stirring to form a smooth slurry. When sauce is boiling, whisk in the slurry and cook just to thicken, about 1 minute. Remove from heat, set aside, and keep warm.

To prepare the oysters, pat them very dry on absorbent paper towels. Dip them first in the beaten egg whites, one at a time, then into the seasoned breadcrumbs, coating well and shaking off excess crumbs. Deep-fry the oysters just until a golden crust forms, about 1½ to 2 minutes. (Do not fry too many oysters at one time, or the temperature of the oil will drop.) Drain on wire racks; set aside and keep warm. Working quickly, place the slices of green onion in a fine-meshed strainer and lower the strainer into the hot oil. Fry the strips until golden brown and crisp, about 2 minutes. Turn out onto absorbent paper towels to drain.

Spoon a portion of the sauce onto each serving plate, covering the bottom. Arrange some of the spinach leaves on each plate. Top with the fried oysters and scatter the fried green onion strips over each plate. Serve hot.

❧ Serves 4 to 6.

SUGGESTED WINES

HIDDEN SPRINGS WINERY BLUSH

LLANO ESTACADO WINERY PASSIONELLE

SISTER CREEK VINEYARDS CHARDONNAY

TEXAS HILLS VINEYARD PINOT GRIGIO

Fish market, Seabrook (upper right)

OYSTER FACTS

Jonathan Swift stated, "He was a bold man that first ate an oyster." Eating one's first oyster has been described as a "gastronomic loss of virginity."

Oysters are bivalve mollusks that grow in brackish (slightly salty) to salt water. Oysters harvested from fresher, brackish waters are called "sweet" oysters. Those from salty waters are called "salty" oysters. Most people prefer the taste of salty oysters. The oyster feeds on tiny, microscopic plankton that it filters out of the water. A single oyster will siphon up to 40 gallons of water a day through its body while filtering out its food supply. It's easy to understand why oysters are so susceptible to contamination from pollution!

When buying oysters in their shells, be sure they're alive—the shell will be tightly closed. When you open an oyster, if the meat is dry and no liquor is present, or if there is an off-odor, discard it. The oyster itself should be plump and full of liquid. The color is usually creamy tan, but it can vary with the season. In the cool season, oysters are tan and referred to as "fat." During the late spring and summer months the tissues become clear and watery.

Many people still believe that oysters can only be eaten in months containing the letter "R" in their names, but they can be safely eaten any time of the year. Like most seafood, oysters are highly perishable and, in the days when refrigeration and transportation were poor or nonexistent, they spoiled quickly in the hot summer months, which, of course, have no "R." Green and sienna-hued pigmentation in oysters is harmless. However, if the meat is pinkish-colored and has an off-odor, bacteria are present. Discard such oysters.

When buying shucked oysters, be sure they're packed in their natural liquor, which should be viscous and clear, with a delicate aroma. When properly stored in their liquor, at 34 to 38 degrees, shucked oysters will keep for up to two weeks. Check the dates on the containers when you purchase them. Live oysters in the shell must be stored at 34 to 38 degrees. They should stay alive for about a week, but the longer they're kept, the less liquor they will have. Never put live oysters in sealed containers or they will suffocate. Never allow them to come in contact with fresh water, which would kill them.

OYSTERS ON THE HALF SHELL WITH CILANTRO-CHILI SAUCE

This baked half-shell oyster dish is one of my favorites. Asian foods have gained immense popularity in Texas in the last ten to fifteen years. Many of the exotic ingredients used in these cuisines have been "borrowed" by chefs for use in other types of food. The resulting blend of various ethnic and native ingredients has been labeled "Fusion Cooking." It's exciting and delicious.

24 oysters on the half shell, liquor drained and reserved

Rock salt

6 large garlic cloves, minced

2 heaping tablespoons minced cilantro

4 green onions, minced, including green tops

2 tablespoons sugar

⅓ cup Oriental chili paste with garlic

½ teaspoon minced lime zest

⅓ cup freshly squeezed lime juice

⅓ cup Thai or Vietnamese fish sauce (see "The Texas Cook's Pantry")

1½ tablespoons minced pickled ginger

Line a baking sheet with rock salt and nest the oysters in their shells in the salt. Refrigerate until ready to use. Combine the reserved oyster liquor and all remaining ingredients in a large bowl. Whisk vigorously to blend well and dissolve the sugar. Allow mixture to sit at room temperature for 1 hour. Preheat oven to 350 degrees.

When ready to bake the oysters, spoon a generous portion of the sauce over each oyster. Bake in preheated oven for 15 minutes, or until sauce is bubbly and oysters are curled around the edges. Serve 6 oysters per person on plates lined with the hot rock salt.

ଔ **Serves 4 as a first course.**

SUGGESTED WINES

FALL CREEK VINEYARDS SAUVIGNON BLANC

HAAK VINEYARDS AND WINERY
BARREL-FERMENTED CHARDONNAY

HIDDEN SPRINGS WINERY MUSCAT CANELLI

SPICEWOOD VINEYARDS SAUVIGNON BLANC

TEXAS HILLS VINEYARD MOSCATO

MESQUITE-SMOKED OYSTERS

In Texas just about anything goes on the barbecue pit. If it can't be grilled, smoked, or barbecued, it's probably not any good anyway. I love oysters, so I just had to try them over mesquite. Mmmmm. They were keepers.

24 oysters on the half shell and their liquor

½ cup unsalted butter, melted

Dash of liquid smoke

2 medium garlic cloves, minced

1½ tablespoons minced sun-dried tomatoes

⅛ teaspoon ground cumin

2 teaspoons minced fresh cilantro

2 teaspoons fresh lime juice

1 teaspoon Worcestershire sauce

¼ teaspoon ground black pepper

Salt to taste

Prepare a mesquite charcoal fire in a smoker pit with a lid. Let the fire burn down until coals are white.

Drain the liquor from the oysters into a heavy saucepan. Add remaining ingredients except salt and cook just to heat. Add salt to taste. Arrange the oysters in the shells on a baking sheet and spoon a potion of the sauce over each. Place the baking sheet on rack in pit and smoke just until oysters are opaque, about 15 to 20 minutes. Serve hot.

ଔ **Serves 4.**

Jetty fishing, Port Bolivar (left)

BAKED OYSTERS IN SPICED TOMATO SAUCE

This light and zesty dish is perfect for the cocktail hour or as a first course. To make preparation easier on the day you wish to serve them, prepare the Spiced Tomato Sauce in advance and refrigerate.

24 live oysters
4 ounces imported proscuitto, minced
Shredded Parmesan cheese
Rock salt

SPICED TOMATO SAUCE

ca **Makes 2 cups.**

1 16-ounce can Italian-style tomatoes, juice reserved
¼ cup extra-virgin olive oil
1 small onion, finely chopped
3 large garlic cloves, minced
½ of a green bell pepper, finely chopped
1 tablespoon minced fresh basil
¾ teaspoon dried leaf oregano
1 tablespoon minced flat-leaf parsley
1 small bay leaf, minced
2 teaspoons freshly squeezed lemon juice
1 teaspoon Worcestershire sauce
½ teaspoon freshly ground black pepper
½ teaspoon salt
2 teaspoons crushed red pepper flakes

Shuck the oysters and discard the flat top shells. Drain off and reserve the oyster liquor. Set oysters aside.

To make the Spiced Tomato Sauce, place tomatoes and their juice in work bowl of food processor fitted with steel blade; puree until smooth. Set aside. Heat olive oil in a heavy 10-inch skillet over medium heat. Sauté onion, garlic, bell pepper, basil, oregano, parsley, and bay leaf until onion is wilted and transparent, about 5 minutes. Stir in the tomato puree and reserved oyster liquor. Add lemon juice, Worcestershire sauce, black pepper, salt, and red pepper flakes. Cook over medium heat, stirring occasionally, until sauce has thickened, about 15 to 20 minutes. Taste for seasonings; adjust if needed. Set aside.

Preheat oven to 400 degrees. Line 2 baking sheets with rock salt. Nest the oysters in their shells in the rock salt. Top each oyster with a portion of the sauce. Scatter minced proscuitto and shredded Parmesan cheese over the sauce. Bake in preheated oven until cheese is golden and sauce is bubbly, about 10 minutes. Serve hot.

ca **Serves 4.**

SUGGESTED WINES

BECKER VINEYARDS ESTATE BOTTLED FUMÉ BLANC
CAP*ROCK VINTNER'S RED
DELANEY VINEYARDS AND WINERY
BARREL-FERMENTED CHARDONNAY
MESSINA HOF WINE CELLARS "TEX-ZIN" ZINFANDEL

Facing page: Mesquite-Smoked Oysters (upper left); Baked Oysters in Spiced Tomato Sauce (top right); Oysters on the Half Shell with Cilantro-Chili Sauce (lower).

BOILED STONE CRAB CLAWS WITH TWO SAUCES

*S*tone crab claws are just too good to describe. I don't know of a word that even comes close to defining the sweet, succulent taste of those fat, meaty chunks of crustacean glory. The best source for stone crab claws, of course, is to trap them yourself. Remember when you do catch stone crabs in your crab trap that you can only keep the large right claw. Just twist it off and put the big guy back in the water to grow another one—and keep only those that measure 2½ inches from the tip of the immovable claw to the first joint. Rush them to the boiling pot without putting them on ice, if possible. If they've been iced before boiling, the meat will stick to the shell and you will really have to dig to get it out. But trust me, they're worth the trouble if you have to purchase them on ice from the seafood market. Be sure to have some crab claw crackers or wooden mallets handy when you plan to serve them. One of my favorite summer meals is to invite a crowd, boil up a bunch of blue crabs and stone crab claws with vegetables, spread newspapers on the patio tables, and just dump the drained crabs and veggies in the middle. Shiner Bock from the Spoetzle Brewery is always a good bet with boiled seafood. Oh, what a feast!

2 cups Zatarin's granulated crab boil, or your personal favorite

12 small red new potatoes

4 fresh ears of corn, each chopped into 3 pieces

24 large stone crab claws

12 small yellow onions

MUSTARD SAUCE

ભ **Makes about 2 cups.**

¾ cup whole-grain mustard

1 cup mayonnaise

2 tablespoons prepared horseradish

2 teaspoons Oriental chili paste with garlic

1 tablespoon minced pickled ginger

DRAWN BUTTER SAUCE

ભ **Makes about 3 cups.**

3½ cups (7 sticks) unsalted butter

1 large garlic clove, crushed with blade of chef's knife

1 teaspoon minced lemon zest

1 tablespoon fresh lemon juice

Salt to taste

Prepare the Mustard Sauce by combining all ingredients in work bowl of food processor fitted with steel blade. Process until smooth. Refrigerate until ready to serve.

To make the Drawn Butter Sauce, clarify the butter by melting it in a heavy 3-quart saucepan over medium heat. Bring the butter to a rapid boil and allow it to boil for about 2 minutes, then remove from heat and set aside. Skim off the foam that rises to the top. When the milky solids have settled to the bottom of the butter, carefully pour off the clear butter. Discard the milky portion at the bottom of the pan.

Place the clarified butter in a saucepan and add remaining ingredients. Simmer gently for 5 minutes. Strain the sauce through a fine strainer; set aside and keep warm.

To prepare the crabs, fill a 12- to 15-quart soup pot three-fourths full of water and put on burner over high heat. Add the crab boil and bring to a rolling boil. When the water is boiling, add the whole potatoes, corn, and crab claws. Boil for 10 minutes, then add the onions. Boil an additional 10 minutes. Drain and serve with the two sauces.

ભ **Serves 4.**

SUGGESTED WINES

COMFORT CELLARS WINERY COMFORT BLUSH

HAAK VINEYARDS AND WINERY SAUVIGNON BLANC

TEXAS HILLS VINEYARD DUE BIANCO

CRAB-STUFFED PORTABELLO MUSHROOMS

Portabello mushrooms, those giant brown beauties, made their debut on the restaurant market in the 1990s and have now become fairly standard items in supermarkets. They have a fabulous, rich flavor and a meaty texture. When selecting portabellos, look for light tan caps, rounded and with a nubby texture and slightly uneven edges. The gills will be very visible on the underside. Flat, dark, wrinkled caps indicate that the mushroom is more mature. Don't pass these by, however, if you love a really intense mushroom taste. Store the mushrooms in paper bags, never plastic, and wipe them with a barely damp paper towel to clean. This sinfully rich dish makes an ideal first course for a meal.

4 medium portabello mushrooms (about 4 inches in diameter)

Olive oil, salt, and freshly ground black pepper for glazing mushrooms

1 pound lump crabmeat

½ cup (1 stick) unsalted butter

2 teaspoons Chef Paul's Seafood Magic or other Cajun-style seafood seasoning

¾ teaspoon freshly ground black pepper

¼ teaspoon red (cayenne) pepper, or to taste

1 teaspoon granulated garlic

2 teaspoons minced fresh parsley

1 large red bell pepper, blistered, peeled, and chopped (see "Basics")

6 ounces Monterey Jack cheese, shredded

Heat a gas grill until hot. Remove the stems from the mushrooms and discard. Brush mushroom caps liberally with olive oil inside and out; season with salt and pepper on both sides. Grill until well marked and slightly softened, turning once, about 3 to 4 minutes per side. Set aside. Preheat oven to 350 degrees.

Pick through the crabmeat to remove any bits of shell or cartilage; set aside. Melt the butter in a heavy 12-inch skillet over medium heat. Add the Seafood Magic, black pepper, red pepper, and granulated garlic. Cook, stirring often, until butter has browned slightly, about 4 minutes. Stir in the parsley and chopped bell pepper. Remove skillet from heat and stir in the crabmeat, coating well with the buttery sauce.

Place the grilled mushrooms on a shallow baking sheet. Divide the crabmeat mixture and butter sauce among the mushrooms. Top each with a portion of the cheese, using all the cheese. Place baking sheet in preheated oven and cook just until the cheese has melted. Transfer to individual serving plates and serve hot.

ᑫ Serves 4.

SUGGESTED WINES

BECKER VINEYARDS VIOGNIER

CAP*ROCK WINERY RESERVE TOSCANO ROSSO

DRY COMAL CREEK VINEYARDS WHITE VERITAGE

FALL CREEK VINEYARDS CHENIN BLANC

HAAK VINEYARDS AND WINERY BLANC DU BOIS

TEXAS HILLS VINEYARD PINOT GRIGIO

CRABMEAT TOSTADO

This dish is just what the body needs on a hot and humid summer's day. It combines the robust flavors of Tex-Mex seasonings, the cool crispness of jicama, and the sweetness of blue crab meat. Paired with Terlingua Tortilla Soup or Poblano Chili Bisque, it makes a big hit when served around the pool at lunchtime. The Jicama Slaw is a great summer treat when used as a side dish with other entrées. I find the flesh of this odd vegetable to have a "cooling" effect on the palate. The jicama is an underground tuber that originated in Mexico. It was taken to the Philippines by the Spanish conquistadors in the seventeenth century. Its use has since spread across Asia and the Pacific. It has crunchy, ivory flesh and a slightly sweet, bland flavor that pairs well, cooked or raw, with fruit or shellfish.

1 pound lump crabmeat

Crabmeat Dressing (see recipe below)

4 white corn tortillas, fried until crisp and drained on absorbent paper towels

Jicama Slaw (see recipe below)

Green (tomatillo-based) picante sauce or salsa

CRABMEAT DRESSING

Makes about ¾ cup.

½ cup mayonnaise

3 tablespoons sour cream

¾ teaspoon sugar

¾ teaspoon curry powder

1 teaspoon ground cumin

¼ teaspoon red (cayenne) pepper

⅓ cup whipping cream

Salt to taste

JICAMA SLAW

1 small jicama, peeled and cut into matchstick strips

1 package prepared coleslaw mix

1 small green bell pepper, finely chopped

1 small red bell pepper, finely chopped

1 Roma tomato, finely diced

2 tablespoons finely chopped onion

1 ear of fresh corn, roasted until browned, kernels removed from cob

1 tablespoon minced cilantro

1 jalapeño, seeds and veins removed, minced

SLAW DRESSING

¼ cup mayonnaise

2 tablespoons sugar

1 tablespoon red picante sauce

⅛ teaspoon granulated garlic

¼ teaspoon freshly ground black pepper

2 teaspoons chili powder

1 teaspoon ground cumin

1 teaspoon Tabasco sauce

1 teaspoon minced lime zest

1 tablespoon freshly squeezed lime juice

Prepare the Crabmeat Dressing. Combine all ingredients in medium bowl and whisk to blend well. Taste for seasoning and adjust as needed. Refrigerate, tightly covered, for 8 hours.

Prepare the Jicama Slaw. Combine all slaw ingredients in a large bowl. Make the Slaw Dressing by whisking together all ingredients in a separate bowl. Add dressing to slaw and toss to blend well. Refrigerate, well covered, until ready to use.

To assemble the tostados, carefully pick through the crabmeat to remove any bits of shell or cartilage. Stir the Crabmeat Dressing into crabmeat.

Place a fried tortilla on each serving plate. Top with a portion of the Jicama Slaw, then a mound of the crabmeat. Drizzle a portion of the green picante sauce over the top.

ca Serves 4.

SUGGESTED WINES

ALAMOSA WINE CELLARS FUMÉ BLANC

DELANEY VINEYARDS AND WINERY TEXAS CHAMPAGNE BRUT

HAAK VINEYARDS AND WINERY SAUVIGNON BLANC

SPICEWOOD VINEYARDS CHARDONNAY

FRIED SOFT-SHELL CRABS WITH CHIPOTLE CHILI KETCHUP

Soft-shell crabs are one of the greatest delicacies on the Gulf Coast. As the blue crab grows, it must shed its shell and grow a bigger one. When soft-shell crabbers recognize the signs of a crab about to burst from its shell, they put the crab in special holding pens until the old shell is shed. Then the crab is sold before the new shell starts to harden. And, yes, you eat the whole thing, except for the gills or "dead man's fingers," which must be removed.

8 to 12 medium to large soft-shell crabs

Seasoned Flour for Frying (see "Basics")

Egg wash made from 5 eggs beaten into 8 cups milk

Japanese (panko) breadcrumbs, seasoned liberally with Chef Paul's Seafood Magic or your favorite Cajun seafood seasoning

Canola oil for deep-frying, heated to 350 degrees

CHIPOTLE CHILI KETCHUP

2 tablespoons canola oil

2 large red bell peppers, seeded and diced

1 medium onion, chopped

3 large garlic cloves, minced

5 large Roma tomatoes, chopped

⅓ cup Champagne vinegar

⅓ cup sugar

¼ cup firmly packed chipotle chilies in adobo sauce, chilies and sauce included

Prepare the Chipotle Chili Ketchup. Heat the canola oil in a heavy 4-quart saucepan over medium-high heat. When oil is hot, add the red bell peppers, onions, garlic, and tomatoes. Cook, stirring often, until vegetables are very wilted, about 25 minutes. Add the vinegar and sugar and cook, stirring often, until sugar has dissolved and liquid is reduced, about 25 minutes. Transfer the mixture to a blender. Add the chipotle chilies and adobo sauce; puree until smooth. Return to heat and simmer the mixture gently for about 30 minutes, or until thickened and deep red in color. Refrigerate until well chilled.

To fry the crabs, snip off the eyes using kitchen shears. Lift the outer pointed flaps of the top shells on both sides and pull off the spongy pointed gills ("dead man's fingers") on each side. Lower the shells back down on top of the crabs. Pat the crabs very dry on absorbent paper towels. Dredge in the seasoned flour, turning to coat well; shake off all excess flour. Next dip the crabs in the egg wash, coating well. Finally dredge them in the seasoned Japanese breadcrumbs, pressing the crumbs into each crab. Shake off all excess crumbs. Fry the crabs in the preheated oil just until they turn medium golden brown, turning often. Fry in batches and do not crowd the deep fryer. Drain crabs on wire cooling rack fitted over baking sheet. Serve hot with the chilled Chipotle Chili Ketchup for dipping.

Serves 4 to 6.

SUGGESTED WINES

CAP*ROCK WINERY CABERNET ROYALE, ROSÉ OF CABERNET SAUVIGNON

DRY COMAL CREEK VINEYARDS SAUVIGNON BLANC

LA BUENA VIDA VINEYARDS SPRINGTOWN MERLOT L'ELEGANCE

MESSINA HOF WINE CELLARS BARREL RESERVE SAUVIGNON BLANC

TEXAS HILLS VINEYARD SANGIOVESE

JAPANESE BREADCRUMBS

Japanese (panko) breadcrumbs make a wonderful, crisp coating for foods to be fried. The crust will stay crisp far longer than regular flour or cornmeal crusts. Because the crisp crumbs have literally no flavor of their own, they readily adopt the flavor of whatever seasonings you use. Panko breadcrumbs can be used to bread just about anything you want to fry—from quail to catfish to shrimp. They can be purchased in Asian markets or specialty food markets.

Crabhouse, Kemah

GRILLED HOT PEPPER CRABS WITH GINGER AND GARLIC

This dish is a great one for summertime gatherings in the back forty with friends. They're spicy, messy to eat, and worth every minute of the trouble. To moderate the heat, cut down on the number of dried chilies in the marinade. Oh, and be sure that the crabs are all completely stunned by the ice-water bath before you try to handle them!

18 live blue crabs, held in an ice-water bath until stunned and completely inactive

MARINADE

12 cups canola oil

20 dried arbol chilies, coarsely chopped, including seeds

1 cup minced pickled ginger

1 large head of garlic, cloves peeled and chopped

1 tablespoon salt

Prepare the marinade by combining all ingredients in an 8-quart soup pot over medium heat. Cook, stirring occasionally, for about 30 minutes, or until garlic is completely soft and the oil is very aromatic. Remove oil from heat and allow it to stand overnight. It should be reddish and very spicy. Strain the oil, discarding solids. Set aside.

To prepare the crabs, remove them, one at a time, from the ice-water bath. Working quickly (before they get warm and frisky), remove the top shell from the crab and rinse under running water to remove all fat and intestines. Lift the outer pointed flaps of the top shells on both sides and pull off the spongy pointed gills ("dead man's fingers") on each side. Then break the crab in half. Repeat with remaining crabs. Place the crabs in a single layer in large, shallow baking dishes. Pour the marinade over the crabs. Turn crabs over several times to coat well. Cover with plastic wrap and refrigerate for 2 hours.

Preheat gas grill to medium-high. Remove crabs from the marinade and grill, turning often with long tongs. Cook for about 8 to 10 minutes, or until meat is opaque and shells are lightly charred. The grill will flare when the oil from the marinade drops onto the flame, so take caution with loose clothing and bare hands.

Serve the crabs hot with crab-cracking tools or small wooden mallets. And lots of napkins.

ॐ **Serves 6.**

SUGGESTED WINES

BECKER VINEYARDS ESTATE BOTTLED CHARDONNAY

DRY COMAL CREEK VINEYARDS SAUVIGNON BLANC

LLANO ESTACADO WINERY CHARDONNAY

MESSINA HOF WINE CELLARS GEWÜRZTRAMINER

Victorian commercial facades of The Strand, Galveston

MATAGORDA DEVILED CRAB

*E*ast Matagorda Bay, accessible from Sargent, is a favorite spot with Gulf Coast fishermen. When conditions are right, you can catch the big reds and specs. (That's redfish and speckled trout for the landlubbers.) You can also set out a couple of crab traps for the weekend and catch yourself a nice mess of blue crabs. When we have more crabs than we know what to do with, I like to make up a dozen or so of these zesty deviled crabs to go in the freezer for those times when I'm craving crab and there's no time to go catch them. After crabs have been boiled and picked, scrub the top shells clean with a brush and put them through the top rack of the dishwasher. If you don't have crab shells, you can spoon the stuffing into individual casserole dishes to bake and serve.

8 ounces lump crabmeat

8 ounces claw crabmeat

2 eggs, well beaten

⅔ cup evaporated milk

4 French bread slices (1 inch thick)

½ cup (1 stick) unsalted butter

1 medium onion

2 celery stalks, chopped

1 large green bell pepper, chopped

4 large garlic cloves, minced

1 tablespoon Worcestershire sauce

2 tablespoons dry sherry

½ teaspoon freshly ground black pepper

1 teaspoon red (cayenne) pepper

Salt to taste

4 green onions, chopped

¼ cup minced flat-leaf parsley

1½ cups (6 ounces) shredded Pepper-Jack cheese

12 cleaned crab shells, if available

Dry breadcrumbs tossed with a small amount of melted butter

Preheat oven to 350 degrees. Carefully pick through the crabmeat; remove and discard any bits of shell and cartilage. Set aside. In a medium bowl, whisk the eggs and milk together until well blended. Tear the French bread slices into small pieces

and stir into the egg mixture. Set aside. In a heavy 12-inch skillet over medium heat, melt the butter. Sauté onion, celery, bell pepper, and garlic, stirring often, until vegetables are wilted, about 10 minutes. Add Worcestershire sauce, sherry, black pepper, cayenne, salt, and crabmeat. Simmer for 10 minutes. Add green onions and parsley, stirring to blend well. Remove from heat and fold in the bread and egg mixture and the shredded cheese. Divide the mixture among the cleaned crab shells. Arrange filled shells on baking sheets. Scatter some of the breadcrumbs over the tops. Bake in preheated oven until golden brown and bubbly on top, about 20 to 25 minutes. Serve hot.

ଔ **Makes 12 stuffed crabs.**

SUGGESTED WINES

BECKER VINEYARDS FUMÉ BLANC ESTATE BOTTLED

FALL CREEK VINEYARDS CASCADE
SEMILLON/SAUVIGNON BLANC

LLANO ESTACADO WINERY CHENIN BLANC

MESSINA HOF WINE CELLARS GEWÜRZTRAMINER

GRILLED KING CRAB LEGS WITH BAYOU BUTTER

*A*lthough native to the icy North Pacific waters, Alaskan king crab legs have become very popular with Texans. The king crab is one of the largest members of the entire crab family, which includes over a thousand species! The largest king crab on record weighed 25 pounds and measured six feet from claw to claw. It was probably a mistake on the part of nature that they wound up in Alaska. Any crab that big should live in Texas! King crab legs are generally served steamed, accompanied by a drawn butter sauce. This dish takes the giant, meaty crustaceans to a Texas Grilled level of dining excitement. The legs are cracked, then dipped in a spicy butter sauce with Cajun undertones and grilled. Decidedly different and certainly a favorite.

10 pounds large king crab legs, cracked

BAYOU BUTTER

    4 cups (8 sticks) unsalted butter
    ½ cup Chef Paul's Seafood Magic (see "The Texas
       Cook's Pantry")
    1 tablespoon freshly ground black pepper
    ½ teaspoon red (cayenne) pepper
    2 teaspoons granulated garlic

Prepare the Bayou Butter. Melt butter in a heavy 4-quart sauce-pan over medium heat. Add remaining ingredients and let the mixture boil for 10 minutes. Remove from heat and set aside.

Heat gas grill to medium-hot. Pour the Bayou Butter in a large bowl and dip the crab legs in the butter mixture. Place legs directly on hot grill and cover them with a large metal mixing bowl. Baste and turn often with long tongs. (The bowl on top creates steam, which self-bastes the crabmeat.) Cook for about 25 minutes. Serve on a large platter with individual side dishes of the Bayou Butter for dipping. Have crab-cracking tools or small wooden mallets for guests to use.

ଓ **Serves 6 to 8.**

SUGGESTED WINES

Cap*Rock Winery Topaz Royale

Haak Vineyards and Winery Sauvignon Blanc

Llano Estacado Winery Chardonnay

Messina Hof Wine Cellars Barrel Reserve
Sauvignon Blanc

Sister Creek Vineyards Pinot Noir

Spicewood Vineyards Chardonnay

FINGER-LICKIN' SPICY PEPPERED SHRIMP

*T*his is one of my favorite foods to serve for informal dinners. I say "informal" because the shrimp are cooked in their shells and eaten with the fingers. It's one of those roll-up-your-sleeves dinners. When we serve the dish at the lodge, we give each diner a bib! They are spicy and buttery and addictive. Serve with some good French bread for sopping up the spicy sauce. And lots of napkins!

    1 cup olive oil
    4 cups (8 sticks) unsalted butter
 1½ cups seafood stock (see "Basics")
    8 large garlic cloves, minced
    5 fresh bay leaves, minced
    1 tablespoon minced fresh rosemary
    1 heaping teaspoon minced fresh basil
    1 teaspoon dried Mexican oregano
    ¾ teaspoon red (cayenne) pepper
 1½ teaspoons freshly grated nutmeg
    1 tablespoon Hungarian paprika
    ⅓ cup finely ground black pepper
    ⅓ cup freshly squeezed lemon juice
 1½ teaspoons salt, or to taste
    5 pounds large (16 to 20 count) unpeeled shrimp

Heat the olive oil in a heavy 8-quart Dutch oven over medium heat. Add the butter and cook to melt it. Add all remaining ingredients except shrimp. Cook, stirring occasionally, for 25 minutes, to brown the butter slightly. Stir in the shrimp and blend them into the buttery sauce. Cook, stirring often, until shrimp are done and have turned a rich coral pink, about 25 minutes. Do not overcook.

To serve, divide the shrimp among individual serving bowls. Ladle an ample portion of the buttery sauce into each bowl.

ଓ **Serves 6 to 8.**

SUGGESTED WINES

Delaney Vineyards and Winery Texas Claret

Hidden Springs Winery Sauvignon Blanc

Messina Hof Wine Cellars Gewürztraminer

Sister Creek Vineyards Pinot Noir

SEARED SHRIMP IN BASIL CREAM SAUCE OVER PASTA

This is a great dish to serve when you don't have much time but you need an impressive entrée. Buy the small peeled and deveined shrimp and fresh pasta to help speed things up. Pair the dish with a salad and pick up some good bread at the bakery. Presto! You're in business. This dish contains another of my favorite chef's "secret ingredients"—Pernod. This anise-flavored liqueur, when used in moderation, can add a really exciting and mysterious taste element to sauces. Remember that moderation is the key word here. Pernod has an aggressive taste and can easily overpower the other flavors in your dish if used with a heavy hand. Cook the pasta al dente (in Italian, "to the tooth," meaning that the cooked pasta will provide slight resistance to the teeth). Pasta will continue to cook even after it has been drained, so when in doubt, it's best to err on the side of undercooking.

2½ pounds small (70 to 90 count) shrimp, peeled and deveined

Chef Paul's Seafood Magic seasoning or other spicy seafood seasoning

Olive oil for searing the shrimp

Your favorite pasta, cooked al dente and drained

Shredded Asiago cheese

BASIL CREAM SAUCE

¼ cup extra-virgin olive oil

3 medium garlic cloves, minced

¼ cup minced fresh basil

2 large red bell peppers, blistered, peeled, and cut into ½-inch dice (see "Basics")

2 tablespoons minced oil-packed sun-dried tomatoes

1 tablespoon Pernod, or to taste

3 cups seafood stock (see "Basics")

3 cups whipping cream

Salt and freshly ground black pepper to taste

3 tablespoons Beurre Manié (see "Basics")

1 teaspoon Tabasco sauce

Wash the shrimp in a colander; shake off excess water. Pat shrimp very dry using absorbent paper towels. Season the shrimp liberally with the seafood seasoning. Heat a thin layer of olive oil in a heavy 12-inch skillet over high heat until very hot. Add the shrimp in 4 batches, searing quickly while stirring (they will not be completely cooked). Set aside and repeat until all shrimp have been seared, adding additional olive oil if needed. Set shrimp aside.

Return the same pan to the heat and add the ¼ cup olive oil over medium heat. Sauté the garlic, basil, diced red bell pepper, and sun-dried tomatoes for about 5 minutes, stirring frequently. Add the Pernod and stir to blend well. Add the stock, stirring to scrape up any browned bits from bottom of skillet. Cook, stirring occasionally, until stock is reduced by half. Add the whipping cream; blend well. Stir in the reserved seared shrimp and season to taste with salt and freshly ground black pepper. Taste for Pernod, adding more if desired (the Pernod taste should be subtle). Simmer slowly for 20 minutes. Bring the mixture to a full rolling boil and whisk in a small amount of the Beurre Manié in small batches. Allow each batch to dissolve and thicken before adding the next. Use just enough to thicken to a good sauce consistency. Stir in Tabasco sauce.

To serve, place a portion of the cooked pasta in each pasta plate and top with a portion of the shrimp and sauce. Scatter shredded Asiago cheese over the top and serve hot.

ᑫ **Serves 4 to 6.**

SUGGESTED WINES

ALAMOSA WINE CELLARS ROSATO DI SANGIOVESE

FALL CREEK VINEYARDS CHARDONNAY

SISTER CREEK VINEYARDS PINOT NOIR

TEXAS HILLS VINEYARD DUE BIANCO

Port of Houston (facing page, top); Fishing at Rollover Pass, Bolivar Peninsula (facing page, bottom).

SAUTÉING

THE WORD <u>SAUTÉ</u> COMES FROM THE FRENCH VERB <u>SAUTER</u>, WHICH MEANS, LITERALLY TRANSLATED, "TO JUMP." THAT'S EXACTLY WHAT SHOULD BE HAPPENING TO THE FOODS IN THE PAN WHEN YOU ARE SAUTÉING THEM. THE FAT SHOULD BE HOT ENOUGH THAT WHEN YOU ADD THE FOODS, THEY JUMP AND SIZZLE IN THE PAN. SAUTÉING IS A FAST, HIGH-HEAT FORM OF COOKING OF SHORT DURATION. IF THE FAT IS NOT HOT ENOUGH WHEN THE FOODS ARE ADDED TO THE PAN, OR IF THE PAN IS TOO SMALL TO COOK THE FOODS IN A SINGLE LAYER, THEY DON'T REALLY SAUTÉ, THEY WILL JUST STEAM IN THEIR OWN JUICES. THERE IS A TASTE DIFFERENCE BETWEEN SOMETHING SAUTÉED AND SOMETHING STEAMED. NOTHING CAN REPLACE THE TASTE OF THE QUICK SEARING WHICH A TRUE SAUTÉ WILL IMPART TO FOODS.

Broiled Shrimp with Lemongrass Pesto, Feta Cheese, and Green Onions

Lemongrass is one of those marvelous herbs that we have borrowed from Southeast Asian cooking. I love to use it in any dish in which I want a really intense lemon flavor. The herb is easy to grow in pots; it is also available in Asian markets. When using lemongrass, use only the lower, white portion and discard the long green tops.

16 large (16 to 20 count) shrimp, peeled, deveined, and butterflied

Lemongrass Pesto (see recipe below)

4 green onions, chopped, including green tops

4 ounces feta cheese, crumbled

Lemongrass Pesto

3 medium garlic cloves, peeled

1 cup firmly packed cilantro sprigs (stems and leaves), coarsely chopped

1 large serrano chili, coarsely chopped

1 lemongrass stalk (white portion only), coarsely chopped

Juice and zest of 1 medium lemon

⅛ cup parsley leaves

1½ tablespoons minced pickled ginger

2 heaping tablespoons toasted pine nuts

1 teaspoon Hungarian paprika

1 teaspoon ground cumin

½ teaspoon salt

¼ teaspoon freshly ground black pepper

⅓ cup extra-virgin olive oil

Preheat broiler and position oven rack 6 inches below heat source. Arrange 4 shrimp in each of 4 individual ovenproof au gratin dishes. Place the shrimp split side down and curl the tail over the body of the shrimp. Set aside.

Make the Lemongrass Pesto. Combine all ingredients in work bowl of food processor fitted with steel blade. Process until ingredients are minced and well blended, about 1 minute. Spoon a portion of the pesto over each dish, covering the shrimp. Broil for 4 minutes, or just until shrimp are almost cooked through. Scatter some of the feta cheese and green onions over each serving. Broil another minute to slightly brown the cheese. Serve hot.

෪ **Serves 4 as a first course.**

SUGGESTED WINES

Becker Vineyards Estate Bottled Chardonnay

Cap*Rock Winery Chardonnay

Dry Comal Creek Vineyards Sauvignon Blanc

Llano Estacado Winery Signature White

Whooping cranes, Aransas National Wildlife Refuge (right); Mouth of the Rio Grande River (facing page).

SWEET P'S EATERY SHRIMP CREOLE

Pam Sparks is a wonderful cook with a background in Cajun food. She developed her love of cooking from her father, who operated a shop for making shrimp nets in Freeport. He would often cook gumbos and jambalayas at the shop's kitchen and invite his friends for lunch. A few years ago, Pam realized her dream of opening her own soup and sandwich shop. Located in a restored old house with an old-fashioned screened porch, her charming restaurant is my favorite spot for lunch in West Columbia.

¼ cup bacon drippings

¼ cup all-purpose flour

1 medium yellow onion, chopped

¾ cup chopped green onions, divided

2 celery stalks and their leafy tops, chopped

1 medium green bell pepper, chopped

2 large garlic cloves, minced

½ cup tomato paste

1 cup diced plum tomatoes and their juice

½ cup tomato sauce

½ cup chicken stock (see "Basics")

½ teaspoon freshly ground black pepper

¼ teaspoon red (cayenne) pepper, or to taste

Tabasco sauce to taste

3 fresh bay leaves, minced

½ teaspoon sugar

1 teaspoon Worcestershire sauce

1 tablespoon freshly squeezed lemon juice

2½ teaspoons salt

2½ pounds small (70 to 90 count) raw shrimp, peeled and deveined

¼ cup minced flat-leaf parsley

6 cups cooked white rice (see "Basics")

In a heavy 6-quart Dutch oven, heat the bacon drippings over medium heat. Add the flour all at once and stir to blend. Make a dark brown roux, stirring constantly. Stir in the yellow onions, half of the green onions, celery, bell pepper, and garlic. Sauté until onions are wilted and transparent, about 20 minutes. Add tomato paste and stir to blend well. Add tomatoes, tomato sauce, stock, black pepper, cayenne, Tabasco sauce, bay leaves, sugar, Worcestershire sauce, and lemon juice. Stir and add salt to taste. Simmer, covered, for 1 to 1½ hours, stirring occasionally. Add the shrimp and remaining green onions. Simmer for 30 minutes. Stir in the parsley just before serving.

To serve, mound hot rice in a 1-cup metal measuring cup and invert in the middle of serving plate. Spoon the shrimp mixture around the rice and serve hot.

℞ **Serves 4 to 6.**

SUGGESTED WINES

ALAMOSA WINE CELLARS ROSATO DI SANGIOVESE

FALL CREEK VINEYARDS GRANITE RESERVE
CABERNET SAUVIGNON

LA BUENA VIDA VINEYARDS SPRINGTOWN RED

SISTER CREEK VINEYARDS PINOT NOIR

PANKO-FRIED FROG LEGS WITH RED PEPPER MAYONNAISE

If you've never been frog gigging at somebody's pond or lake after dark on a summer evening, you have missed a Texas rite of passage. Just sitting out there listening to the deep, ominous-sounding croaking of the big bullfrogs is quite an experience. An even greater loss, though, would be if you've never tasted fried frog legs. Even if you don't have a frog gigger in your house, most large seafood retailers and specialty markets can get frog legs. Bullfrogs can grow to enormous size with legs weighing in at half a pound per pair or more. The taste is quite unique and sensuously, subtly musky. Japanese (panko) breadcrumbs are one of my favorite breading ingredients for fried foods. I like them because they produce an ultimately crispy crust and also because they add no distinctive flavor of their own to the breading. You can create your own crust flavor by the seasonings you add to the panko crumbs.

12 pairs 4- to 6-ounce frog legs

 2 cups Seasoned Flour for Frying (see "Basics")

 5 eggs, whisked into 4 cups milk

 8 cups Japanese (panko) breadcrumbs, seasoned with 3 tablespoons Chef Paul's Seafood Magic seasoning (or other spicy seasoning blend) and 1 tablespoon salt

Canola oil for deep-frying, heated to 350 degrees

RED PEPPER MAYONNAISE

❧ **Makes about 2 cups.**

 2 large garlic cloves, peeled

 2 egg yolks

 1 tablespoon whole-grain mustard

 1 teaspoon salt

 ½ teaspoon red (cayenne) pepper

 2 tablespoons red wine vinegar

1¼ cups canola oil

 ¼ cup extra-virgin olive oil

Prepare the Red Pepper Mayonnaise. In work bowl of food processor fitted with steel blade, mince the garlic cloves by dropping them through the feed tube. Stop processor and scrape down side of work bowl. Add remaining ingredients except for the canola and olive oils. Process until mixture is thickened and smooth, about 2 minutes. Combine the canola and olive oils. With processor running, add the combined oils in a slow, steady stream through the feed tube to form a smooth mayonnaise. After all oil has been added, process an additional 15 to 20 seconds. Refrigerate until ready to use, but do not keep longer than 3 days.

To prepare the frog legs, pat the legs dry using absorbent paper towels. Dredge them in the seasoned flour, coating well and shaking off any excess flour. Next dip them in the egg wash, coating well. Finally, dredge them in the seasoned panko breadcrumbs. Shake off excess crumbs. Lower the frog legs into the hot oil a few at a time, taking care not to crowd the fryer. Fry until golden brown, turning once, for a total cooking time of about 5 minutes. Drain on wire racks. Serve hot with the chilled Red Pepper Mayonnaise.

❧ **Serves 4.**

SUGGESTED WINES

ALAMOSA WINE CELLARS VIOGNIER

BECKER VINEYARDS PROVENCE

FALL CREEK VINEYARDS CHARDONNAY

MESSINA HOF WINE CELLARS JOHANNESBURG RIESLING

MESSINA HOF WINE CELLARS PINOT GRIGIO

GRILLED SCALLOPS ON STIR-FRIED KALE WITH BALSAMIC GLAZE

*S*callops are generally misunderstood, abused, and underutilized critters. And what a shame because, when properly cooked, they are wonderful. Scallops are bivalve mollusks with a highly developed adductor muscle, which they use to open and close their shells, propelling them through the water. Because scallops cannot fully close their shells, they die soon after they're taken from the water. Therefore, we rarely find them in their shells with roe at the market. They are shucked, trimmed, and iced aboard the fishing boats as soon as they're caught. In case you've never seen one, the ribbed shell of the scallop is the logo for the Shell Oil Company.

SCALLOPS AND MARINADE

2 pounds large scallops (U-10's)

2 large lemongrass stalks, white bottom portion only, trimmed of tough outer fronds and minced

2 large garlic cloves, minced

1 large French shallot, minced

1 tablespoon minced cilantro

1 large serrano chili, seeds and veins removed, minced

¼ cup Thai or Vietnamese fish sauce

1 teaspoon Oriental chili paste with garlic

1 tablespoon freshly squeezed lime juice

1 tablespoon dark sesame oil

Salt and black pepper to taste

STIR-FRIED KALE WITH BALSAMIC GLAZE

1 tablespoon good-quality balsamic vinegar

1 teaspoon soy sauce

2 teaspoons hoisin sauce

1 teaspoon peach schnapps

2 tablespoons peanut oil

2 large garlic cloves, peeled and crushed with the side of a chef's knife

4 French shallots, sliced

2 bunches fresh kale, washed and dried, stems and thick mid-ribs discarded

Salt to taste

Remove adductor muscles from the sides of the scallops, if present. Arrange the scallops in a single layer in a non-aluminum baking dish. Combine all marinade ingredients and whisk to blend well. Pour the marinade over the scallops, turning to coat them well. Cover with plastic wrap and marinate, refrigerated, for about 4 hours.

Preheat gas grill to medium high. Prepare the Stir-Fried Kale with Balsamic Glaze. Stir the balsamic vinegar, soy sauce, hoisin sauce, and peach schnapps together, blending well; set aside. Place a Chinese wok in its ring on a burner over high heat. When the wok is very hot, pour the peanut oil around the sides of the wok. When oil is hot, toss in the crushed garlic cloves. Cook until the cloves are browned and fragrant. Remove garlic with a slotted spoon and discard. Add the sliced shallots and stir-fry for about 30 seconds. Add the kale leaves and stir-fry just until they are barely wilted, about 2 minutes. Pour the balsamic vinegar mixture into the wok and toss rapidly to coat the greens. Remove from heat and divide the kale among the serving plates, arranging a bed of the greens in the center of each plate. Set aside and keep warm.

Remove the scallops from the marinade and grill. Cook just until they have lost their translucent appearance and are opaque throughout, about 3 to 4 minutes, turning once. Do not overcook. Set the scallops atop the greens on each serving plate. Serve hot.

ॐ **Serves 4 to 6.**

SUGGESTED WINES

BECKER VINEYARDS VIOGNIER

CAP*ROCK WINERY SPARKLING BLANC DE NOIR

HAAK VINEYARDS AND WINERY BLANC DU BOIS

SPICEWOOD VINEYARDS SAUVIGNON BLANC

Things with Wings

Texas is a bird hunter's paradise. The state lies at the end of the great Central Flyway for migrating birds. This is where they winter—on the coastal plains and inland waterways you find ducks, geese, and sandhill cranes. Wild turkeys roam the Hill Country. Quail are found from the East Texas Pineywoods region to the arid deserts and mountains of the Trans-Pecos and the regions in between. The magnificently plumed pheasant, which introduced itself to the Panhandle around the time of World War II, thrives in this grain-growing area and is a highly prized game bird. Dove, perhaps the most widely hunted bird in Texas, occurs in all areas of the state. Doves are a challenge to the hunter because they are fast and difficult targets.

The meat of poultry and fowl is one of Mother Nature's most delicious achievements, ranging from the delicate taste and light meat of the Texas bobwhite quail, to the slightly more assertive taste of pheasant and white-winged dove, to the darker meat and more musky taste of ducks, geese, and wild turkey.

As with domesticated chickens and turkeys, game birds pair well with the bold and assertive seasonings we love in Texas. Roasted quail arranged on a bed of sauce made from chilies, onions, tomatoes, and herbs simmered slowly in rich stocks. Duck breasts grilled just so, after being marinated in a rich and sassy, garlic-

Bobwhite quail in bromegrass, Hartley County; Migratory geese, Chambers County (pages 134–35).

infused glaze. Wild turkey slow-smoked to juicy perfection. Doves simmering in a rich cream sauce, seasoned with fresh herbs. Smoked goose breast napped with a sauce made from native persimmons. Roasted free-range chicken, its crisp skin glistening from its baste of butter and native Mexican mint marigold. Poached turkey, sliced and robed in exotic mole sauce.

One of the most important things to remember about cooking game birds is that they have very little fat. If cooked too fast (with too much heat) or too long, the meat will be dry and tasteless. The breast meat, especially, should be covered with fat during cooking. Be mindful of the fact that older birds will be particularly tough if overcooked.

Even if you're not a hunter, you can enjoy game birds. Many species are now farm-raised and available frozen at specialty markets or from mail-order sources (see "The Texas Cook's Pantry"). Organic free-range chickens are also available from upscale markets, and their intense chicken taste and tender, juicy meat make them worth their premium price.

Whatever flavor of bird your appetite hankers for, Texas has one for you.

Mated wooducks, Lower Colorado River; Sunrise on the Lower Sabine River (pages 138–39).

GRILLED DUCK BREAST WITH TAMARIND GLAZE AND MANGO-PAPAYA SALSA

Duck is such a marvelous meat around which to create a spectacular entrée. It seems to have an exotic flair, yet it is not difficult to cook. The skin contains rich fat that renders into the meat during cooking, producing a crisp skin and succulent, moist meat. My hands-down favorite wild duck is mallard. It has a slightly musky taste. If you buy farm-raised duck or duck breasts, they will have a milder taste. One variety sold through retail outlets is the mild White Pekin. Two varieties with a more pronounced flavor are Muscovy and Moulard, a cross between a male Muscovy and a female White Pekin. When cooking duck breast, never overcook it. Ideally, it should be cooked medium-rare but never past medium. This recipe is excellent with Orange and Saffron Couscous with Ancho Chilies (see "Sides").

4 skin-on duck breasts, about 8 ounces each
   (serve 2 per person if breasts are small ones from
   wild ducks)

TAMARIND GLAZE

¼ cup tamarind pulp (see next page)

4 cups chicken stock (see "Basics")

½ cup sugar

1 teaspoon Chinese five-spice powder

¼ cup minced cilantro

MANGO AND PAPAYA SALSA

4 whole cloves

¾ teaspoon whole cumin seeds

¾ teaspoon Szechuan peppercorns

1 chipotle chili in adobo sauce

1 large Roma tomato, chopped

3 medium garlic cloves, minced

2 French shallots, chopped

1 tablespoon minced pickled ginger

¼ cup rice wine vinegar

¼ cup freshly squeezed lime juice

1 large mango, peeled, pitted, and finely chopped

1 large papaya, peeled, seeds removed, and finely
   chopped

1 tablespoon honey

¼ teaspoon freshly ground black pepper

Salt to taste

¼ cup firmly packed cilantro leaves

Prepare the Tamarind Glaze. Combine all ingredients, except cilantro, in a 2-quart saucepan over medium-low heat. Bring the liquid to a boil, then reduce heat and simmer gently for 30 minutes until liquid is reduced and thickened. It should be very aromatic. Stir in the cilantro and remove pan from heat. Set aside to steep for 15 minutes. Strain the glaze, pressing the solids to remove all liquid. Discard solids and set the glaze aside.

Prepare the Mango and Papaya Salsa. In a small skillet over high heat combine the cloves, cumin seeds, and Szechuan peppercorns. Toast the spices, tossing the pan, until very fragrant, about 3 minutes. Do not burn the spices. Remove the toasted spices from the pan and set aside. In a heavy 10-inch skillet over medium heat, combine the chipotle chili, tomato, garlic, shallots, ginger, vinegar, and lime juice. Cook until the chopped tomato has become pulpy, about 10 minutes. Stir in the mango and papaya, honey, salt, black pepper, and toasted spices. Bring to a boil over medium-high heat, then reduce heat and simmer until the fruit is very soft, about 25 minutes. Remove from heat and set the mixture aside to cool. When the salsa has cooled, transfer it to blender container. Add the cilantro to the container and puree until smooth. Serve at room temperature.

To cook the duck, heat gas grill to medium-high. Baste the duck breasts with the Tamarind Glaze and place on grill rack, skin side down. Grill, basting often, for about 7 minutes. Brush with the glaze, turn, and cook an additional 3 minutes.

To serve, slice the breasts into thin diagonal slices. Place a bed of the Mango and Papaya Salsa on each serving plate. Fan the slices out on the salsa. Serve hot.

☙ Serves 4.

SUGGESTED WINES

ALAMOSA WINE CELLARS VIOGNIER

BECKER VINEYARDS CLARET ESTATE BOTTLED

COMFORT CELLARS WINERY ORANGE CHARDONNAY

TEXAS HILLS VINEYARD MOSCATO

TAMARIND

Tamarind pods, from which the pulp is extracted, grow in clusters on a beautiful evergreen tree originally native to Africa. It is often referred to as the Indian date tree. The tree now grows throughout the tropical and subtropical regions of the world. Tamarind is used in Indian, Asian, Indonesian, Chinese, African, and Central American cooking and in the West Indies. The pulp itself is somewhat acidic, or sweet-sour, and is generally combined with sugar or sweet fruit to make a syrup. Dried tamarind pods can often be found in the produce section at the supermarket. The pulp is sold in Asian and Indian markets or in ethnic food sections of larger markets. Tamarind is the secret ingredient in Worcestershire sauce. It can add a very interesting taste note to bold-flavored dishes.

Gothic-style Methodist church, Colorado City

COUNTRY-STYLE BRAISED WILD DUCK

Our state is one of the nation's leading areas for waterfowl shooting. The West Texas High Plains is prime duck hunting territory due to the millions of acres of grain harvested there. Ponds, lake, and stock tanks in the East Texas Pineywoods abound with ducks. The rice fields of the coastal prairies are among the state's best duck hunting regions. During the long duck hunting season, hunters are in duck hunter's heaven. Mallards, teals, pintails, gadwalls, canvasback, widgeons, ringnecks, and black ducks go home to stew pans, barbecue grills, oven roasters, and gumbo pots. I love this preparation for wild duck. The exotic musky taste of the ducks lends subtle hints to the gravy in the pan. The aroma alone entices.

4 large wild ducks, about 2 to 2½ pounds each, cleaned

2 yellow onions, quartered

8 large garlic cloves, peeled

¾ pound andouille sausage, cut into 1-inch slices

Canola oil for glazing

Salt and freshly ground black pepper

GRAVY

3 medium yellow onions, chopped

4 large garlic cloves, minced

1 medium green bell pepper, chopped

3 celery stalks, chopped, including leafy tops

¼ cup minced flat-leaf parsley

½ pound andouille sausage, sliced into bite-size pieces

1 pound mushrooms, sliced

1 teaspoon red (cayenne) pepper

⅓ cup Worcestershire sauce

3 fresh bay leaves, minced

2 teaspoons minced fresh thyme

2 teaspoons minced fresh sage

1 cup Cabernet Sauvignon

2 cups beef stock (see "Basics")

1 14-ounce can artichoke hearts (not marinated), drained and quartered

Salt and freshly ground black pepper to taste

Additional beef stock as needed

Brown roux made with 3 tablespoons bacon drippings and 3 tablespoons all-purpose flour (see "Basics")

4 green onions, chopped, including green tops

Cooked Texmati rice or other basmati-style rice (see "Basics")

Remove and discard the tail knob from the ducks. Stuff each duck with the onion quarters, garlic, and andouille sausage. Rub each duck with canola oil and season with salt and pepper. Heat a thin glaze of canola oil over medium heat in a Dutch oven or flameproof roasting pan. When the oil is hot, place the ducks in the pan, breast side down, and sear on all sides. Remove pan from heat and carefully pour off all fat. Place the ducks on their backs in the pan.

To prepare the gravy, scatter the onions, garlic, bell pepper, celery, parsley, ½ pound andouille sausage, and mushrooms in the pan. Combine the red (cayenne) pepper, Worcestershire sauce, bay leaves, thyme, sage, and Cabernet Sauvignon, whisking to blend well. Pour the wine mixture into the pan. Set the pan over medium-low heat and cook to reduce the wine by about half, approximately 30 minutes. Add the beef stock, cover the pan, and simmer gently for 1 hour. The juices should run light pink when the breast is pierced. Add the artichoke hearts and cook an additional 15 minutes. Remove the ducks from the pan; set aside and keep hot. Return the pan to medium heat and add 1 cup additional stock. Bring the liquid to a full, rolling boil. Add the brown roux all at once and stir to blend; cook until thickened, about 5 minutes. Stir in the green onions.

To serve, cut the ducks in half lengthwise through the breastbone, discarding the backbone. Place a portion of the cooked rice on each serving plate and arrange duck, cut side down, on the rice. Spoon vegetables and gravy from the pan over and around the ducks. Serve hot.

ଲ Serves 6 to 8.

SUGGESTED WINES

ALAMOSA WINE CELLARS SANGIOVESE

DELANEY VINEYARDS AND WINERY MERLOT

DRY COMAL CREEK VINEYARDS WHITE VERITAGE

LLANO ESTACADO WINERY PASSIONELLE

SISTER CREEK VINEYARDS CHARDONNAY

GRILLED GOOSE BREAST WITH PERSIMMON SAUCE

In the late fall and early winter Texas skies fill with the V formations of migrating geese. These tourists make themselves right at home in the grain fields of the coastal prairies and marshes. It is an awesome sight to see a flight of 25,000 to 50,000 snow geese lift off from a rice field at the same time. The beating of the wings is like an angry roaring wind. Combined with the cacophonous honking, it makes for a truly awesome experience. Wild geese can be roasted whole, but I prefer to keep only the breast. The size of geese will vary with the variety, so you will have to use common sense in determining how many breasts you will need to serve your guests.

8 boneless wild goose breasts, skin on
2 cups Muscat Canelli wine
1 tablespoon balsamic vinegar
2 fresh sage sprigs, bruised
2 teaspoons freshly ground black pepper
½ cup olive oil

Dry Rub

2 teaspoons salt
3 tablespoons firmly packed light brown sugar
½ teaspoon freshly ground black pepper
1 teaspoon minced fresh thyme
1 teaspoon minced fresh sage
2 tablespoons minced onion

Persimmon Sauce

1 tablespoon minced French shallots
½ cup Muscat Canelli wine
2 cups peach nectar
1 serrano chili, seeds and veins removed, minced
2 teaspoons minced orange zest
3 persimmons, peeled, seeded, and chopped
¼ cup whipping cream

Place the goose breasts in a single layer in a non-aluminum baking pan. Combine the wine, vinegar, sage, and black pepper and pour over the breasts. Cover with plastic wrap and marinate in the refrigerator for 4 hours.

Make the dry rub by combining all ingredients and blending well.

Remove the breasts from the marinade and pat dry using absorbent paper towels. Brush the breasts with olive oil and rub the dry rub onto both sides; set aside at room temperature.

Prepare the Persimmon Sauce. Combine the shallots and wine in a 2-quart saucepan over medium heat. Cook to reduce the liquid to a syrup. Add the peach nectar and serrano chili. Cook until reduced by half, about 10 minutes. Add the orange zest and chopped persimmons. Simmer to thicken slightly. Transfer the mixture to blender and puree. Return the puree to saucepan and stir in the whipping cream. Cook just to heat through; keep warm.

To grill the goose breasts, preheat gas grill on medium heat. Grill breasts, skin side up first. Cook for 4 to 7 minutes per side, depending on size, turning once. They should be served medium-rare.

To serve, slice the breasts diagonally into thin slices. Place a bed of the Persimmon Sauce on each serving plate and fan a sliced breast out on the sauce.

ভ **Serves 4 to 6.**

SUGGESTED WINES

ALAMOSA WINE CELLARS ROSATO DI SANGIOVESE
FALL CREEK VINEYARDS SAUVIGNON BLANC
HAAK VINEYARDS AND WINERY CABERNET SAUVIGNON
SISTER CREEK VINEYARDS CHARDONNAY

Tallgrass prairie remnants at Fairview Cemetery, Bastrop

QUAIL IN COUNTRY HAM WITH PEPPERED COFFEE GRAVY ON DIRTY RICE

Nathalie Dupree is an accomplished southern cook and cookbook author. She is also my mentor and a person to whom I owe a great deal for her guidance in this crazy business of food. One of her many books is a wonderful tome on southern food, Southern Memories. She created a recipe for quail wrapped in country ham. It is a grand, elegant, typically southern entrée. I have always loved the dish. I "Texanized" Nathalie's dish to serve at Maner Lake Lodge, pairing it with a bold, wake-up-your-face gravy and real country-style dirty rice. I have also served the dish on a bed of scrambled eggs for brunch with great results. Farm-raised quail are available with the backbone and breastbone removed, making for much easier eating, or ask your butcher to do the task. Encourage your guests to eat the tiny legs and wings with their fingers. What tasty little morsels they are—and finger licking is certainly permitted.

12 semi-boneless quail (backbone and breastbone removed)

Melted unsalted butter

Salt and freshly ground black pepper

12 thin-cut Smithfield country-cured ham slices (see "The Texas Cook's Pantry")

DIRTY RICE

1 pound chicken or turkey gizzards

½ pound chicken, duck, or turkey livers

1 cup bacon or sausage drippings (or substitute solid vegetable shortening)

2 medium onions, chopped

1 green bell pepper, chopped

2 celery stalks, chopped, including leafy tops

2 garlic cloves, minced

3 cups chicken stock (see "Basics")

½ teaspoon red (cayenne) pepper, or to taste

Salt and freshly ground black pepper to taste

¼ cup minced flat-leaf parsley

5 green onions, chopped, including green tops

4 cups cooked white rice (see "Basics")

PEPPERED COFFEE GRAVY

½ cup bacon drippings (or substitute solid vegetable shortening)

2 Smithfield "Virginia" country-cured ham slices, ¼ inch thick

1 teaspoon freshly ground black pepper

4 tablespoons all-purpose flour

1 cup strong black coffee

1½ cups beef stock (see "Basics")

Preheat oven to 350 degrees. Brush each quail liberally with some of the melted butter. Season with salt and freshly ground black pepper. Wrap each quail in a slice of the ham, leaving the wings exposed on top of the ham slice. Place the quail in a single layer in a heavy baking pan with the loose ends of the ham slices tucked underneath them. Roast in preheated oven for 45 minutes, or until quail are just cooked through.

Prepare the Dirty Rice while quail are roasting. Using a small sharp knife, remove the tough outer skin from the gizzards by scraping the meat from the skin, leaving the blade of the knife against the skin on the cutting board. Place the gizzards and livers in the work bowl of food processor fitted with steel blade and process to puree the meats. Scrape the puree out of the bowl with a rubber spatula and set aside.

Heat the drippings in a heavy 12-inch frying pan over medium-high heat. When the fat is hot, add the pureed meats and cook, stirring often, until well browned. Be sure the meat does not cook into clumps. Add the onion, bell pepper, garlic, and celery, blending well. Continue to cook until vegetables are wilted, about 8 minutes. Add the stock and seasonings, scraping the bottom of the pan to release any browned bits of meat glaze. Cook over medium heat until liquid is reduced and thickened, about 45 minutes. Stir in the parsley, green onions, and rice, mixing well. Cook, stirring often, for 10 minutes, or until rice is slightly sticky.

While quail and rice are cooking, prepare the Peppered Coffee Gravy. Heat the bacon drippings in a heavy, 10-inch cast-iron skillet over medium heat. Add the ham slices and cook until they are very crisp. Remove and set aside. Add the pepper and flour to the bacon drippings; stir to blend well. Cook for about 5 minutes, stirring constantly, to give the gravy greater depth of flavor. Add the coffee and stir rapidly to blend well. Bring to a boil and cook for 3 to 4 minutes. Stir in the beef stock. Chop the reserved ham slices into crumb-size pieces and add to the gravy. Cook, stirring, until thickened.

To serve, place a bed of the Dirty Rice in the center of each serving plate. Nest two quail in the center and spoon a portion of the Peppered Coffee Gravy over the quail. Serve hot.

ର Serves 6.

SUGGESTED WINES

Alamosa Wine Cellars Sangiovese

Cap*Rock Winery Merlot

Fall Creek Vineyards Granite Reserve
Cabernet Sauvignon

Hidden Springs Winery Sauvignon Blanc

Sister Creek Vineyards Pinot Noir

Contour plowing, Briscoe County

COUNTRY HAM

COUNTRY HAMS ARE AMERICA'S VERSION OF ITALY'S FAMED PROSCUITTO DI PARMA AND SPAIN'S TANGY SERRANO HAM. THE AMERICAN COUNTRY HAM TRADITION HAD ITS BEGINNINGS IN SMITHFIELD, VIRGINIA, WHICH WAS SETTLED IN 1619. THE RECIPE FOR CURING A COUNTRY HAM WAS BORROWED FROM THE INDIANS OF THE AREA, WHO PRESERVED VENISON FOR THE WINTER BY RUBBING IT WITH "MAGIC WHITE SAND" (SALT) AND SMOKING IT SLOWLY OVER A FIRE. THE RECIPE WAS APPLIED TO THE HIND LEGS OF THE PIGS THAT RAN WILD IN THE FORESTS SURROUNDING THE TOWN. MALLORY TODD BEGAN CURING HAMS IN SMITHFIELD IN THE LATE 1700S, AND HAMS FROM SMITHFIELD BECAME AN IMPORTANT EXPORT. THEY WERE A FEATURED ITEM ON THE ROYAL DINING TABLE AT WINDSOR CASTLE DURING THE REIGN OF QUEEN VICTORIA. THESE DRY-CURED, COLD-SMOKED HAMS ARE AGED FOR AS LONG AS A YEAR. THE MUSKY TASTE AND FIRM TEXTURE OF THE MEAT IS DELICIOUS AND UNIQUE. ALWAYS SLICE COUNTRY HAM PAPER THIN. THERE REALLY IS NO SUBSTITUTE FOR THE TASTE OF AMERICAN COUNTRY HAM.

SLOW-SMOKED QUAIL ON SAVORY BREAD PUDDING
WITH THREE-CHILI SAUCE

Whether wild or farm-raised, the quail is adaptable to a wide variety of cooking methods and pairs well with all manner of other flavors and seasonings. This recipe contains a lot of steps, but they can be broken down into a doable project. Marinate the quail the day before you plan to serve the dish. The next day, smoke the quail and get the Savory Bread Pudding ready to bake, then refrigerate it. You can make the sauce several days ahead of time and reheat it when ready to serve. On the day you intend to serve the dish, bake the Savory Bread Pudding and fry the quail. There—not such a forbidding dish when you spread it out!

12 quail
Canola oil for deep-frying, heated to 350 degrees
Savory Bread Pudding (see next page)
Three-Chili Sauce (see next page)

MARINADE

½ cup real maple syrup
¼ cup canola oil
2 canned chipotle chilies in adobo sauce
¼ cup Oriental hoisin sauce
¼ cup Chinese rice wine or sake

BATTER

2 eggs, beaten until frothy
2½ cups ice water, or more as needed
2 cups all-purpose flour
1 cup cornstarch
1 teaspoon salt
1 tablespoon baking powder

Whisk together all marinade ingredients in a bowl, blending well. Arrange quail in a shallow baking dish in a single layer and pour the marinade over them, turning to coat well. Cover and marinate in refrigerator overnight, or for a minimum of 8 hours.

To cook the quail, prepare a fire in a barbecue pit or smoker and let it cook down until heat registers 100–125 degrees. Drain the quail, discarding marinade. Smoke indirectly over prepared charcoal fire for 45 minutes. Remove and refrigerate until ready to complete and serve. The quail will be barely cooked.

To fry the quail, heat canola oil for deep-frying to 350 degrees. Prepare the batter by whisking together the eggs and ice water; set aside. Combine the flour, cornstarch, salt, and baking powder, tossing with a fork to blend well. Whisk the flour mixture into the ice water just to blend. Add additional water if needed to make a smooth batter. (Do not prepare the batter until you are ready to use it.) Dip the quail into the batter, coating well and plunge at once into the heated oil. Fry only a few at a time just until they are golden brown on both sides, turning once. Drain on a wire cooling rack placed over a baking sheet. Repeat until all quail have been fried.

Serve each quail on a triangle of Savory Bread Pudding and drizzle a portion of the Three-Chili Sauce over the top.

ରେ Serves 6.

SCAMORZA CHEESE

SCAMORZA CHEESE IS A VERY UNIQUE AND DELICIOUS CHEESE MADE BY THE MOZZARELLA COMPANY IN DALLAS. FRESH MOZZARELLA IS FORMED INTO ROUNDS, THEN GENTLY SMOKED OVER PECAN SHELLS. THE SMOKED CHEESE IS SEALED IN WAX TO PROTECT THE DELICATE SMOKED FLAVOR. SCAMORZA CHEESE IS AVAILABLE AT SPECIALTY MARKETS OR BY MAIL ORDER (SEE "THE TEXAS COOK'S PANTRY) IF YOU WANT TO EXPERIENCE THIS WONDERFUL CHEESE.

SAVORY BREAD PUDDING

  4 ounces French bread, cut into ½-inch dice
  ½ cup whipping cream
  ½ cup Thai coconut milk
  ½ teaspoon ground cinnamon
1½ teaspoons minced fresh thyme
  2 large shallots, sautéed in butter until wilted
  2 eggs, beaten
  7 ounces of smoked scamorza cheese, shredded, or other shredded smoked mozzarella
  ½ teaspoon salt
  ½ teaspoon ground black pepper

Preheat oven to 350 degrees and thoroughly butter bottom and sides of a 9-by-13-inch baking dish; set aside. Place the bread cubes in a large bowl; set aside. Combine whipping cream and coconut milk in a small saucepan and heat just until tiny bubbles begin to appear at side of pan. Stir into the bread. Add the seasonings, sautéed shallots, and beaten eggs, blending well. Fold in the cheese, distributing evenly. Turn out into prepared baking dish and bake in preheated oven until set, about 25 to 30 minutes. Cut into 6 squares, then cut the squares in half diagonally to form 12 triangles. Serve hot.

❧ **Serves 6.**

THREE-CHILI SAUCE

❧ **Makes about 3 cups.**

  2 tablespoons peanut oil
  5 Roma tomatoes, chopped
  2 cascabel chilies
  1 pasilla chili
  ¼ teaspoon crushed red arbol chilies
  1 onion, chopped
  3 garlic cloves, minced
  1 quart plus 1 cup chicken stock (see "Basics")
  2 tablespoons minced fresh cilantro

Heat the peanut oil in a medium saucepan over medium heat. Sauté the tomatoes, chilies, onions, and garlic over medium heat until browned, about 15 minutes. Add the stock, stirring to blend well. Cook sauce over medium-low heat until reduced, about 30 to 45 minutes. Puree the sauce in blender and strain through a fine strainer. Return to heat, add the cilantro, and reduce slightly until sauce has thickened, about 10 minutes. Serve hot.

SUGGESTED WINES

ALAMOSA WINE CELLARS ROSATO DI SANGIOVESE

DELANEY VINEYARDS AND WINERY SAUVIGNON BLANC

HAAK VINEYARDS AND WINERY
BARREL-FERMENTED CHARDONNAY

LLANO ESTACADO WINERY ZINFANDEL

Prairie warbler on Maximilian sunflowers, Kaufman County

Cheese- and Jalapeño-Stuffed Barbecued Quail

*T*exans are serious quail hunters. The season is long, stretching from November through late February. Three species of quail in Texas can be hunted—bobwhite, Gambel's, and scaled or blue quail. The bobwhite quail is my personal favorite. It has slightly sweet, white meat and a delicious taste. Quail that you purchase will most likely be pharaoh quail from the eastern United States. They are larger than the Texas quail and have dark meat (about the color of dark chicken meat). The taste of the pharaoh quail is very good, though, so don't hesitate to cook with them.

8 slices applewood-smoked bacon or other good-quality smoked bacon

8 semi-boneless quail (backbone and breastbone removed), patted dry on absorbent paper towels

Baste

ଔ **Makes about 2 cups.**

12 ounces Italian salad dressing

1 tablespoon plus 1 teaspoon freshly squeezed lime juice

1 teaspoon minced lime zest

2 tablespoons honey

1 tablespoon Worcestershire sauce

1 tablespoon Dijon-style mustard

½ teaspoon crushed red pepper flakes

¼ teaspoon ground cumin

1 teaspoon granulated garlic

¼ teaspoon chili powder

1 tablespoons minced green onion

Stuffing

½ cup (2 ounces) shredded Asiago cheese

½ cup (2 ounces) shredded Monterey Jack cheese

½ cup (2 ounces) shredded Fontina cheese

⅓ cup Italian-seasoned breadcrumbs

2 eggs, well beaten

1 pickled jalapeño, minced

1 chipotle chili in adobo sauce, minced

2 tablespoons minced cilantro

Prepare a fire in a barbecue pit with an indirect heat source. Let fire cook down until temperature in cooking chamber is about 250 degrees.

Place the bacon strips between two pieces of plastic wrap. Using a rolling pin, roll the bacon until it is thin; set aside. Prepare the baste by combining all ingredients in a bowl. Whisk to blend well and set aside.

Prepare the stuffing by mixing all ingredients in a bowl. Stuff the interior cavity of each quail with a portion of the stuffing. Wrap each quail in a slice of the bacon, tucking the bacon under the wings. Secure bacon slices firmly with toothpicks.

Place the birds on grill in barbecue pit and brush with the baste. Cook, turning often and basting with each turn, until birds are done, about 1½ hours. Remove the toothpicks and serve quail hot, 2 per person.

ଔ **Serves 4.**

SUGGESTED WINES

Fall Creek Vineyards Chenin Blanc

Messina Hof Wine Cellars Gewürztraminer

Sister Creek Vineyards Pinot Noir

Spicewood Vineyards Merlot

Braised Doves in Shiitake Mushroom Cream

There are five species of doves in the state, three of which can be hunted. The best known is the mourning dove with its familiar woeful song. The other two species are the white-winged dove and the white-tipped dove. The white-winged dove is the largest of the three species—about 25 percent larger than the mourning dove. Doves are tender—with fine-grained and flavorful dark meat—but very small, weighing on the average a little over 4 ounces in feather and undrawn, so allow three per person. The birds are quite lean and therefore are at their best when cooked by moist-heat methods like braising (cooking in a liquid) or basting and broiling. When roasted, they tend to dry out to the point of being rather unpalatable. You may also substitute quail or even Cornish hens in this delicious recipe. Sometimes I serve the Shiitake Mushroom Cream sauce with rice (or pasta) as a side dish with other meats or with a simple broiled or baked fish.

12 doves, dressed

Salt, freshly ground black pepper, and granulated garlic

½ cup Sauvignon Blanc

½ cup beef stock (see "Basics")

½ cup chicken stock (see "Basics")

¼ cup canola oil

Cooked Texmati rice or another basmati-style rice (see "Basics")

Shiitake Mushroom Cream

5 French shallots, finely chopped

4 fresh shiitake mushrooms, thinly sliced

3 tablespoons minced fresh tarragon

1 teaspoon freshly ground black pepper

1½ cups beef stock (see "Basics")

1½ cups chicken stock (see "Basics")

2 cups whipping cream

Salt to taste

Beurre Manié, as needed (see "Basics")

Preheat oven to 325 degrees. Season the doves with salt, pepper, and granulated garlic; set aside. Heat the canola oil in a heavy 12-inch skillet over medium heat. Cook the doves, turning them on all sides just to brown them. Remove pan from heat and transfer doves to a 10-by-14-inch open roasting pan. Reserve the pan drippings. Add the Sauvignon Blanc, ½ cup beef stock, and ½ cup chicken stock to the roasting pan. Cover the pan with aluminum foil. Place pan in preheated oven and cook for 35 to 40 minutes.

Make the Shiitake Mushroom Cream. Place the pan with reserved drippings over medium heat. Add 1 tablespoon or more canola oil as needed to equal the original ¼ cup. When oil is hot, add the shallots, mushrooms, tarragon, and black pepper. Sauté until shallots are wilted and transparent, about 10 minutes. Add the beef and chicken stocks, scraping bottom of pan to release the browned bits of meat glaze. Lower heat and simmer for 30 minutes, stirring occasionally. Add the cream and cook an additional 15 minutes.

When the doves are cooked, remove them from the oven; set aside and keep warm. Add ½ cup of the roasting pan drippings to the sauce; stir to blend well. Add salt to taste. Bring the sauce to a full boil. Add 1 tablespoon Beurre Manié while stirring vigorously. Continue to add 1 tablespoon at a time until the sauce is slightly thickened.

To serve, place a portion of the rice in the center of each serving plate. Spoon a portion of the mushrooms and sauce over the rice. Nest 2 or 3 of the doves in the center of the rice and serve hot.

❧ Serves 4 to 6.

SUGGESTED WINES

Becker Vineyards Cabernet Sauvignon Reserve
Estate Bottled

La Buena Vida Vineyards Springtown Chardonnay

Messina Hof Wine Cellars Barrel Reserve Chardonnay

Sister Creek Vineyards Pinot Noir

Northwestern rim of Palo Duro Canyon

ROAST PHEASANT WITH CARAMELIZED PEARS ON SEARED FOIE GRAS

This recipe is one of the most regal in the book and costly to prepare, but well worth the expense. The combination of flavors is wonderful—the gratifying "wild chicken" taste of the pheasant is paired with fois gras, one of the most deletable tastes on earth. You can prepare the dish, of course, without the fois gras and substitute another bird or even chicken.

3 pheasants, dressed and cleaned (about 2 to 2½ pounds each)

¼ cup honey

¼ cup Oriental hoisin sauce

1 cup canola oil

¼ cup bourbon whiskey

Freshly ground black pepper

Salt and additional freshly ground black pepper

12 applewood-smoked bacon strips

CARAMELIZED PEARS

4 pears, peeled, cored, and sliced in half

½ cup light brown sugar

⅓ cup finely chopped pickled ginger

¼ cup chicken stock

SEARED FOIE GRAS

1 piece Grade AA Moulard duck liver (see "The Texas Cook's Pantry")

Salt and freshly ground black pepper

CHILI-CORIANDER SAUCE

⅓ cup finely minced pickled ginger

¾ cup jalapeño pepper jelly, melted and strained

¼ heaping cup whole coriander seeds, toasted

1 cup water

1 tablespoon chili paste with garlic

¼ cup sherry wine vinegar

1 bunch fresh cilantro leaves and stems

2 cups chicken stock

Tie the legs of the pheasant together with butcher's (cotton) twine and tuck the wing tips under the bodies, securing them with poultry pins. Place in a large baking dish. Combine honey, hoisin sauce, canola oil, whiskey, and black pepper, whisking to blend well. Pour the marinade over the birds, turning to coat well. Marinate in refrigerator for 8 hours or overnight.

Preheat oven to 350 degrees. Remove birds from marinade and arrange them, breast side up, in a roasting pan, not touching. Salt and pepper the birds, then cover each breast with 4 bacon slices. Cover the pan and place in preheated oven. Roast for 40 minutes, then uncover and roast an additional 15 minutes to brown the pheasants.

While birds are roasting, prepare the Caramelized Pears. Place the brown sugar in a heavy 12-inch sauté pan; heat until melted and syrupy. Add the ginger and chicken stock, stirring over medium-high heat until the sugar has melted into the stock and the mixture is smooth and thick. Add the pear halves and cook until they are lightly caramelized but still crisp and tender. Set aside and keep warm.

Prepare the Chili-Coriander Sauce. Combine the pickled ginger, jalapeño jelly, coriander seeds, water, and chili paste with garlic. Cook over medium-high heat until the coriander becomes very fragrant. Add the sherry vinegar and cilantro. Cook to reduce the liquid by half. Add the chicken stock and reduce until slightly thickened and syrupy, about 25 minutes. Strain the sauce through a fine strainer, discarding solids. Set aside and keep warm.

When ready to serve, prepare the Seared Foie Gras. Salt and pepper the duck liver. Heat a dry, heavy skillet over medium-high heat, then sear the liver until crisp and glazed, about 3 minutes per side, turning once. It should be medium-rare to medium. Set aside and keep warm.

Remove bacon strips from pheasant and discard. Slice the pheasants in half. Slice the foie gras into ⅜-inch-thick slices and fan a few slices on each serving plate. Top with the pheasant halves and arrange 2 pear halves around the birds. Drizzle a portion of the sauce over each serving. Serve at once.

જ Serves 4 to 6. SUGGESTED WINES

BECKER VINEYARDS CLARET ESTATE BOTTLED

FALL CREEK VINEYARDS "SWEET JO" JOHANNESBURG RIESLING

HIDDEN SPRINGS WINERY MUSCAT CANELLI

LLANO ESTACADO WINERY ZINFANDEL

SISTER CREEK VINEYARDS PINOT NOIR

BRINED AND ROASTED TURKEY WITH GIBLET GRAVY

*B*rining poultry before roasting is one of those secret tricks used by chefs to make food more delicious than you know how to make it. This simple maneuver will assure you a very moist, tender, and amazingly tasty bird. The method also works very well for chicken. Serve with Country Cornbread Dressing (see "Sides"). For general information about purchasing and cooking turkey, see "Basics."

18-pound turkey, preferably fresh

Melted unsalted butter

  6 sprigs fresh thyme

Salt and freshly ground black pepper

  8 slices good-quality bacon, preferably applewood-smoked

  1 quart chicken stock (see "Basics")

BRINE

1½ quarts water

¾ cup kosher salt

¼ cup plus 2 tablespoons sugar

4½ quarts ice water

GIBLET GRAVY

Giblets and neck from turkey

  1 quart chicken stock (see "Basics")

½ cup pan drippings from turkey

  1 large celery stalk, finely chopped

  1 small onion, finely chopped

Salt and freshly ground black pepper to taste

½ cup all-purpose flour

  1 hard-cooked egg, chopped

Prepare the brine by combining 1½ quarts of water with the salt and sugar in a 3-quart saucepan over medium heat. Cook to dissolve salt and sugar. Remove from heat and set aside to cool.

Remove the giblets and neck from turkey and reserve for Giblet Gravy. Rinse the turkey well and drain. Stand turkey in a 20-quart, non-metal storage container. (A squeaky-clean 5-gallon bucket will work.) Combine the cooled brine syrup with 4½ quarts of ice water. Pour over the turkey, completely covering it. Cover and refrigerate for 24 hours, or ice down the container in an ice chest for 24 hours.

To roast the bird, remove it from the bucket and discard the brine. Rinse the turkey thoroughly, inside and out, and pat dry with paper towels. Preheat oven to 500 degrees. Place the turkey in a roasting pan large enough that the flesh does not touch the sides or ends of the pan. Baste the turkey all over with a liberal amount of the melted butter. Place 2 of the thyme sprigs inside the turkey cavity. Season with salt and pepper. Arrange the remaining thyme sprigs over the breast area and lay the bacon slices, slightly overlapping, over the breast. Pour the chicken stock into the bottom of the pan, cover, and place turkey in preheated oven, legs first. Roast for 2 hours and 20 minutes, or until the leg joint near the backbone wiggles easily. Baste with the pan drippings every 20 minutes. Uncover the bird for the last 20 minutes of cooking to brown the skin.

While the turkey is roasting, prepare the Giblet Gravy. Simmer the giblets and necks in the chicken stock, covered, for 1 hour. Drain, reserving the broth for the gravy. Cool the giblets and chop finely. Pull the meat from the neck and chop it also. Set meats aside.

Remove turkey from roasting pan and allow it to rest for 20 minutes before carving. After the bird has been removed from the roasting pan, pour ½ cup of the fat from the pan into a heavy 10-inch skillet; set aside. Skim any remaining fat from the roasting pan. Pour the reserved stock from giblets into the roasting pan. Place pan over high heat and scrape up any browned bits from bottom of pan. Strain through fine strainer and set aside.

Heat the fat in the skillet over medium heat. Add the celery and onions; cook until limp, about 10 minutes. Add salt and pepper to taste and stir in the flour all at once. Cook, stirring, for 3 to 4 minutes. Pour in the reserved broth in a slow, steady stream while stirring. Bring to a boil to thicken. Add the chopped giblets, neck meat, and hard-cooked egg. Pour Giblet Gravy into a gravy bowl and pass separately with the turkey.

☙ **Serves 10 to 12.**

SMOKED WILD TURKEY

*T*urkey hunting has always been of great importance in Texas. One of the first bird species recorded in the state was a Rio Grande turkey captured by the Long Expedition on its way from Colorado through the Panhandle Plains in 1820. Around the turn of the twentieth century, the population of wild turkeys declined sharply in the state because of changing land use, rampant deforestation, and unrestricted hunting. By 1941 the Pineywoods region of East Texas had fewer than 100 wild turkeys. With the cooperation of privately funded organizations, the Texas Parks and Wildlife Department has put the wild turkey on the comeback trail. Today Texas has more wild turkeys than any other state. Hunting wild turkeys is a true test of a hunter's skill. Ask any hunter who's missed a shot at one of the wily critters. Wild turkeys have extraordinary hearing and eyesight to warn them of any impending danger. Thus warned, they can hightail it out of sight at speeds up to 20 miles an hour—as fast as a deer! Or they can take flight, reaching flight speeds of 50 miles an hour within seconds. But hang in there because smoked wild turkey is one of nature's premier taste treats. The best way to smoke a whole turkey is to use one of the electric smokers with a water pan between the wood chips and the meat rack. Don't be disappointed to learn that the wild turkey does not have a huge, roly-poly breast like a domestic turkey. The taste will more than compensate.

To determine how many your wild turkey will serve, weigh the dressed bird. Turkeys weighing 12 pounds or less will feed 1 person per pound. Larger birds will feed 1 person per ¾ pound.

1 wild turkey

Melted unsalted butter

½ cup light brown sugar blended with 2 teaspoons freshly ground black pepper, 2 teaspoons ground cumin, and 1½ teaspoons salt

2 onions, coarsely chopped

3 celery stalks, coarsely chopped

Port wine

Beef stock (see "Basics")

Soak hardwood chips in water to cover for 1 hour. My favorites are pecan, applewood, and oak. Drain the chips and place in the bottom pan of an electric meat smoker. Turn the smoker on and wait for it to produce a good head of smoke before putting the turkey on.

When the smoker is ready, brush the turkey liberally with the melted butter. Using your hands, rub the brown sugar mixture all over the turkey; set aside. Place the onions and celery stalks in the middle pan of the smoker. Add port wine and beef stock to almost fill the pan. Place the turkey on the top rack of the smoker and place the lid securely on the top. Smoke the turkey for about 6 hours. Baste often with the liquid from the pan below the turkey. Add additional port wine and beef broth as needed during cooking.

Preheat oven to 325 degrees. Remove the turkey from the smoker and place in a roasting pan. Cover the pan and roast the turkey until an instant-read thermometer inserted in the thick portion of the thigh registers 160 degrees. Allow the turkey to rest for 20 minutes before carving. Smoked wild turkey is also delicious when served cold.

◀ SUGGESTED WINES

ALAMOSA WINE CELLARS ROSATO DI SANGIOVESE

HAAK VINEYARDS AND WINERY BARREL-FERMENTED CHARDONNAY

MESSINA HOF WINE CELLARS BARREL RESERVE SAUVIGNON BLANC

TEXAS HILLS VINEYARD MERLOT

SUGGESTED WINES

ALAMOSA WINE CELLARS SANGIOVESE

CAP*ROCK WINERY RESERVE CABERNET SAUVIGNON

DELANEY VINEYARDS AND WINERY CABERNET FRANC

FALL CREEK VINEYARDS GRANITE RESERVE CABERNET SAUVIGNON

LLANO ESTACADO WINERY SIGNATURE RED MERITAGE

Turkey Melt Sandwiches

A good sandwich is hard to beat. Especially in Texas. I like to think we have a more laid-back, casual kind of lifestyle than a lot of other places in the country. So it stands to reason that we would have more occasions to eat laid-back things like sandwiches. But if I'm going to eat something, even casual, I want it to be equal in taste to the calories going into my mouth. This creation, with its exotic taste, courtesy of the toasted fennel seeds, is a mighty deserving sandwich. Deserving of being savored to the last bite.

1 heaping teaspoon fennel seeds

2 tablespoons extra-virgin olive oil

3 ounces sliced mushrooms

1 large green bell pepper, sliced into thin julienne strips

1 large red bell pepper, sliced into thin julienne strips

1 small yellow onion, halved lengthwise, then sliced thin

Salt and freshly ground black pepper to taste

4 hoagie buns

Mayonnaise

1 pound roasted turkey breast, sliced thin

4 ounces sliced pepperoni

Shredded provolone cheese

Spread the fennel seeds out in a small skillet over medium-high heat. Toast the seeds, shaking the pan constantly, until they become very aromatic. Remove from heat and place the seeds between two sheets of plastic wrap. Using a meat pounder, crush the seeds. Set aside.

Heat olive oil in a heavy 10-inch skillet over medium-high heat. Sauté the mushrooms, bell peppers, onions, and crushed fennel seeds until vegetables are wilted and mushroom liquid has evaporated, about 10 minutes. Strain the vegetables through a fine strainer to remove all oil. Season to taste with salt and freshly ground black pepper. Set aside.

Preheat oven to 350 degrees. Spread both sides of the buns with mayonnaise. Place 4 ounces of turkey on each bun. Spread a portion of the sautéed vegetables on top of the meat. Arrange a row of the pepperoni slices, slightly overlapping, down the center. Top with a generous amount of the shredded provolone. Place the tops on the sandwiches and compress them with the flat of your hand. Place sandwiches on a baking sheet and cover tightly with aluminum foil. Bake in preheated oven until cheese is melted and sandwiches are hot, about 15 to 20 minutes. Slice sandwiches in half diagonally and serve.

☙ Serves 4.

SUGGESTED WINES

Becker Vineyards Chardonnay Estate Bottled

Cap*Rock Winery Reserve Toscano Rosso

Delaney Vineyards and Winery Barrel Fermented Chardonnay

Messina Hof Wine Cellars Chenin Blanc

Back door of the old mercantile, Bronte (left); Quarterhorses, Bandera County (facing page).

WILD TURKEY OR DEER JERKY

I have always loved good jerky. The practice of drying strips of meat to remove moisture, thereby preserving the meat indefinitely, is one that our ancestors learned from the American Indians. They called it pemmican. Today, we don't have to dry our meat for the trail, but it sure is nice to munch on some good jerky while driving down the road. There used to be a funky little place on Lake Travis in the Central Texas Hill Country where you could go drink some cold beer, play a game or two of pool, and enjoy the lake view. They made and sold incredible jerky. Sadly, the little place is gone. I'm sure the land value was worth more than another 20 years of beer and jerky. Robert Crumpler, a hunting and fishing guide from Rockport, shared this recipe with me. It makes a really good jerky. I've tried it using all sorts of meats—beef, chicken, deer, even ostrich (which was one of my favorites, by the way.) Make lots, though, because everybody will want some. Shiner Bock from the Spoetzle Brewery in Shiner is my hands-down favorite beverage with a nice hunk of good jerky.

2½ pounds of wild turkey or deer meat, cut into ½-inch-thick strips

1 tablespoon Adolph's Meat Tenderizer

½ teaspoon red (cayenne) pepper, or less for a milder jerky

1½ tablespoons finely ground black pepper

½ teaspoon Lawry's Seasoning Salt

¼ cup soy sauce

⅓ cup Worcestershire sauce

2 tablespoons liquid smoke

½ teaspoon granulated garlic

3 tablespoons light brown sugar

Trim all tendons from meat. Place the strips in a non-aluminum, shallow baking dish. Combine the remaining ingredients and whisk to blend well. Pour the mixture over the meat strips, covering them well. Cover and refrigerate for 12 hours. (The longer the meat is marinated, the spicier the finished jerky will be.) Stir several times while marinating, but be sure that the strips remain submerged in the liquid. Remove the meat from the marinade and place strips on the racks of a dehydrating oven. (You can also smoke the jerky over a wood fire, maintained at 125 degrees.) Dehydrate or smoke for about 8 to 10 hours, or until meat has dried. Cool on wire cooling racks. Store the jerky in airtight containers or zip-sealing plastic bags.

Roast Free-Range Chicken with
Mexican Mint Marigold Butter and White Wine Sauce

There is an art to roasting the perfect chicken. The perfect roast chicken has browned, crisp skin, yet it is lusciously juicy and tender inside. The perfect roast chicken reminds us that the most humble thing can often be the most wonderful. When roasting a chicken, keep in mind that you are dealing with two types of meat—the soft and tender but less fatty breast meat, which must remain moist during cooking, and the denser, tougher, fattier meat of the thighs and legs.

A suitable chicken for roasting is under 8 months old and weighs 3½ to 5 pounds. A free-range, or "organic," chicken will provide the best flavor. They haven't been fed on hormone- or antibiotic-laced feed, and they're allowed to run around the compound and develop some taste in their muscles. (Look for free-range chickens at speciality markets.) When buying a chicken, look for moist, light pinkish skin and a flexible breastbone. Beware of a chicken with a purplish tinge or a very rigid breastbone. Both are signs that the chicken is past its prime. If you roast it, it will be a tough and dry old bird. Remember when cooking chicken that deep red coloration close to the bones does not mean the bird is not cooked thoroughly. In young chickens, red blood cells seep out of the bone marrow (which has not fully hardened and sealed) into the adjacent flesh during cooking. Pink meat is underdone.

2 free-range chickens, 3½ to 5 pounds
1 cup (2 sticks) unsalted butter, softened
2 tablespoons minced Mexican mint marigold
1 teaspoon freshly ground black pepper
1½ teaspoons salt
2 cups chicken stock (see "Basics")

White Wine Sauce

Pan drippings from roasted chicken
3 French shallots, finely chopped
Freshly ground black pepper
⅔ cup Sauvignon Blanc wine
4 cups chicken stock (see "Basics")
4 tablespoons Beurre Manié (see "Basics")
Salt to taste

Preheat oven to 400 degrees. Spray a shallow flameproof roasting pan with non-stick spray. Wash each chicken well and pat very dry with absorbent paper towels; set aside. Combine the butter, Mexican mint marigold, pepper, and salt in work bowl of small food processor fitted with steel blade. Process until smooth and well blended. Transfer butter mixture to a bowl using a rubber spatula.

Using your fingers, loosen the skin of the chicken from the meat all around the breast. Carefully sever the tissue attached to the middle of the breastbone, using your index finger like a hook. Separate the skin down the rib cage on the sides and all the way to the tailbone and down to the leg joint. Your hand will be completely under the skin. Take care not to tear the skin over the breast meat.

Using your hands, spread the butter mixture under the loosened skin of the chicken, distributing evenly. Pat the skin back into place, evening out the buttery lumps. Smear the remaining butter on the outside skin of the chicken, tie the legs together with butcher's (cotton) twine, and place in prepared roasting pan, breast side up. Pour the 2 cups of chicken stock around the chicken.

Loosely cover the chicken with parchment paper and roast for 20 minutes per pound in preheated oven. After the first 15 minutes, turn the chicken onto one side and baste with pan juices, using a bulb baster or spoon. Repeat the turning and basting every 15 minutes, until chicken is once again on its back. Remove the parchment paper for the last 15 minutes of roasting. The chicken should be nicely browned with crisp skin on all sides. To test for doneness, pierce the flesh of the thigh near bone with a skewer. The liquid that runs out should be clear with no traces of pink. Place chicken on cutting board and cover loosely with aluminum foil. Allow the chicken to rest for 15 minutes.

Prepare White Wine Sauce. Place the roasting pan directly on burner over high heat. Add the shallots and black pepper; sauté until shallots are wilted and transparent. Add the white wine and stir, scraping up all browned bits from bottom of pan. Cook until pan juices and wine are reduced to a glaze. Add the chicken stock and cook to reduce by half. Strain the sauce into a 2-quart saucepan. Place saucepan over medium-high heat and bring to a full, rolling boil. Whisk in the Beurre Manié, one small chunk at a time, until desired thickness has been reached.

To serve, carve each chicken into 4 pieces (2 breast-wing portions, 2 thigh-leg portions). Arrange the pieces on serving platter. Pass the White Wine Sauce separately in a sauceboat.

ॐ **Serves 4.**

SUGGESTED WINES

Alamosa Wine Cellars Fumé Blanc
Comfort Cellars Winery Chenin Blanc
Spicewood Vineyards Chardonnay
Texas Hills Vineyard Pinot Grigio

MEXICAN MINT MARIGOLD

Mexican mint marigold, also known as "yerba anise," is the Gulf Coast's answer to true French tarragon, which simply will not grow in our humidity. I find it to be identical in taste to real tarragon. (Perhaps I actually like it a little better because it seems to have a more well-rounded flavor.) Mint marigold is a very hardy evergreen in our region in all but the harshest winters.

It will grow to gargantuan proportions in your herb garden and reward you with thousands of brilliant yellow blooms that you can use in salads or as a garnish.

If the herb gets "bitten" by a moderate freeze, simply cut it back to about 2 inches from the ground and wait until spring. It will come back even fuller than it was the year before.

Rocking on the hotel porch, Turkey (right); Wheat harvesting, Perryton (pages 160–61).

ROGER'S CHICKEN-FRIED CHICKEN WITH TEXAS GRAVY

Roger Canales, one of my sous-chefs, has brought the rich heritage of the wonderful, exotic foods of his native El Salvador to our kitchen. Roger has that all-important talent that separates a great chef from a merely adequate chef—an inherent sense of seasoning foods. It comes from somewhere deep inside a person. Over the years it manifests itself as a highly refined palate. This is the talent that guides a chef in pairing foods with the perfect seasonings and sauces or pairing entrées with the perfect sides. When Roger has day duty in our kitchen, he often prepares this dish for "staff lunch." A humble chicken breast takes on new flavor dimensions with a few simple seasonings. Topped with Texas Gravy, a.k.a. "Cream Gravy," it's a mighty memorable meal. (The gravy is also mucho bueno *on Terry's Tender, Flaky, Lighter-Than-Air Biscuits.) If you want to serve beer with this quintessentially Texas dish, Shiner Bock from the Spoetzle Brewery in Shiner is always a great choice.*

4 6- to 8-ounce boneless, skinless chicken breasts

2 teaspoons freshly ground black pepper

4 tablespoons light brown sugar

1½ cups good-quality pineapple juice

Seasoned Flour for Frying (see "Basics")

Egg wash made from beating 3 eggs into 4 cups of milk

Canola oil for frying

TEXAS GRAVY

⌘ Makes about 5 cups.

½ cup bacon or sausage drippings

½ cup all-purpose flour

½ teaspoon freshly ground black pepper

2 teaspoons chicken base paste (see "The Texas Cook's Pantry")

4 cups whole milk, or more as needed

Salt to taste

Place the chicken breasts, one at a time, inside an open zip-sealing bag. Using the flat side of a meat pounder, pound the breasts until thin. Place the chicken breasts in a single layer in a non-aluminum baking dish. Scatter the black pepper and brown sugar evenly over the breasts. Pour the pineapple juice around them, cover with plastic wrap, and marinate, refrigerated, for 2 hours.

Prepare the Texas Gravy. Heat the drippings in a 12-inch cast-iron skillet over medium heat. When the drippings are hot, add the flour all at once and whisk to blend well. Cook, whisking constantly, for 3 to 4 minutes. Add the pepper and chicken base; stir to blend well. Add the milk and whisk until smooth. Bring the gravy to a full boil and boil until thick, about 1 minute. Add additional milk if gravy is too thick. Lower heat and season to taste with salt. Keep hot over low heat.

To cook the chicken, remove breasts from marinade, shaking off liquid. Dredge the breasts in the seasoned flour, turning to coat both sides well. Shake off all excess flour. Next dip them in the egg wash. Finally, dredge them in the seasoned flour again, coating well and shaking off all excess flour. In a heavy 12-inch skillet, add the oil to a depth of 1½ inches and preheat to 350 degrees. Lower the breasts into the preheated oil and fry, turning once, until golden brown, about 12 to 15 minutes. Drain on wire rack set over baking sheet.

To serve, place a chicken breast on each serving plate and top with a portion of the Texas Gravy.

⌘ Serves 4.

SUGGESTED WINES

BECKER VINEYARDS CHARDONNAY ESTATE BOTTLED

LA BUENA VIDA VINEYARDS SPRINGTOWN SAUVIGNON BLANC

MESSINA HOF WINE CELLARS BARREL RESERVE "TEX-ZIN" ZINFANDEL

TEXAS HILLS VINEYARD PINOT GRIGIO

Mole Guanajuato con Pollo

*N*o book dealing with Texas foods would be complete without a recipe for mole. Moles are a category of complicated sauces that have traveled to Texas from Mexico. The word comes from an Aztec word, molli, meaning a sauce flavored with chilies. The most famous of these dishes is Mexico's national holiday dish, Mole Poblano de Guajolote (Turkey in Pueblan Sauce). There are controversies about the origins of mole sauces. Some say the sauce was invented in the sixteenth century in the Spanish convent of Santa Rosa in the city of Puebla. However, most scholars believe it was a native Aztec dish discovered by the Spanish conquistadors. Today there are many versions of mole with the ingredients characterized by the region, but all are a combination of dried chilies, toasted seeds and nuts, spices and herbs, vegetables, and Mexican chocolate. Mexican chocolate is very different from regular chocolate, so don't substitute. Mexican chocolate is available in Hispanic markets or in the ethnic section of specialty markets. Although the sauce is complicated, the taste is sublime. The pride in accomplishment is also immense. If you wish to tackle a mole dish, I recommend preparing the time-consuming sauce a day or two in advance. Finish the dish by braising the chicken on serving day. Prepare some white rice cooked in chicken stock with a pinch of saffron and sautéed onions to serve with the dish. This particular recipe calls for dried avocado leaves. These are literally the dried leaves of the avocado tree, which have a leathery texture and an anise-like aroma and flavor. They aren't sold commercially, so if you don't have an avocado tree, you may substitute bay leaves and a pinch of anise seeds. In keeping with the Mexican theme, you may serve the dish with a Mexican beer like Tecate, Corona, or Dos Equis.

8 6- to 8-ounce boneless chicken breast halves, skin on

Salt and freshly ground black pepper

Canola oil

3 celery stalks, coarsely chopped, including leafy tops

2 small onions, coarsely chopped

2 carrots, peeled and coarsely chopped

2 dried bay leaves

4 large garlic cloves, crushed

1 tablespoon whole black peppercorns

2 quarts chicken stock (see "Basics")

8 cups cooked white rice with saffron (see "Basics")

Mole Guanajuato

¼ pound dried mulato chilies, seeds and veins removed

¼ pound dried pasilla chilies, seeds and veins removed

¼ pound dried ancho chilies, seeds and veins removed

3 cups hot water

½ cup sesame seeds

2 dried avocado leaves, or dried bay leaves and 5 or 6 anise seeds

1 bolillo or a small, hard French roll (petit pan), cut into cubes

2 corn tortillas, torn into small pieces

Lard for frying

3 ounces each of sliced almonds and raw peanuts (skin on)

¼ cup golden raisins

1 4-inch cinnamon stick

3 whole cloves

4 whole allspice

½ teaspoon each of dried marjoram, thyme, and Mexican oregano

2 onions, chopped

1 whole garlic head, unpeeled

¼ pound tomatillos, peeled and washed

½ pound Roma tomatoes

Canola oil

4 ounces Mexican chocolate, coarsely chopped

2 teaspoons sugar

Salt to taste

1 quart chicken stock (see "Basics")

Prepare the Mole Guanajuato. Toast all of the chilies in a dry cast-iron skillet until fragrant, then soak in the hot water for 15 to 20 minutes, or until they are very pliable. Place the chilies and soaking liquid in blender and puree. Set puree aside.

Toast the sesame seeds, avocado leaves, bread, and tortillas in a dry skillet until browned. Set aside.

Heat ¼ cup lard in a 12-inch cast-iron skillet. Sauté the nuts, raisins, cinnamon, cloves, allspice, herbs, and onion until onion is wilted and transparent, about 10 minutes. Drain off all fat and set aside.

Place the garlic, tomatillos, and tomatoes in a small baking dish and coat with canola oil. Roast in a 350-degree oven until well browned. When cool enough to handle, squeeze the pulp out of the garlic cloves. Set aside with tomatillos and tomatoes.

Combine all the reserved ingredients except the chilies in work bowl of food processor fitted with steel blade and process until smooth. Add a little chicken stock if needed to keep the mixture moving. It will be fairly thick.

Heat ½ cup of lard in a 12-inch cast-iron skillet. Add the processed mixture and cook over very low heat for about 1 hour. Add the pureed chilies and cook an additional hour.

Add the chocolate to the skillet, stirring until melted. Stir in the sugar and add salt to taste.

Gradually add the chicken stock, stirring. Simmer the sauce on very low heat for 25 minutes. The mole should be thick, but if it is too thick for your preference, add additional chicken stock. (At this point the mole is ready to use, or you may refrigerate it for several days.)

To cook the chicken, salt and pepper both sides of the breasts. Heat a glaze of the canola oil in a heavy Dutch oven over medium-high heat. Quickly sear the breasts on both sides, browning well. Pour off the oil from the pan. Add the remaining ingredients except rice to the pan and braise the breasts over medium-low heat until done, about 30 minutes.

To serve, transfer the breasts to the skillet with the mole sauce and simmer for about 10 minutes. Place some saffron rice on each serving plate. Spoon a portion of the sauce over the rice and place a chicken breast in the center. Serve hot.

ର Serves 8.

SUGGESTED WINES

Haak Vineyards and Winery Chardonnay
Hidden Springs Winery Muscat Canelli
Llano Estacado Winery Passionelle
Sister Creek Vineyards Chardonnay
Spicewood Vineyard Sauvignon Blanc

Quilters, Cuero

Meat, Tame and Wild

There's probably not a cowboy or cowgirl around that won't agree that Texas is red-meat country. We raise it, we hunt it, and we like to eat it. We also include pork in the category of red meat, even though it's technically whitish in color! We like our meat roasted, fried (sautéed, if you're into fancy frying), braised, broiled, grilled, barbecued, smoked, dry-cured into jerky, or any other way we can think of to cook it up.

Red meat and the raising of it are all wound up in our history. Texas history is rich with tales of the early Texas ranches and the legendary cattle drives where huge herds of cattle were driven north to be sold to the cattle markets in the Midwest. Fort Worth grew up around the huge stockyards where thousands of head of cattle were processed for sale. Today Fort Worth is still sometimes referred to as "Cowtown" even though it has grown into a large and sophisticated city. Those early cattle ranchers set a standard for quality beef that still exists in Texas today. Nothing makes a cowboy smile wider than a well-marbled rib-eye cut about an inch and a quarter thick and sizzled on the grill.

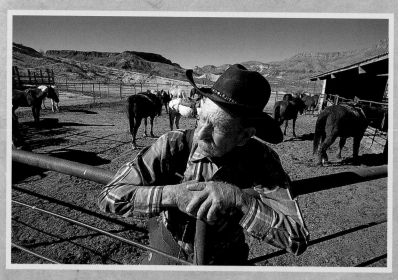

Trailrider and remuda, Lajitas; Whitetails, Kerr County (pages 168–69).

Texas boasts an abundant supply of game animals. Squirrel, rabbit, wild hogs and their cousin, the javelina, and deer of many varieties are avidly hunted. Many Texas families count on deer season to fill the freezer with meat, to be augmented by other small game the remainder of the year. Hunting skills are passed on from one generation to another. It's a rite of passage for Texas youngsters when they bag their first deer.

My first introduction to game meat was at my wedding reception. I married a country cowboy and ours was a "cowboy style" wedding. It was held outside and everybody dressed western. There were coon dogs and guinea hens and peacocks milling around among the wedding guests. The barbecue pits had been blazing all night cooking the feast of wild boar and venison that was served along with pinto beans and greens and a lethal concoction called "Coon Dog Punch" that was ladled out of a large plastic trash can packed in a tub of ice. It was wonderful—succulent, tender meat with an exotic, slightly wild taste. That was the moment I was hooked on game meat and became an honorary cowgirl.

Barbecueing for the roundup near Concepcíon; Vaqueros, Jim Hogg County (pages 172–73).

CATTLEMAN'S CHOICE GRILLED RIB-EYE STEAKS WITH TEXAS BUTTER

In Texas, steaks are king. The two most popular backyard foods are grilled rib-eye steaks and smoked brisket. Without question, the rib-eye is the most naturally flavorful and desirable steak. Rib-eye steaks are cut from the whole rib-eye muscle, which is a continuation of the tender muscle that runs along the back from the shoulder to the hip of the steer. The rib-eye has more marbling than other cuts of meat, and therefore it will have more flavor, since fat and flavor go together. Rib-eye steaks are expensive, so treat them well when you cook them. By well, I don't mean well done. If you must cook your steaks well done, then I suggest buying a cheaper cut of meat. When the rib-eye is cooked past medium-rare to medium, all of its wonderful fat is cooked out, leaving it tougher and with far less taste than it started out with. When grilling steaks, you will get the optimum taste and texture by using a gas grill rather than a charcoal fire. Save the barbecue pit for the brisket.

4 12-ounce rib-eye steaks

Red Meat Dip and Baste (see recipe for Grilled Medallions of Venison Backstrap with Ancho Chili and Honey Sauce)

Freshly ground black pepper

TEXAS BUTTER

ଔ **Makes ½ pound.**

1 cup (2 sticks) unsalted butter, softened

1 heaping tablespoon minced flat-leaf parsley

1 teaspoon minced lemon zest

1 tablespoon Worcestershire sauce

½ teaspoon Tabasco sauce

¼ teaspoon salt, or to taste

1 teaspoon freshly ground black pepper

Make the Texas Butter. Cut the butter into small cubes and place in work bowl of food processor fitted with steel blade. Add remaining ingredients and process until smooth. Roll the butter into cylinders in parchment paper and freeze it. (You can cut off individual portions from the frozen logs and they keep forever in the freezer.)

Heat a gas grill to medium-hot. Brush both sides of the steaks with some of the Red Meat Dip and Baste. Liberally pepper both sides. Place the steaks on the hot grill and cook to desired degree of doneness, about 3 to 4 minutes per side for medium-rare. Use chef's tongs to turn the steaks. Never puncture them with a fork, which would cause them to lose their delicious juices. Just before the steaks are done, place a ½-inch-thick slice of the Texas Butter in the center of each steak. As soon as the butter has begun to melt, transfer steaks to serving plates and enjoy.

ଔ **Serves 4.**

SUGGESTED WINES

ALAMOSA WINE CELLARS EL GUAPO, TIO PANCHO RANCH

BECKER VINEYARDS CABERNET SAUVIGNON RESERVE ESTATE BOTTLED

COMFORT CELLARS WINERY MERLOT

DRY COMAL CREEK VINEYARDS SAUVIGNON BLANC

LLANO ESTACADO WINERY SIGNATURE RED MERITAGE

TEXAS CHICKEN-FRIED RIB-EYE WITH TABASCO CREAM GRAVY

Chicken-fried steak with white cream gravy is one of the most traditionally Texan dishes in the state. You won't find anything quite like it anywhere else in the country. Many restaurants have made their reputations around the quality of their chicken-fried steaks—the bigger the better! This is the ultimate chicken-fried steak, made from the tender and very flavorful rib-eye and topped off with a genuine kick-ass, get-in-your-face gravy laced with Tabasco pepper sauce. Serve it with another Texas tradition, Shiner Bock from the Spoetzle Brewery in Shiner.

4 to 6 well-trimmed rib-eye steaks, cut ⅝-inch thick (approximately 7 ounces each)

3 cups Seasoned Flour for Frying (see "Basics")

Egg wash made from 3 eggs well beaten with 4 cups milk

4 cups Japanese (panko) breadcrumbs, seasoned with 2 teaspoons salt and 2 teaspoons Chef Paul's Meat Magic or other Cajun-style meat-seasoning blend

Canola oil for deep-frying, heated to 350 degrees

TABASCO CREAM GRAVY

½ cup bacon or sausage drippings

½ cup all-purpose flour

½ teaspoon ground black pepper

2 teaspoons chicken base paste (see "The Texas Cook's Pantry")

4 cups whole milk, or more as needed

2 tablespoons Tabasco sauce

Salt to taste

Pat steaks dry using absorbent paper towels. Place each steak between two sheets of plastic wrap and pound to about half their thickness with a meat-tenderizing mallet. Dredge the steaks in the seasoned flour, coating well and shaking to remove all excess flour. Dip steaks in the egg wash, coating well. Then press the steak into the seasoned Japanese breadcrumbs, coating well on both sides and shaking off excess crumbs. Refrigerate steaks until you are ready to fry them.

Make the Tabasco Cream Gravy. Heat the drippings in a heavy cast-iron skillet over medium heat. When the drippings are hot, add the flour all at once and whisk to blend well. Cook, whisking constantly, for 3 to 4 minutes. Add the pepper and chicken base paste, stirring to blend well. Add the milk and whisk until smooth. Bring the gravy to a *full boil* to thicken; boil for about 1 minute. Lower heat and season to taste with salt and additional black pepper, if needed. Stir in Tabasco sauce. Thin gravy with additional whole milk as needed.

Deep-fry the breaded steaks in the preheated oil. Cook only until the crust is crisp and medium-golden brown, about 4 minutes, turning once. Do not overcook the steaks; they should be served medium-rare to medium so they are fork tender. Place the steaks on individual plates and top with a liberal amount of the gravy.

ର Serves 4 to 6.

SUGGESTED WINES

DRY COMAL CREEK VINEYARDS CABERNET SAUVIGNON

HAAK VINEYARDS AND WINERY ZINFANDEL

HIDDEN SPRINGS WINERY BLUSH

MESSINA HOF WINE CELLARS BARREL RESERVE SHIRAZ

Main Street mural, Martindale

Texas-Style Roast Prime Rib Au Jus

*S*tanding rib roast is a regal dish. It is the supreme cut of meat for the serious beef lover. Roasted to medium-rare perfection and served with a thin, rich broth made from its own meat drippings, it makes a hard act to follow. Select a standing rib roast of a size appropriate to serve the number of guests. Allow about 14 ounces of meat per person. When purchasing the roast, ask for the small end, which is the tenderest portion. It may be a bit more expensive, but the taste will compensate for the small difference in price. When you have an occasion with a large crowd that calls for a really spectacular creation, buy the whole, lip-on rib-eye and roast it, adjusting the quantities in this recipe relative to the weight of the rib-eye.

Boneless standing rib roast, about 6 pounds

1 small onion, quartered

1 large carrot

2 celery stalks, including leafy tops

4 cups beef stock (see "Basics")

Prepared horseradish

Dry Rub

¼ cup granulated garlic

2 tablespoons Lawry's seasoning salt

2 tablespoons ground black pepper

⅓ cup sugar

2 teaspoons crushed red pepper flakes

¼ cup beef stock (see "Basics")

1 tablespoon teriyaki marinade or Worcestershire sauce

Au Jus

Strained and de-fatted drippings from roasting pan, combined with enough additional beef stock to make 3 cups, if needed

2 garlic cloves, crushed with side of chef's knife

2 tablespoons dry red wine

Preheat oven to 350 degrees. Place oven rack in middle position. Combine all Dry Rub ingredients and whisk into a smooth paste. Spread the paste evenly over the top fat layer and sides of the roast. Put the onion, carrot, celery stalks, and beef stock in a heavy open roasting pan. Place a wire rack in the pan and set the roast on the rack, fat side up. Place in hot oven for 1 hour. Reduce heat to 250 degrees and roast an additional 1 hour and 15 minutes. An instant-read meat thermometer should read 135–140 degrees for medium-rare to medium. (Cooking time is 19 minutes per pound from the time the meat goes in the oven.) Set the meat aside to rest for 15 minutes.

Prepare the Au Jus. Combine the de-fatted beef drippings and stock, garlic cloves, and red wine in a 2-quart saucepan and bring to a boil. Lower heat and simmer for 10 minutes. Strain and keep hot.

Slice the roast into 6 portions. Serve with the Au Jus and prepared horseradish.

ᐓ **Serves 6.**

SUGGESTED WINES

Alamosa Wine Cellars Sangiovese

Fall Creek Vineyards Merlot

Haak Vineyards and Winery Cabernet Sauvignon

Sister Creek Vineyards Cabernet Blend

SLOW-SMOKED BRISKET WITH HELLFIRE AND BRIMSTONE SAUCE

*B*arbecue is a very serious subject in Texas. There are all sorts of bragging rights associated with cooking the best at the various barbecue competitions around the state. There is one thing that all Texas barbecuers agree on, however: barbecue in Texas means beef, and the brisket is king. The brisket is a homely-looking piece of beef, but when cooked properly the taste can bring tears to a cowboy's eyes. Brisket is the underside chest muscle from the beef cattle. It has a thick end called the point cut, or nose, and a thin end called the flat cut. One side of the brisket has a layer of fat, and another, larger layer of fat extends inside the point end. These fats act as a natural baste for flavor and moisture during the long cooking process. The fat should never be trimmed away prior to cooking. Remember, fat equals flavor. The drawback to brisket is that it is one of the toughest cuts of meat on the steer. The secret to cooking tender and juicy brisket is "low and slow." A general rule of thumb is to cook brisket 1¼ hours per pound at a pit temperature of around 220 degrees. For serious brisket cooking, you really need a barbecue rig with a separate firebox so that the meat is cooked by the indirect heat method. To get the best smoke flavor, supplement the charcoal fire with hardwood chunks (not chips). My favorites are oak, pecan, applewood, and maple. Soak the chunks in water for a couple of hours before using so that they smolder and make smoke instead of just burning up. And never, never use charcoal lighter. It gives off a vapor of petroleum-like taste that will flavor the meat. Beer is always a good bet for Texas barbecue. Shiner Bock from the Spoetzle Brewery in Shiner just happens to be my personal favorite. It's brewed in the European style—like real beer should be!

Beef brisket, 10 to 12 pounds, untrimmed
Sliced yellow onions
Hamburger-sliced dill pickles

DRY RUB

◪ **Makes 1 cup.**

⅓ cup light brown sugar
1 tablespoon plus 1 teaspoon salt
1 tablespoon plus 1 teaspoon granulated garlic
1 tablespoon plus 1 teaspoon granulated onion powder
1 tablespoon plus 1 teaspoon celery salt
2 tablespoons plus 2 teaspoons paprika
1 tablespoon medium-hot chili powder
2 teaspoons finely ground black pepper
1 teaspoon lemon-pepper seasoning
1 teaspoon dry mustard
1 teaspoon dried thyme
¼ teaspoon ground red (cayenne) pepper

BIG YELLOWBACK BASTING SAUCE

◪ **Makes about 1 quart.**

1 cup Italian salad dressing
1 cup apple cider vinegar
1 cup yellow mustard
1 tablespoon freshly squeezed lime juice
2 teaspoons pureed garlic
2 teaspoons pureed onion
½ teaspoon crushed red pepper flakes
2 teaspoons medium-hot chili powder
2 teaspoons ground cumin
¼ cup Worcestershire sauce
1½ teaspoons freshly ground black pepper
¼ teaspoon salt

(continued)

HELLFIRE AND BRIMSTONE BARBECUE SAUCE

Makes 2 quarts.

- 4 tablespoons unsalted butter
- 4 green onions, minced, including green tops
- 2 tablespoons granulated garlic
- ¼ cup dark red chili powder
- 1 tablespoon finely ground black pepper
- 6 cups tomato ketchup
- ⅓ cup firmly packed light brown sugar
- ½ cup granulated sugar
- 1 cup apple cider vinegar
- ¾ cup beer
- ⅓ cup dry red wine
- 1½ teaspoons dried Mexican oregano
- 1 teaspoon red (cayenne) pepper
- ½ cup Worcestershire sauce
- 2 tablespoons Tabasco sauce

Prepare the fire by building a charcoal or wood fire in firebox of barbecue pit. When the coals are glowing red, add soaked hardwood chunks. Allow the fire to cook down until temperature in the cooking chamber is around 220 degrees.

While the fire is cooking down, prepare the Dry Rub by combining all ingredients and blending well; set aside.

Make the Big Yellowback Basting Sauce by combining all ingredients and whisking to blend well.

Rub the Dry Rub into the meat, coating it well on all sides. Let meat sit at room temperature until the temperature in the pit is right. Place meat on cooking rack in pit, fat side up, and baste with the Big Yellowback Basting Sauce. Cook the meat for about 12½ to 15 hours, depending on size of brisket. Turn and baste often. Maintain a temperature of 220 degrees in the pit, adding more charcoal and wood chunks as needed. For the last hour of cooking, wrap the brisket tightly in aluminum foil.

While the brisket is cooking, make the Hellfire and Brimstone Barbecue Sauce. Combine all ingredients in a 4-quart soup pot. Stir over medium heat until butter has melted. Simmer, covered, for 1 hour. Cool and store in refrigerator, reheat when ready to use. Never use the barbecue sauce on the meat while it is cooking. It will cause the "bark," or outside crust, of the meat to char and have a bitter taste.

When ready to serve the meat, unwrap it and trim off the surface fat. Cut the nose end loose from the layer of fat under it and cut out the fat layer. Slice the meat across the grain into thin slices. (Thin slices are tenderer than thick ones.) Serve hot with sliced onions and hamburger pickles. Pass the hot Hellfire and Brimstone Barbecue Sauce separately.

Serves 8 to 10.

SUGGESTED WINES

CAP*ROCK WINERY CABERNET ROYALE, ROSÉ OF CABERNET
SAUVIGNON

COMFORT CELLARS WINERY COMFORT BLUSH

LA BUENA VIDA VINEYARDS SPRINGTOWN MIST

SPICEWOOD VINEYARDS CABERNET CLARET

TEXAS HILLS VINEYARD CABERNET SAUVIGNON

Cowboy leather, Quitaque; Spanish dagger near Terlingua (pages 182–83).

Roast Beef Tenderloin with Two-Mushroom Essence Sauce

The beef tenderloin is the tenderest cut of meat on a steer and offers optimum taste when cooked medium-rare to medium. The sauce for this dish uses only the concentrated juices of mushrooms. I love to pair their musky, very sensuous taste with beef, but the unique sauce is also wonderful with veal and chicken dishes.

1 whole beef tenderloin, trimmed of silverskin, about 4 to 6 pounds

8 large garlic cloves, minced

1 teaspoon minced fresh thyme

2 teaspoons freshly ground black pepper

1½ teaspoons salt

½ cup extra-virgin olive oil

Two-Mushroom Essence Sauce

2 ounces dried morel mushrooms

2 pounds fresh white mushrooms

2 large French shallots, coarsely chopped

½ teaspoon minced fresh thyme

3 cups beef stock

½ cup whipping cream

½ teaspoon freshly ground black pepper

Salt to taste

2 tablespoons unsalted butter, softened

Prepare the Two-Mushroom Essence Sauce. Soak the morel mushrooms in 2 cups hot water for about 20 minutes, or until they are softened and pliable. Remove them from the water and squeeze all of the liquid out of them back into the water. Reserve ½ cup of the water.

Combine the morels and 4 cups of the white mushrooms in work bowl of food processor fitted with steel blade. Process until finely chopped, about 1 minute. Add the shallots, thyme, and 1 cup of the beef stock, the reserved mushroom soaking liquid, and another 4 cups of the mushrooms. Process until finely chopped, scraping down side of bowl as needed. Transfer to a separate bowl.

Add the remaining mushrooms and remaining beef stock. Process until finely chopped. Stir into the first batch of mushrooms, blending well. Place a fine strainer over a large bowl and add the mushroom puree. Press hard on the mushroom mixture with a wooden spoon to remove as much of the liquid as possible. Place the pulpy mushroom puree in a clean cloth and gather up the corners, twisting them together. Squeeze excess liquid out of the mushrooms into the bowl with the rest of the liquid. Keep twisting the cloth until no more liquid comes out. Discard the pulp. Transfer the liquid (about 4 to 5 cups) to a medium saucepan and bring to a gentle boil. Lower heat and simmer gently until the liquid is reduced to 1½ cups, about 45 minutes. Keep skimming off the grayish foam that will rise to the top. Set aside.

Preheat oven to 425 degrees. Cut the thin, tapered end off the tenderloin. Save it for another use. Combine the minced garlic, thyme, black pepper, salt, and olive oil. Spread the mixture all over the tenderloin, coating it well. Place tenderloin in roasting pan and cook uncovered in the preheated oven for 45 to 60 minutes, or until an instant-read meat thermometer inserted into the thickest part of the meat registers 135 degrees. Remove the meat from the oven and set aside to rest for 15 minutes to redistribute the juices.

When ready to serve the meat, reheat the reduced mushroom liquid. Add the whipping cream and bring to a boil. Add the black pepper, lower heat, and simmer for 10 minutes. Add salt to taste and remove pan from heat. Set aside and keep warm.

Slice the tenderloin into ½-inch-thick medallions. Whisk the 2 tablespoons of butter into the sauce, off the heat. Serve 3 or 4 slices of the meat per person, topped with a portion of the Two-Mushroom Essence Sauce.

ॐ **Serves 6 to 8.**

SUGGESTED WINES

Alamosa Wine Cellars Sangiovese

Delaney Vineyards and Winery Merlot

Fall Creek Vineyards Granite Reserve Cabernet Sauvignon

Hidden Springs Winery Cabernet Sauvignon

Llano Estacado Winery Cellar Select Cabernet Sauvignon

BORDER BURGERS

*H*amburgers are one of the most popular foods in Texas. And, fast-food outlets withstanding, there are some really good hamburger joints in the state. One of the best is in Austin, a very unique city that is deeply enmeshed in the culinary heritage of the state. Although Austin is growing uncontrollably, there are a few places in the city that never really change. They retain the soul of the Austin of the sixties. One of those places is Hut's Hamburgers on Sixth Street. I recently revisited Hut's after 30 years. It was like stepping back in time. Even the same music was playing! If you can't get to Hut's, try this one. All it's missing is the atmosphere. With this burger, I like the tangy taste of a really cold Mexican beer like Tecate or Corona.

4 pounds lean ground beef

2 tablespoons Worcestershire sauce

½ cup dehydrated onions

1½ teaspoons fine-grind black pepper

¾ teaspoon salt

Red Meat Dip and Baste (see recipe for Grilled Medallions of Venison Backstrap with Ancho Chili and Honey Sauce)

Serrano Chili Guacamole (see separate recipe)

Thinly sliced red onion

Tomato slices

Sliced pickled jalapeño chilies

Sliced Monterey Jack cheese

Good-quality hamburger buns

To make the burger patties, combine ground beef, Worcestershire sauce, onions, black pepper, and salt in a large bowl and blend well, using your hands. Form into 10 patties, approximately 6 to 7 ounces each.

To cook the burgers, heat a gas grill to medium-hot and spray the grill with non-stick vegetable spray. Place the patties on the hot grill and baste with the Red Meat Dip and Baste. Cook the burgers for 20 minutes, turning 3 or 4 times and basting with the dip. Preheat oven to 350 degrees. When the burgers are done, place them on a baking sheet. Top each with a portion of the Serrano Chili Guacamole, then a few slices of red onion and tomato slices. Pile desired amount of jalapeños on the tomatoes and top with a slice of cheese. Place baking sheet in oven and cook just until cheese begins to melt, about 5 minutes. While cheese is melting, lightly toast both halves of the buns on the grill. Place the burgers on the buns and serve hot.

ଓ **Makes 10 burgers.**

SUGGESTED WINES

COMFORT CELLARS WINERY COMFORT BLUSH

DELANEY VINEYARDS AND WINERY ROSÉ

LA BUENA VIDA VINEYARDS SPRINGTOWN MIST (BLUSH)

LLANO ESTACADO WINERY SIGNATURE RED MERITAGE

MESSINA HOF WINE CELLARS "TEX-ZIN" ZINFANDEL

SUGGESTED WINES ▶

CAP*ROCK WINERY TOPAZ ROYALE

COMFORT CELLARS WINERY COMFORT BLUSH

HAAK VINEYARDS AND WINERY BLANC DU BOIS

LLANO ESTACADO WINERY PASSIONELLE

SPICEWOOD VINEYARDS CABERNET SAUVIGNON

Pecan Street architectural detail, Bastrop

Tequila Beef Fajitas with Pico de Gallo

*T*he grilled fajita as we know it in Texas is a Texas invention that has taken the whole country by storm. Fajitas are one of the most fun—and easiest—dishes to prepare for a large outdoor party. For really great fajitas, you must use the real fajita meat—inside skirt steak. The word *fajita actually means "little girdle," which describes the skirt steak. There are only two skirts per beef, one on the inside of each forequarter. Before the popularity of fajitas, it was almost impossible to find this great cut of meat because nobody knew what to do with it, except the butcher who took them home to savor! A Mexican beer like Tecate or Corona is always a good taste match for this fun Tex-Mex food.*

5 pounds beef inside skirt steak
Sour cream
Shredded Monterey Jack cheese
Picante sauce
8- or 9-inch flour tortillas

Marinade

1 8¼-ounce jar Rogelio Bueno mole paste
⅔ cup fresh lime juice
1 teaspoon ground cumin
1 teaspoon freshly ground black pepper
½ teaspoon red (cayenne) pepper
1½ tablespoons minced garlic
1 can 7-Up soda
1 fifth tequila

Pico de Gallo

ભ **Makes about 3 cups.**

4 ripe Roma tomatoes, diced small
1 small red onion, finely chopped
4 green onions, chopped, including green tops
1 medium cucumber, unpeeled, seeds removed, cut into small dice
10 serrano chilies, seeds and veins removed, minced
⅓ cup roughly chopped cilantro
2 tablespoons freshly squeezed lime juice
1 large avocado, peeled, pitted, and diced
Salt to taste

Vegetables

2 large red bell peppers, cut into thin julienne strips
2 large green bell peppers, cut into thin julienne strips
2 yellow onions, halved lengthwise, then sliced
Salt to taste
1 tablespoon dark chili powder
1 teaspoon dried Mexican oregano
2 teaspoons ground cumin
2 teaspoons ground coriander
Lard or bacon drippings

Trim the skirt steak, removing any silverskin or traces of fat. Cut off any ragged edges; set aside. Make the marinade by combining all ingredients in a large, non-aluminum bowl; whisk to blend well. Immerse the skirt steak in the marinade, cover with plastic wrap, and marinate, refrigerated, overnight.

To prepare the Pico de Gallo, combine all ingredients in non-aluminum container and toss to blend well. Season to taste with salt. Refrigerate, tightly covered, until ready to serve.

When ready to cook the fajitas, preheat gas grill or prepare charcoal fire. Remove the meat from the marinade; discard marinade. Grill the skirt steaks until they are about medium, searing well on both sides. Set aside to keep warm while cooking the vegetables.

Place vegetables in a large bowl and toss with the seasonings, taking care to season all vegetables; set aside. In a large cast-iron skillet, melt the lard or heat bacon drippings until smoking. Add a portion of the vegetable mixture and toss until browned and seared. Remove with tongs and set aside to keep warm. Repeat with remaining vegetables.

Slice the skirt steak into ¾-inch-wide strips. Toss the sliced fajitas with the vegetables. Serve hot with Pico de Gallo, sour cream, shredded cheese, picante sauce, and flour tortillas.

ભ **Serves 8.**

Texas-Style Eggs Benedict

The brunch concept was originally introduced to America by the British, who celebrated the end of a hunt with a lavish spread of food around the noon hour. Brunch did not really catch on in this country until around 1930. The practice was slower to evolve in Texas because the whole idea seemed to have sissified connotations. Today leisurely Sunday brunches are a commonplace form of entertaining in Texas. All major hotels and many restaurants offer Sunday brunches with lavish spreads of meats and seafood, fruits, egg dishes, and endless varieties of breads and pastries. We created this dish to serve for brunch at Maner Lake Lodge. It has been deemed worthy of being eaten by manly men.

4 7-ounce rib-eye steaks, sliced about ⅝-inch thick
Olive oil
Salt and freshly ground black pepper
4 slices Texas Toast (see separate recipe)
Tomato slices
4 poached eggs (see "Basics")
Paprika

Béarnaise Sauce

4 tablespoons finely chopped shallots
2 tablespoons dried tarragon
2 tablespoons dried chervil
⅔ cup tarragon vinegar
6 egg yolks
¼ teaspoon salt
¼ teaspoon red (cayenne) pepper
2 cups (4 sticks) unsalted butter, melted and hot

Preheat gas grill to medium-hot. To make the Béarnaise Sauce, combine the shallots, tarragon, chervil, and tarragon vinegar in a small saucepan. Cook over medium heat until the liquid is reduced to about 2 tablespoons. (It will be almost dry.) Set aside to cool slightly. Combine the reduced herb mixture, egg yolks, salt, and cayenne pepper in work bowl of food processor fitted with steel blade. Process about 2 minutes, or until egg yolks are thickened and light lemon yellow in color. With the machine running, pour the hot butter through the feed tube in a very slow, steady stream until all has been added. Process an additional minute to form a strong emulsion. Strain the mixture through a fine strainer, stirring the herb mixture with a wooden spoon to extract all excess sauce. Discard solids. Cover the sauce and set aside to keep warm. (Do not leave the sauce over direct heat, or it will break.)

Brush the steaks with olive oil and season with salt and freshly ground black pepper. Grill the steaks to medium doneness.

To assemble the dish, place a slice of Texas Toast on each serving plate. Top with a grilled steak. Place 2 tomato slices on each steak. Top with a poached egg, then spoon a generous amount of the Béarnaise Sauce over the top. Garnish with a dusting of paprika. Serve hot.

ᴄ❧ **Serves 4.**

SUGGESTED WINES

Alamosa Wine Cellars Sangiovese
Becker Vineyards Chenin Blanc
Delaney Vineyards and Winery Texas Champagne Brut
Fall Creek Vineyards Merlot

Chisos Mountains, Big Bend National Park

CHILIES RELLENOS WITH PORK PICADILLO AND RANCHERO SAUCE

A really good chili relleno is a very satisfying thing. They are difficult to prepare, and so few Mexican restaurants offer them, which is a shame. To make a real chili relleno, you must use the poblano chili—never green bell peppers! The poblano chili is one of the most widely used in Mexican and southwestern cuisines. It is a dark green chili with a purple-black tinge. The chili tapers from the shoulders (stem end) to a point at the bottom. Poblanos usually measure about 4 to 5 inches in length. The chili is usually not eaten raw but rather roasted and peeled before use. It is the ideal chili for chili rellenos because the flesh is so thick. Poblanos range in strength from medium to hot. It is a good idea to taste a small portion of the chili to make sure that it's not too hot. If your poblanos are too piquant, soak them in a vinegar and water solution for 30 minutes to moderate the bite of the capsaicin, or hot chili oil. Poblanos are commonly available in the produce section of most full-service markets in the state. A good Mexican beer, served well chilled, such as Tecate, Corona, or Dos Equis, is a great match to this spicy Tex-Mex dish.

6 unblemished poblano chilies, blistered and peeled (see "Basics"), stems intact

1 cup all-purpose flour plus 1 additional tablespoon for eggs

3 eggs, room temperature, separated

½ teaspoon salt

2 inches of canola oil in a heavy 12-inch skillet, heated to 375 degrees

PICADILLO

1 package pork tenderloin (about 2½ pounds)

1 tablespoon red wine vinegar

2 tablespoons prepared mole sauce

½ teaspoon salt

½ teaspoon freshly ground black pepper

2 tablespoons lard or solid shortening

1 medium onion, chopped

1 fresh jalapeño chili, seeds and veins removed, minced

2 large Roma tomatoes, peeled, seeded, and chopped

1 teaspoon dried Mexican oregano

2 teaspoons chili powder

1 teaspoon ground cumin

¼ teaspoon red (cayenne) pepper

1 tablespoon minced cilantro

¾ cup (3 ounces) shredded Monterey Jack cheese

RANCHERO SAUCE

2 tablespoons lard or solid shortening

1 medium onion, chopped

1 medium green bell pepper, chopped

1 celery stalk, chopped

2 large garlic cloves, minced

1 16-ounce can plum tomatoes, drained and cut into small dice

½ teaspoon freshly ground black pepper

½ teaspoon ground cumin

1 fresh bay leaf, minced

½ teaspoon ground coriander

1½ teaspoons chili powder

1½ teaspoons paprika

2 cups chicken stock (see "Basics")

Prepare the Ranchero Sauce. Melt the lard or shortening in a heavy 3-quart saucepan over medium-high heat. Add onions, bell pepper, celery, and garlic. Cook until onions are wilted and transparent, about 10 minutes. Add remaining ingredients and stir to blend. Lower heat and simmer the sauce until thickened, about 25 minutes. Puree the sauce in blender and pass through a fine strainer. Press down on the solids with a wooden spoon to remove all excess liquid. Return the sauce to a clean saucepan and keep warm over low heat.

Prepare the Picadillo. Trim the tenderloin of any fat and silverskin. Cut into large chunks. Coarsely chop the meat in small batches in food processor fitted with steel blade. Combine the meat with the vinegar, mole sauce, salt, and pepper, blending well. Set aside.

Heat the lard or shortening in a heavy, deep, 12-inch

skillet over medium-high heat. Add the onions and jalapeños; sauté until onions are wilted and slightly browned, about 8 minutes. Stir in the pork mixture and cook until meat is done, stirring frequently. Add tomatoes, oregano, chili powder, cumin, and cayenne pepper. Cook, stirring often, until tomato liquid has evaporated slightly, about 10 minutes. Remove pan from heat and stir in the cilantro. Set the mixture aside to cool completely. When it is cool, stir in the Monterey Jack cheese. Refrigerate until ready to stuff the chilies.

Prepare the chilies. Using a small, sharp knife, make a slit in the side of each chili, from the shoulder down about two-thirds of the length of the chili. With your index finger, carefully scrape out the seeds and discard them. Take care to leave the top of the chili, the part around the base of the stem, intact. Very carefully rinse the chilies under running water to flush out the seeds, then drain and pat the chilies dry on absorbent paper towels.

Stuff the chilies with the chilled Picadillo until they are filled out, leaving room to reclose the opening. If a chili tears, use toothpicks to hold it together, to be removed after cooking. Set aside while preparing the batter. Place the cup of flour in a shallow pan. Combine the egg whites and salt in a clean, grease-free mixing bowl and beat with electric mixer with wire whisk attachment just until they are stiff enough to hold a peak. Add the egg yolks, one at a time, beating just to blend. Finally add the 1 tablespoon of flour and beat just to blend. Holding the stuffed chilies by the stem, dredge them first in the flour, shaking off all excess flour. Next dip them completely into the egg batter and draw them out quickly. Be sure that all of the chili is covered. If you have missed any spots, pat some batter on the spots with your fingertips. Carefully slide the chilies into the preheated oil and fry until golden brown, turning once. Drain on wire racks and keep hot while frying remaining chilies. Do not crowd the pan.

To serve, spoon a portion of the Ranchero Sauce on each serving plate. Set a chili in the center of the sauce. Serve hot.

❧ Serves 6.

SUGGESTED WINES

CAP*ROCK WINERY CHARDONNAY

HIDDEN SPRINGS WINERY BLUSH

LA BUENA VIDA VINEYARDS SPRINGTOWN
MERLOT L'ELEGANCE

LLANO ESTACADO WINERY ZINFANDEL

Gypsum flats below Guadalupe Mountains, Hudspeth County

HERB-ROASTED PORK LOIN WITH TEXAS PORT WINE GLAZE

Port wine and pork are natural partners. When preparing the port wine glaze for this recipe, use a good-quality port. I love Messina Hof's Papa Paulo port. The dried cranberries in the glaze add a rousing hint of tartness that is smoothed out by the red current jelly.

Boneless, center-cut pork loin roast, 3 to 4 pounds
Extra-virgin olive oil

 2 tablespoons minced fresh rosemary

 2 tablespoons minced fresh sage

 3 garlic cloves, minced

 1 teaspoon salt

 1 teaspoon freshly ground black pepper

TEXAS PORT WINE GLAZE

 2 tablespoons extra-virgin olive oil

 3 French shallots, minced

 1 tablespoon minced fresh sage

 ½ teaspoon minced fresh rosemary

 ½ cup dried cranberries

 2 cups Messina Hof Papa Paulo port wine

 ⅓ cup beef stock (see "Basics")

 ⅓ cup red wine vinegar

 ½ cup red currant jelly

1½ tablespoons cornstarch stirred into 2 tablespoons cold beef stock

Preheat oven to 350 degrees. Place roast in an open roasting pan; set aside. In a small bowl combine the rosemary, sage, garlic, salt, and pepper. Brush the roast with olive oil. Pat the herb mixture onto the roast. Roast the pork in preheated oven for 1 hour to 1 hour and 20 minutes, or until an instant-read thermometer inserted in meat registers 145–150 degrees.

While meat is roasting, make the Texas Port Wine Glaze. Heat the olive oil in a heavy 10-inch skillet over medium heat. When oil is hot, add shallots, sage, rosemary, and cranberries. Sauté until shallots are wilted and transparent, about 8 minutes. Add the port wine, beef stock, vinegar, and red currant jelly. Cook over medium-low heat, stirring often, until mixture is slightly thickened, about 20 minutes. Bring to a boil and quickly stir in the cornstarch mixture. Cook until thickened.

To serve, remove pork from oven and set aside to rest for 15 minutes. Slice the meat into ½-inch-thick slices. Place 2 or 3 slices on each serving plate and spoon a portion of the Texas Port Wine Glaze over each serving. Serve hot.

❧ Serves 6.

SUGGESTED WINES

FALL CREEK VINEYARDS SAUVIGNON BLANC

HIDDEN SPRINGS WINERY CRYSTAL RED TABLE WINE

LA BUENA VIDA VINEYARDS WALNUT CREEK CELLARS VIDA DEL SOL PORT

LLANO ESTACADO WINERY CELLAR SELECT CHARDONNAY

SISTER CREEK VINEYARDS PINOT NOIR

COOKING PORK

TODAY'S LEAN PORK MUST BE COOKED VERY DIFFERENTLY FROM THE WAY OUR MOTHERS COOKED THE GOOD OLD FAT KIND OF PORK, WHICH WAS COOKED TO 180 DEGREES OF INTERNAL TEMPERATURE. PORK TODAY SHOULD BE SERVED MEDIUM — AT ABOUT 145–150 DEGREES — SO THE MEAT WILL BE FLAVORFUL AND JUICY. FOR THOSE WHO FEAR THE DREADED TRICHINA PARASITE, KEEP IN MIND THAT THE ORGANISM IS KILLED IF THE PORK HAS BEEN FROZEN FOR 72 HOURS. ALL MEAT PURCHASED AT THE MARKET HAS BEEN FROZEN FOR AT LEAST THAT AMOUNT OF TIME.

CHILI-SPICED BARBECUED PORK TENDERLOIN

Pork tenderloin is a delicious meat. It has an intense pork taste, adapts itself to a variety of cooking methods, and pairs well with a wide assortment of seasonings and sauces. Because it is so lean, it is important to avoid overcooking pork tenderloin. It should not be cooked past medium. This is a fast and easy main dish with a wonderful, slightly spicy taste. With this boldly seasoned pork, I love the hearty, two-fisted taste of Shiner Bock from the Spoetzle Brewery in Shiner.

2 pieces pork tenderloin, about 2½ pounds

2 tablespoons chili powder

1 tablespoon ground cumin

2 teaspoons dried Mexican oregano

4 large garlic cloves, minced to a paste

1 tablespoon freshly squeezed lime juice

Olive oil

Build a smoky fire in the barbecue pit, using hardwood chunks that have been soaked in water for 1 hour. Trim all fat and silverskin from the meat; set aside.

Combine the remaining ingredients, except olive oil, in a small bowl and blend well. Stir in just enough olive oil to form a loose paste. Spread the paste on all sides of the meat.

Place the meat on the cooking rack of barbecue pit and cook until an instant-read thermometer inserted in meat registers 145–150 degrees, about 30 to 45 minutes. Remove the meat and set aside to rest for 10 minutes before slicing. Slice the meat on a baking sheet with sides. Slice about ¾ inch thick. Fan slices out on serving plates and drizzle a portion of the drippings from the baking sheet over each serving. Serve hot.

ଓ **Serves 4.**

SUGGESTED WINES

CAP*ROCK WINERY RESERVE CABERNET SAUVIGNON

DELANEY VINEYARDS AND WINERY TEXAS CLARET

MESSINA HOF WINE CELLARS MAMA ROSA ROSÉ

SPICEWOOD VINEYARDS MERLOT

TEXAS HILLS VINEYARD MERLOT

NEW BRAUNFELS PORK AND SAUSAGE BRAISED WITH SAUERKRAUT AND APPLES

Any ethnic cuisine that I can think of has at least one marvelous one-dish meal for which the cuisine is known. This dish was a common one among the early German settlers in the New Braunfels area. Sauerkraut was a staple, and the cook would add bits of sausage or whatever meat was on hand, almost always pork. This German-style dish is a perfect match for a hearty, European-style beer like Shiner Bock.

1 rack of pork baby back ribs, cut into individual ribs

1½ pounds kielbasa sausage or other smoked sausage, cut into bite-size pieces

3 tablespoons bacon drippings

2 medium onions, chopped

2 cups Gewürztraminer wine

2 32-ounce jars refrigerated sauerkraut, drained

1 cup chicken stock (see "Basics")

1½ teaspoons freshly ground black pepper

8 juniper berries, well crushed

4 Granny Smith apples, peeled, cored, and sliced

Salt to taste

Preheat oven to 350 degrees. Place the rib pieces and sliced sausage on a large flameproof baking sheet. Bake in preheated oven until ribs are lightly browned, about 30 minutes. Remove from oven and drain off all fat. Set meats aside, reserving brown glaze on the baking sheet.

In a heavy 8-quart soup pot over medium heat, melt the bacon drippings. When fat is hot, add the onions and sauté until they are very wilted and transparent, about 10 minutes. Place the pan with the reserved glaze over high heat. Pour in about ½ cup of the Gewürztraminer and cook, scraping up the browned bits of meat glaze in the pan. The wine should start to take on a nice brown color from the meat glaze. Add additional ½ cup of wine. Pour the wine from the baking sheet into the onions. Add the remaining cup of wine, sauerkraut, and the reserved meats. Cook, stirring often, until wine is reduced by three-fourths, about 20 minutes. Add the chicken stock, black pepper, and juniper berries. Cover the pot and cook for 30 minutes. Stir in the apples and add salt to taste. Cook, uncovered, for about 20 minutes. Turn out into a large bowl and serve family style.

ଓ **Serves 4 to 6.**

VENISON AND RED WINE STEW OVER EGG NOODLES

*D*eer hunting is one of the state's largest outdoor participation sports, with more than half a million hunters every year. Venison is very good meat, although some people have a great aversion to its taste. I usually suspect that these folks have had venison that was killed during a stressed breeding season, improperly field-dressed, or not cold-hung to relax and tenderize the meat and allow the animal's enzymes to moderate the bold, gamy taste of the meat. It is also very important to remove any traces of fat from venison. Although the animal is very lean, any fat left on the meat will be very strongly flavored when cooked. Also remember that the longer the meat is cooked, the stronger it will taste. Venison cooked no more than medium-done or closer to medium-rare will produce the optimum taste. For those who do not hunt but would like to experience the taste of venison, see "The Texas Cook's Pantry" for a wonderful Texas source for deer meat.

7 dried morel mushrooms

5 pounds venison stew meat, cut into 1½-inch cubes

Black pepper

Extra-virgin olive oil

1 medium onion, halved lengthwise, then sliced

1 large carrot, peeled and sliced

5 cups beef stock (see "Basics")

1½ tablespoons unsalted butter

8 ounces white mushrooms, sliced

3 French shallots, minced

1½ cups Cabernet Sauvignon

1 tablespoon tomato paste

1 minced chipotle chili in adobo sauce and a little of the sauce

4 tablespoons Beurre Manié (see "Basics")

Salt and freshly ground black pepper to taste

1¼ cups pearl onions

4 tablespoons unsalted butter

4 tablespoons canola oil

Egg noodles, cooked al dente, drained, and tossed with melted butter

Minced parsley as garnish

Preheat oven to 350 degrees. Place the morel mushrooms in a bowl and add hot water to cover. Set aside until mushrooms are soft and pliable, about 20 minutes. Squeeze the moisture out of the mushrooms and slice them; set aside. Pat the meat cubes dry on absorbent paper towels. Season liberally with black pepper. Heat a thin layer of the olive oil in a deep 14-inch skillet until very hot. Add the venison in small batches and cook, turning constantly, to sear and brown the outside. Remove meat and repeat until all has been seared. Set meat aside. Reduce the heat and add the onion and carrot. Cover the pot and cook gently for 10 minutes, or until vegetables begin to brown. Carefully drain off all fat from the pan and return it to the heat. Add the seared venison cubes and pour in the beef stock. Scrape bottom of pan to release any browned bits of meat glaze. Cover the pan first with aluminum foil, then a lid, and bring to a boil. Place pan in preheated oven and braise for 45 minutes.

Meanwhile, melt the 1½ tablespoons of butter in a heavy skillet over medium heat. Cook the morels and sliced mushrooms until mushroom liquid has evaporated. Stir in the shallots and cook for about 10 minutes, then add the red wine and cook to reduce by half. Stir in the tomato paste and minced chipotle chili. Remove skillet from heat.

Melt the remaining 4 tablespoons of butter in a heavy 12-inch skillet over medium heat; add the canola oil and heat. When oil-butter mixture is very hot, add the pearl onions and cook, tossing often, until onions are uniformly browned. Remove from heat, strain out fat, and set the onions aside.

When the meat has finished cooking, remove pan from oven and strain the sauce into a clean Dutch oven. Set meat aside and keep warm. Stir the mushroom and wine mixture into the sauce and bring to a full boil. Add the Beurre Manié, a tablespoon at a time, and whisk rapidly to blend and thicken the sauce. Add additional Beurre Manié as needed to thicken the sauce to desired consistency. Season to taste with black pepper. Return the meat to the sauce and stir in the browned pearl onions. Cook to heat through.

Serve the stew over hot egg noodles. Garnish with minced parsley.

ભ **Serves 6 to 8.**

SUGGESTED WINES

DELANEY VINEYARDS AND WINERY CABERNET FRANC

HIDDEN SPRINGS WINERY CABERNET SAUVIGNON

LLANO ESTACADO WINERY CABERNET SAUVIGNON

MESSINA HOF WINE CELLARS BARREL RESERVE MERLOT

TEXAS HILLS VINEYARD SANGIOVESE

GRILLED MEDALLIONS OF VENISON BACKSTRAP
WITH ANCHO CHILI AND HONEY SAUCE

*A*ny serious hunter will tell you that the choicest cut on the deer is the backstrap. It has the same texture as beef tenderloin, only with the savory, rich taste of venison. It really is a sacrilege to cook the backstrap past medium-rare—you lose the tender texture, and the delicate taste turns more intensely wild.

The Ancho Chili and Honey Sauce is good on just about any red meat. The Red Meat Dip and Baste is borrowed from my friend Merle Ellis, whose syndicated column and TV show, "The Butcher," taught legions of Americans all about meat, and it's great on your favorite steak, too. Ancho chilies are the dried version of the poblano chili and are available wherever dried chilies are sold. The toasting of the cumin and coriander seeds in the sauce is a common practice in making the robust sauces of cowboy and southwestern cooking. It really cranks up the taste of the spices a few notches, so don't be a recipe cheat and leave out the step! For an ideal side dish, try Sweet Potato Pone (see "Sides").

1 large whole venison backstrap, trimmed of all silverskin

Crushed black pepper

RED MEAT DIP AND BASTE

ભ **Makes 1 quart.**

8 ounces firmly packed light brown sugar

1 teaspoon granulated garlic

1 teaspoon onion powder

½ teaspoon fine-grind black pepper

3 tablespoons French's yellow mustard

1 teaspoon Tabasco sauce

1 teaspoon celery salt

10 ounces soy sauce

5 ounces Worcestershire sauce

5 ounces A-1 sauce

5 ounces Heinz 57 sauce

1 teaspoon freshly squeezed lemon juice

ANCHO CHILI AND HONEY SAUCE

7 whole cumin seeds

1 teaspoon whole coriander seeds

2 tablespoons canola oil

4 large dried ancho chilies, seeds and veins removed

1 small onion, chopped

3 large garlic cloves, minced

6 Roma tomatoes, cut into wedges

4 cups chicken stock (see "Basics")

6 whole cilantro sprigs

¼ cup clover honey

¼ cup freshly squeezed lime juice

Salt and freshly ground black pepper to taste

Prepare the Red Meat Dip and Baste. Combine the first 8 ingredients in a medium, non-aluminum bowl. Blend the ingredients together with a large spoon until the mixture is smooth. Add remaining ingredients, one at a time, whisking vigorously after each addition. Transfer to storage container and refrigerate until ready to use.

Prepare the Ancho Chili and Honey Sauce. Combine the cumin and coriander seeds in a small skillet. Toss over medium-high heat to toast, about 2 to 3 minutes, or until a strong aroma develops. Do not burn the seeds! Remove from skillet and set aside. Heat the canola oil in a heavy 4-quart saucepan over medium heat. Add the ancho chilies, onions, garlic, and tomatoes. Cook, stirring often, until chilies are very soft and all vegetables are wilted, about 25 minutes. Add the chicken stock and reserved toasted seeds. Cook for 30 minutes, reducing the liquid slightly. Remove from heat and add the cilantro sprigs; puree in blender. Pass the puree through a fine strainer into a clean saucepan, stirring with back of a spoon to extract all excess liquid. Stir the honey and lime juice into the sauce. Season to taste with salt and black pepper. Simmer gently for 20 to 30 minutes to make a smooth, medium-thick sauce. Keep warm while grilling the venison.

Preheat gas grill or prepare charcoal fire in barbecue pit. Baste the backstrap liberally with the Red Meat Dip and Baste, then season heavily with cracked black pepper. Grill the meat to medium-rare, or until an instant-read meat thermometer

(continued)

registers about 135 degrees. Turn often to form a seared crust, basting often with the Red Meat Dip and Baste.

   Remove the backstrap to a carving board and cover loosely with foil. Allow the meat to rest for 10 minutes. To serve, slice the meat into round medallions about ½ inch thick. Spoon a portion of the Ancho Chili and Honey Sauce onto each serving plate. Fan 3 or 4 slices of the venison out on the sauce and serve hot.

ର **Serves 4.**

SUGGESTED WINES

Alamosa Wine Cellars El Guapo, Tio Rancho Ranch
Llano Estacado Winery Cabernet Sauvignon
Messina Hof Wine Cellars Barrel Reserve Shiraz
Sister Creek Vineyards Merlot
Texas Hills Vineyard Sangiovese

Venison and Mango Enchiladas with Black Bean Sauce

*E*nchiladas are one of the most popular of all the Tex-Mex dishes. These are dishes that had their roots in Mexican cuisine. As Hispanic families lived in Texas for many generations, the foods began to change subtly. They adapted to the ingredients available here and to the more modern cooking methods they found in America. Gradually, a new cuisine was unofficially born and has been referred to as "Tex-Mex." This is the type of food that is served in most Mexican restaurants in the state. Enchiladas can be filled with anything from simply cheese and onions to scraps from the hunt. They can be served with cheese only, with chili-type sauces, or with an innovative sauce like this one made from black beans. The secret to making good enchiladas is softening the corn tortillas before filling and rolling. If they are not softened, they will crack and fall apart. To soften a tortilla, heat a glaze of lard or solid shortening in a skillet. Place the tortillas, one at a time, in the hot oil and cook, turning once, until they are soft and pliable, about 5 seconds. They may now be rolled without tearing. I further enhance the taste of the tortilla by dipping it in a chili puree before glazing it in the oil.

Enchiladas

  2 tablespoons olive oil
  2 small to medium onions, chopped fine
  2 tablespoons minced garlic
  ½ teaspoon freshly ground black pepper
  2 pounds deer meat, well trimmed and finely chopped
  3 tablespoons minced cilantro
  ¼ cup pureed Marinated Ancho Chilies (see recipe for Roasted Red Bell Pepper Bisque)
  1 large mango, seeded and finely chopped
  4 poblano chilies, roasted, peeled, seeded, and finely chopped (see "Basics")
Salt to taste
  ¾ pound Monterey Jack cheese, shredded
  20 white corn tortillas
Additional pureed Marinated Ancho Chilies, diluted with a little chicken stock

Canola oil for softening tortillas
Sour cream, at room temperature, thinned with a little whipping cream

Black Bean Sauce

  1 cup black beans, soaked overnight in water to cover
  1 small ham hock
  1 small onion, finely chopped
  2 garlic cloves, minced
  ½ teaspoon ground cumin
Beef stock to cover beans by 2 inches
  1 canned chipotle chili in adobo sauce, minced
  ¼ cup Madeira
Salt to taste

Make the Black Bean Sauce. Drain the beans after they have soaked overnight and place in a heavy 4-quart saucepan over medium heat. Add the ham hock, onion, garlic, cumin, and beef stock. Bring to a boil. Reduce heat and simmer for 1 hour. Strain the beans, reserving cooking liquid. Remove the ham hock and trim any meat from the bones. Discard rind and fat. Finely chop the meat. Scoop out 1 cup of the black beans. Transfer to blender with the meat from the ham hock and the chipotle chili. Add a little of the reserved cooking liquid. Puree the beans until smooth. Transfer the puree to a saucepan and stir in the remaining reserved cooking liquid and the Madeira. Add salt to taste. Cook over low heat to reduce until slightly thickened. Set aside.

Heat the olive oil in a heavy, deep, 14-inch skillet over high heat. When oil is almost smoking, sauté the onions and garlic for 2 minutes, or until lightly browned. Add the black pepper and deer meat; continue to cook until meat is evenly browned. Add the cilantro, ancho chili puree, mango, and poblano chilies. Add salt to taste. Cook for 1 minute, then remove from heat and add half of the shredded cheese. Stir to blend well. Transfer meat to a bowl and refrigerate until well chilled.

Preheat oven to 350 degrees. Pour enough of the canola oil into a heavy skillet to measure a depth of ½ inch. Heat the oil until almost smoking. Dip each tortilla, one at a time, in the pureed Marinated Ancho Chilies, then submerge in the hot oil for about 5 seconds each, just to soften. Drain on absorbent paper towels and keep warm.

Working quickly, spread a portion of the venison mixture down the center of each softened tortilla. Roll up the tortillas and place them snugly in a baking pan, seam side down. When all tortillas have been filled and fitted into the pan, scatter the remaining cheese over the top. Cover with aluminum foil and bake in preheated oven for 15 minutes, or until heated through and cheese has melted.

To serve, place a portion of the Black Bean Sauce in the center of each serving plate. Place two enchiladas on the sauce and drizzle some of the sour cream over the top. Serve hot.

ॐ **Makes 20 enchiladas.**

SUGGESTED WINES

BECKER VINEYARDS MERLOT

CAP*ROCK WINERY CABERNET ROYALE, ROSÉ OF CABERNET SAUVIGNON

LLANO ESTACADO WINERY ZINFANDEL

SISTER CREEK VINEYARDS PINOT NOIR

Main Street, McLean

SMOKED WILD BOAR RACKS WITH PASILLA DE OAXACA CHILI SAUCE

Feral hogs make mighty good eating. They are often hunted on deer leases as an adjunct to the deer hunting. I've come across quite a few Texas hunters who actually prefer the taste of wild hog meat to that of domestic pork. The rib rack with its sweet, slightly musky little chops is my favorite cut. The rack consists of 8 ribs and the chops are small, so you need to allow about 4 to 5 ribs per person. I've found that slow smoking to medium doneness brings out the optimum flavor in wild boar. Sauces made from dried chilies pair fabulously with the taste of wild hog. This particular sauce owes it primary flavor notes to the wonderful pasilla de Oaxaca chili and its smoky spice. Its development was a joint effort with my head sous-chef, Cecilio Solis, a talented young chef who graduated from the New England Culinary Institute. The sauce is also good with smoked or roasted domestic pork. A great side dish for this meal is Orange and Saffron Couscous with Ancho Chilies (see "Sides"). And with any type of smoked meat, I love a cold Shiner Bock from the Spoetzle Brewery in Shiner.

4 wild boar racks, fat removed

Olive oil

Dry Rub (see recipe for Slow-Smoked Brisket with Hellfire and Brimstone Sauce)

PASILLA DE OAXACA CHILI SAUCE

1 large red bell pepper, coarsely chopped, seeds discarded

1 stalk celery, including leafy top, coarsely chopped

Olive oil

2 tablespoons peanut oil

16 Roma tomatoes, quartered

5 garlic cloves, peeled and crushed

1 4-ounce can sliced pineapple, coarsely chopped

4 pasilla de Oaxaca chilies, stems removed, coarsely torn (see "The Texas Cook's Pantry")

½ cup toasted, sliced almonds (skin on)

½ cup beef stock (see "Basics")

1½ cups pineapple juice

Salt and freshly ground black pepper to taste

Build a fire in a barbecue pit with a separate firebox. Let the fire cook down until the temperature in the cooking chamber registers about 300 degrees. Brush the boar racks with olive oil and rub the Dry Rub into the meat on all sides. Place the meat on grilling rack in the pit and smoke for 2 hours, basting often with additional olive oil, or until an instant-read meat ther-mometer inserted in the thickest part of the chop registers about 145–150 degrees.

While meat is smoking, prepare the Pasilla de Oaxaca Chili Sauce. Preheat oven to 450 degrees. Place the chopped red bell pepper and celery on a small baking sheet and drizzle with olive oil. Place the pan in preheated oven and roast the vegetables until they are well browned, about 30 minutes. Remove and set aside.

Heat the peanut oil in a heavy 4-quart saucepan over medium heat. Add the tomatoes, garlic, pineapple, and chilies. Cook, stirring occasionally, until the tomatoes are very pulpy, about 20 minutes. Stir in the roasted vegetables, almonds, and beef stock. Cook to reduce beef stock slightly, about 10 minutes. Transfer the mixture to a blender and puree. Return the puree to a clean saucepan and add the pineapple juice and salt and pepper to taste. Cook the sauce over medium-low heat for 30 minutes. Strain the sauce through a fine strainer, stirring the puree with a wooden spoon to extract all excess liquid.

To serve, slice the boar racks into individual chops. Spoon a portion of the sauce on each serving plate and arrange the chops on the sauce, slightly overlapping. Serve hot.

❧ Serves 4 to 6.

SUGGESTED WINES

ALAMOSA WINE CELLARS ROSATO DI SANGIOVESE

DRY COMAL CREEK VINEYARDS CABERNET SAUVIGNON

FALL CREEK VINEYARDS RESERVE CABERNET SAUVIGNON

HAAK VINEYARDS AND WINERY ZINFANDEL

SISTER CREEK VINEYARDS CABERNET SAUVIGNON BLEND

HILL COUNTRY RABBIT STEW

*R*abbits are one of the most populous small game animals in the state, yet they are largely ignored. We have three types of rabbits in Texas—the familiar cottontail, jackrabbits, and swamp or marsh rabbits. Rabbit is very lean with virtually no fat. The meat has a subtly earthy taste and is slightly sweet. Pen-raised rabbit is generally available frozen in specialty markets if you don't care to hunt them. This dish is similar to the classic German Hasenpfeffer prepared by the early German settlers in the Texas Hill Country. The name translates as "hare pepper" and denotes a thick, highly seasoned stew of rabbit meat. This great game dish was always served with good bock beer like Shiner Bock from the Spoetzle Brewery in Shiner.

2 whole rabbits (about 2 to 2½ pounds each)

12 bacon slices

Canola oil as needed

All-purpose flour

1½ cups Becker Vineyards Cabernet Franc or other dry red wine

1 tablespoon honey

¼ cup whole-grain mustard, such as Dusseldorf

1 cup chicken stock (see "Basics")

1½ teaspoons freshly ground black pepper

½ cup sour cream

Buttered egg noodles, cooked al dente

MARINADE

1½ cups apple cider vinegar

1½ cups water

2 tablespoons extra-virgin olive oil

4 large garlic cloves, minced

6 juniper berries, crushed

1½ teaspoons dried Mexican oregano

3 dried bay leaves

8 whole cloves

1 tablespoon mixed pickling spices

1 teaspoon dry mustard

2 teaspoons salt

2 large onions, sliced

4 large French shallots, sliced

Cut up each rabbit into 10 pieces. Disjoint the forelegs from the body at the shoulder and remove. Disjoint the hind legs at the hip and remove. Separate the rib section from the loin. Then separate the hind legs at the knee to make 2 pieces. Cut the loin, or rable, and the rib sections in two crosswise, and trim off the lower portion of the ribs, which are mostly bone, with kitchen shears. Arrange the pieces in a single layer in non-aluminum baking dishes; set aside.

To make the marinade, combine all ingredients except onions and shallots in a bowl and whisk to blend. Scatter the onion and shallot slices around the rabbit and pour the marinade over the top. Cover the baking dishes with plastic wrap and marinate, refrigerated, for 2 days. Turn the pieces often.

To cook the stew, remove the rabbit pieces from the marinade and pat dry using absorbent paper towels. Strain the marinade, reserving both the liquid and the vegetables separately; set aside.

Cook the bacon slices until crisp; set aside. Reserve the bacon drippings, adding enough canola oil to make 2 cups of fat. Transfer to a heavy 14-inch skillet over medium heat. When oil is hot, dredge the rabbit pieces in all-purpose flour and quickly sear them on each side until nicely browned. Remove from pan and set aside. Preheat oven to 350 degrees.

Pour off all fat from the skillet and return pan to medium-high heat. Add the Cabernet Franc and scrape the bottom of the pan to release any browned bits of meat glaze. Add the reserved marinade liquid, honey, mustard, chicken stock, and black pepper. Bring to a boil, lower heat, and simmer for 10 minutes.

Arrange the rabbit pieces in a large Dutch oven or roasting pan. Scatter the marinated vegetables around the rabbit. Crumble the reserved bacon slices and scatter over the rabbit. Pour the mixture from the skillet over the rabbit. Cover the pan and bake in preheated oven for 1 hour.

Remove pan from oven. Transfer the rabbit pieces to a large serving platter and cover to keep warm. Place the pan over medium heat and whisk in the sour cream, blending well. Cook just to heat through. Strain the sauce and pour it over the rabbit. Serve the rabbit with buttered egg noodles.

ରୁ **Serves 6 to 8.**

ALTON AND VIRGINIA ANDERSON'S BRAISED SQUIRREL AND DUMPLINGS

Alton Anderson is my idea of a real-life, true-blue Texan. He is a recently retired State of Texas game warden, a two-fisted drinker, a wonderful two-stepper on the dance floor, a master at the barbecue pit, and an avid and very adept hunter. Alton and his wife, Virginia, have become great game cookers over the years. Squirrel is one of their favorites.

Squirrels feed on nuts and seeds, satisfying their calcium needs by gnawing on shed deer antlers, bones, and abandoned turtle shells. The meat of the squirrel has a pleasingly musky, nut-like taste. Squirrels are most often cooked in braised dishes, but they are also very good grilled or slow-smoked after an initial short blanching to draw out some of the gamy taste.

6 squirrels, dressed and quartered, ribs discarded
2 heaping teaspoons baking soda
1 small onion, coarsely chopped
1 small carrot, coarsely chopped
2 small celery stalks, coarsely chopped
Chicken stock (see "Basics)
Salt and freshly ground black pepper to taste
1 cup milk
4 tablespoons unsalted butter

DUMPLINGS

2 cups all-purpose flour
3 tablespoons solid shortening
½ teaspoon salt
Hot chicken stock, as needed (see "Basics")

Place the quartered squirrels in an 8-quart soup pot. Add water to cover and stir in the baking soda. Bring the water to a full boil over high heat and parboil the squirrels for about 4 minutes. Drain the squirrels, discarding the liquid, and rinse under running water.

Place squirrel pieces back in soup pot with the onion, carrot, and celery. Add chicken stock to cover by about 4 inches. Season to taste with salt and black pepper. Bring the stock to a full boil, then reduce heat to a simmer. Cook until the meat is falling off the bones, about 1½ hours.

Strain the stock into a clean 8-quart pot; set aside. When squirrels are cool enough to handle, pull all meat from the bones and set aside. Discard vegetables.

To make the dumplings, cut the shortening into the flour with a pastry blender until the mixture resembles coarse meal. Add the salt and enough hot stock to make a smooth, cohesive dough. Stir just until the dough comes together. Remove from bowl and knead 3 or 4 times by hand. Roll the dough out on a lightly floured work surface until thin. Cut into 2-inch squares. Bring the reserved broth to a low, rolling boil and drop in the dumplings. Cook until they are soft but not chewy, about 10 minutes.

Stir the reserved squirrel meat into the stock. Add the milk and butter. Cook just to heat the meat through and melt the butter. Serve hot in soup plates or bowls.

℞ Serves 4.

SUGGESTED WINES

BECKER VINEYARDS CLARET ESTATE BOTTLED
CAP*ROCK WINERY MERLOT
DRY COMAL CREEK VINEYARDS CABERNET SAUVIGNON
FALL CREEK VINEYARDS SAUVIGNON BLANC

◄ SUGGESTED WINES

BECKER VINEYARDS CLARET ESTATE BOTTLED
HIDDEN SPRINGS WINERY MUSCAT CANELLI
MESSINA HOF WINERY JOHANNESBURG RIESLING
SISTER CREEK VINEYARDS MERLOT

SIDES

*I*f you're a vegetable and grain lover like I am, you're just as interested in what's on the side of your plate as in what's in the middle. I love to go to covered dish suppers to sample the dozens and dozens of side dishes—garden-fresh vegetables, pots of pinto beans seasoned with an amazing range of creativity, a yummy macaroni casserole, rice casseroles, and perhaps dishes made from other delicious grains such as polenta, couscous, quinoa, white corn grits. Sometimes I never make it to the meat!

When selecting a side to go with your entrée, mentally pair the flavors, using your "mind's tongue." I

Sorghum farmer, Caldwell County; Cottonwoods at ranch headquarters, Hutchison County (pages 202–3).

love to experiment. It's a great way to form a relationship with a new food. Pick a vegetable or grain you've never cooked before and have a go at it. There are some very exciting and exotic tastes out there in the world of vegetables and grains, just waiting for your creativity to turn them into masterpieces of flavor.

Don't overdo the sides. Remember that the entrée is the real star, so side dishes should complement but never overpower that entrée, either in taste or quantity. They should be used to make the main course a harmonious, well-matched, and very satisfying experience.

Wheat harvesting, North Plains

WHITE KIDNEY BEAN RAGOUT WITH SMOKED TOMATOES

The white kidney bean, known in Italy as the cannellini bean, is a great bean to have in your culinary repertoire. The cannellini bean is the signature bean of Tuscan cooking and is used in soups, such as the classic minestrone, and other dishes. Ironically, the cannellini bean originated in America. Serve this hearty dish with roasted or grilled meats. If there's any left over the next day, heat it up in a nice soup plate, tear off a big chunk of crusty bread, pour a chilled glass of Pinot Grigio or Sangiovese, and have yourself a little feast.

½   pound dried white kidney beans

5   cups chicken stock (see "Basics")

½   teaspoon dried Mexican oregano

3   medium garlic cloves, minced

1   small onion, chopped

½   teaspoon freshly ground black pepper

Salt to taste

SMOKED TOMATOES

8   Roma tomatoes, blistered (see "Basics")

3   tablespoons olive oil

¼   cup finely chopped red onion

2   teaspoons minced fresh basil

½   teaspoon salt, or to taste

1   teaspoon crushed red pepper flakes

Soak the beans in water to cover overnight. Drain the beans and place in a 4-quart saucepan with remaining ingredients. Bring to a full boil and cook at a bubbling low boil for 30 minutes, or until the beans are soft and have formed a thickened gravy.

While beans are cooking, prepare Smoked Tomatoes. Chop the tomatoes into chunks, reserving all juice; set aside. Heat the olive oil in a heavy 10-inch skillet over medium-high heat. When the oil is hot, add the tomato chunks and their liquid, red onion, basil, salt, and crushed red pepper flakes. Cook, stirring often, until tomato liquid has evaporated. Stir the tomato mixture into the cooked beans. Serve hot.

❧ Serves 4 to 6.

REFRIED BEANS

The term "refried beans" is actually a mistranslation of the Spanish frijoles refritos, or well-fried beans. The dish is usually made from cooked pinto beans that are mashed to a pulpy consistency, then fried, usually in lard. Refried beans are a common side dish to Mexican entrées. They're also used to make every teenager's favorite snack food, the bean and cheese burrito. Don't try to make them healthy by substituting for the lard or bacon drippings. They'll be limp-flavored.

3   15-ounce cans pinto beans and their liquid

1   large onion, chopped

1½   teaspoons minced garlic

⅓   cup bacon drippings or lard

1¼   cups (5 ounces) shredded Colby cheese

⅓   cup sliced green onions

Combine the beans and their liquid, onions, and garlic in a large saucepan over medium heat. Cook, stirring often, until mixture has thickened and onions are very soft, about 30 minutes. Remove from heat and mash the beans until fairly smooth. Heat the bacon drippings in a heavy, 12-inch cast-iron skillet over medium heat. Add the mashed beans and cook, stirring often, until the mixture is very thick and creamy and the beans have absorbed the bacon drippings. Do not allow the beans to stick to the bottom of the skillet. Serve hot, topping each portion with some of the shredded cheese and sliced green onions.

❧ Serves 6 to 8.

FRIJOLES BORRACHOS

*T*he bean reigns supreme in Texas Cuisine. It would be unheard of to have a barbecue without cooking beans. This recipe for "Drunken Beans" is a good example of the cowboy-style of cooking the beloved pinto bean. Pinto beans, with their earthy flavor, are common throughout the American Southwest. Pinto means "painted" in Spanish, perhaps because it turns reddish brown when cooked. My husband, Roger, never met a bean he didn't like, so often when we have a day of working in the yard, we'll put on a pot of beans to simmer. When we come inside in the evening, we'll throw some cornbread in the oven, ladle up a couple of big bowls of those beans, and feast.

¼ cup bacon drippings or lard

1 medium onion, chopped

2 large garlic cloves, minced

1 pound dried pinto beans, sorted and rinsed to remove rocks and dirt particles

2 meaty ham hocks

1 10-ounce can of beer

1 10½-ounce can Ro-Tel Diced Tomatoes with Chilies

Chicken stock to cover beans by 2 inches, or more as needed (see "Basics")

8 ounces Mexican chorizo sausage, casings removed

¼ cup cilantro

Heat bacon drippings in an 8-quart soup pot over medium heat. Sauté the onions and garlic until onions are wilted and transparent, about 15 minutes. Add beans, ham hocks, and all remaining ingredients except chorizo and cilantro. Stir to blend well. Bring the beans to a full boil, then lower heat and simmer for about 1 hour, or until beans are tender. Sauté the chorizo in a separate skillet until it is cooked thoroughly. Drain off fat and stir the chorizo into the beans. Remove the ham hocks and pull off all meat; chop the meat. Return meat to bean pot and stir. Cook the beans for an additional 30 to 45 minutes, or until a thickened gravy has formed. Stir in the cilantro just before serving.

&ca; Serves 6 to 8.

Plowing patterns near Lamesa

REFRIED BLACK BEANS WITH TOMATILLO AND MASCARPONE SALSA

*T*he black bean is more often associated with Spanish cooking than Mexican, which is generally paired with the pinto bean. Black beans take longer to cook than many other beans, so it's best to soak them overnight to cut down on the cooking time. But it's fine to use canned beans in a pinch. I love them with grilled red meats and game dishes.

    3 15-ounce cans black beans and their liquid
    1 large onion, chopped
 1½ teaspoons minced garlic
 ⅓ cup bacon drippings or lard

TOMATILLO AND MASCARPONE SALSA

☞ Makes about 1½ cups.

    1 fresh jalapeño, stem removed
    1 small onion, coarsely chopped
    2 large garlic cloves, peeled
    6 tomatillos, husks removed and discarded, washed thoroughly
 ¾ cup (loosely packed) cilantro leaves and tender stems
Juice of 1 lime
    1 tablespoon good-quality real maple syrup
Salt to taste
 ½ cup mascarpone cheese

Prepare the Tomatillo and Mascarpone Salsa. Combine jalapeño, onion, and garlic in a heavy 4-quart pot over medium heat. Simmer until onion is very wilted and transparent and jalapeño is tender, about 10 minutes. Add the tomatillos and cook until they are almost ready to burst, about 10 minutes. Drain and set aside to cool. When tomatillo mixture is cool, puree in food processor fitted with steel blade just until chunky. Add the cilantro, lime juice, and maple syrup. Process until smooth. Turn the mixture out into a medium bowl and add salt to taste. Whisk in the mascarpone cheese. Chill before serving.

To make the beans, combine the beans and their liquid, onions, and garlic in a 3-quart saucepan over medium heat. Cook, stirring often, until mixture has thickened, about 20 minutes. Remove from heat and puree the beans until fairly smooth. Heat bacon drippings or lard in a large skillet over medium heat. Add the mashed beans and cook, stirring often, until mixture is very thick and creamy, about 30 minutes. All bacon drippings or lard should be absorbed. Do not allow beans to stick to bottom of pan. Serve hot, topping each portion with some of the Tomatillo and Mascarpone Salsa.

☞ Serves 6 to 8.

MEXICAN RICE

*M*exican Rice is ubiquitous in Texas. On any plate in a Mexican restaurant, you're likely to get some Mexican Rice. Some of it's good; some just takes up space on the plate. The secret to cooking really good Mexican rice is to first fry the raw rice, as with paella. Really good Mexican Rice is a complementary side dish with other types of food, too. I love it with grilled shrimp. A key ingredient in this recipe is Mexican oregano, which is very robust in taste and more flavorful.

 ½ cup bacon drippings or lard
    1 medium onion, finely chopped
    2 garlic cloves, minced
 ⅓ cup finely chopped pitted ripe olives
    2 cups uncooked rice
    2 small carrots, peeled and finely chopped
 ¼ cup chopped pickled jalapeños
Salt and black pepper to taste
 ½ teaspoon ground cumin
 ½ teaspoon dried Mexican oregano
    2 medium Roma tomatoes, peeled and diced
 ½ cup green peas
 1½ cups chicken stock (see "Basics")

Heat bacon drippings or lard in a heavy, deep skillet over medium-high heat. When fat is very hot, add onion, garlic, olives, rice, carrots, jalapeños, salt and pepper, cumin, and oregano. Cook, stirring often, until vegetables are wilted and rice is lightly and uniformly browned, about 10 minutes. Stir in the tomatoes and peas; cook 2 to 3 minutes. Add the chicken stock and stir to blend well. Cover pan and lower heat. Cook until liquid is absorbed and rice is tender, about 30 minutes. Serve hot.

☞ Serves 4 to 6.

Arroz Roja

Mexican "red rice" is a classic side dish for Tex-Mex entrées such as enchiladas, chilies rellenos, and tamales. The saffron in the dish is reminiscent of the classic Spanish paella. Saffron is the world's most costly spice, worth more than gold by weight. The spice is actually the dried stigmas from a certain species of crocus. There are only 3 stigmas per flower and they are picked by hand. Fortunately, only a pinch or a few threads are needed to flavor a recipe. To bring out the greatest depth of flavor from the saffron threads, grind them in a small mortar and pestle. Rinse out the bowl with some of the liquid from the recipe to make sure you don't waste a grain of the precious spice.

4 cups chicken stock (see "Basics")
3 or 4 saffron threads
2 cups long-grain white rice
2½ tablespoons canola oil
1 large onion, chopped
1 15-ounce can plum tomatoes, drained and chopped
½ teaspoon chili powder
½ teaspoon ground cumin
Salt to taste

Combine the chicken stock and saffron threads in a heavy 4-quart saucepan over high heat. Bring the stock to a boil and stir in the rice. Cover pan and turn heat to lowest setting. Cook for 15 minutes; remove pan from heat and set aside.

While rice is cooking, heat the canola oil in a heavy 12-inch skillet over medium heat. Sauté the onions until they are wilted, about 6 minutes. Stir in the tomatoes, chili powder, and ground cumin. Cook until mixture is very wilted, about 8 minutes. Remove from heat.

When the rice is done, stir onion and tomato mixture into the rice, blending well. Serve hot.

∞ Serves 4 to 6.

Almond Rice Pilaf

Pilaf, which originated in the Middle East, made the migration to the American South because of the influence of the spice trade and the vast rice plantings in America. The dish was a popular delicacy in French Louisiana, from where it possibly migrated to Texas. A native version of pilaf was also popular with Greek Americans who settled on the Texas Gulf Coast. Today any rice dish with vegetables and seasonings is referred to as a pilaf. The dish makes an excellent side dish for just about any type of entrée—poultry, game, beef, fish, or shellfish.

4 cups beef or chicken stock, depending on entrée (see "Basics")
1 tablespoon unsalted butter
Pinch of salt
2 cups long-grain white rice
2 tablespoons additional unsalted butter
2 small carrots, peeled and minced
3 green onions, minced, including green tops
2 tablespoons wheat germ
3 tablespoons chopped sliced almonds (skin on)
2 teaspoons minced flat-leaf parsley
1 teaspoon minced fresh sage
¼ teaspoon curry powder
½ teaspoon sugar
Salt and freshly ground black pepper to taste

Combine stock, 1 tablespoon butter, and pinch of salt in a 3-quart saucepan and bring to a rapid boil. Add the rice, stir, cover, and reduce heat to lowest setting. Cook for 15 minutes, then remove pan from heat and set aside.

Melt the additional 2 tablespoons of butter in a heavy 10-inch skillet over medium heat. Add remaining ingredients except salt and pepper. Sauté until green onions are wilted, about 8 minutes, stirring often. Stir the vegetables into the cooked rice, blending well. Season to taste with salt and freshly ground black pepper. Serve hot.

∞ Serves 4 to 6.

QUINOA WITH LENTILS AND CURRY

*T*his calcium-rich, vitamin-loaded grain (pronounced "KEEN-wah") is a cross between mustard and millet. It originated high in the Andes where it was grown by the Incas, who called it "The Mother Grain" and believed it was sacred, since a steady diet of it seemed to promote long, healthy lives. Today we know that there is scientific merit to this belief. The grain is packed with lysine and healthy amounts of the other amino acids that make a complete protein. It is also rich in phosphorus, calcium, iron, vitamin E, and assorted B vitamins. One cup of cooked quinoa has as much calcium as a quart of milk. It's also a very tasty grain, and this recipe is fabulous with game birds and red meats. For a special presentation, serve this dish in a baked winter squash.

1 cup quinoa

2 tablespoons unsalted butter

½ cup finely chopped onion

2 cups hot chicken stock (see "Basics")

1 teaspoon curry powder

½ teaspoon ground cumin

1 tablespoon minced cilantro

⅔ cup hot cooked lentils

Rinse the quinoa under running water. Shake to expel water. Place the quinoa in a dry cast-iron skillet over medium-high heat. Toast, shaking the pan back and forth constantly, until the quinoa gives off a fragrant aroma. Do not allow it to burn. Turn out into a small bowl and set aside.

Melt the butter in a heavy 3-quart saucepan over medium heat. Sauté the onion until wilted and transparent, about 5 minutes. Pour in the hot chicken stock, curry powder, cumin, and quinoa. Bring to a rapid boil. Reduce heat to medium-low, cover pan, and cook until liquid is absorbed, about 12 to 15 minutes. Remove from heat and stir in the cilantro and lentils. Serve hot.

ର Serves 4 to 6.

STORING GRAINS

QUINOA, LIKE MANY OTHER WHOLE GRAINS, IS A PRIME TARGET FOR SPOILAGE. WHOLE GRAINS RETAIN THEIR GERMS, OR SEEDS, AND ALL OF THEIR ESSENTIAL OILS, WHICH BECOME RANCID QUICKLY. THE RICH GRAINS ALSO ATTRACT CRAWLING CRITTERS. STORE THESE WHOLE GRAINS IN THE FREEZER, TIGHTLY SEALED, TO AVOID BOTH HAZARDS. QUINOA, ESPECIALLY, HAS A SHORT SHELF LIFE, ESPECIALLY IN HOT WEATHER. JUST BE SURE TO TOAST THE QUINOA GRAINS BEFORE USE TO EXPEL THE MOISTURE THEY WILL ABSORB IN THE FREEZER.

Log replica of church, Mission Tejas State Historical Park near Weches

ORANGE AND SAFFRON COUSCOUS
WITH ANCHO CHILIES

Couscous is a marvelous grain to cook with. Its nutty taste pairs so well with a myriad of seasonings. I was delighted to discover that it is a great match for dried chilies. The ancho chili, which is the name given to dried poblano chilies, has been used in Mexico since before the arrival of the Spaniards. It is the sweetest of the dried chilies with a mild fruit flavor and tones of raisins and dried plums. Serve this dish with grilled red meats and game meats.

2 ancho chilies

½ cup freshly squeezed orange juice

¾ teaspoon balsamic vinegar

1 tablespoon honey

1⅓ cups instant or precooked couscous

2½ cups boiling chicken stock (see "Basics"), flavored with 6 or 7 saffron threads

1 tablespoon olive oil

2 large French shallots, minced

Zest of 1 small orange, minced

1 tablespoon minced cilantro

1 tablespoon minced flat-leaf parsley

2 tablespoons chopped, toasted sliced almonds (skin on)

Salt and freshly ground black pepper to taste

Place the chilies in a bowl and add hot water to cover. Set aside until chilies are very soft and pliable. Drain and remove veins and seeds from chilies. Chop the chilies fine and place in bowl. Stir in the orange juice, balsamic vinegar, and honey, blending well; set aside.

Place the couscous in a large bowl and add the boiling stock. Stir vigorously to blend in the stock. Set aside until couscous has expanded and absorbed the stock.

Meanwhile, heat the olive oil in a heavy 10-inch skillet over medium heat. Add the remaining ingredients and sauté until shallots are wilted and transparent, about 8 minutes. Add the ancho chili mixture to the skillet and cook until liquid is reduced by about one-third, about 8 to 10 minutes. Stir the mixture into the couscous, blending well. Serve hot.

ભ Serves 4 to 6.

COUSCOUS AND GOAT CHEESE FLAN

Wash day on a Blacklands farm, Comal County

*C*ouscous, not really a grain unto itself, is made from steamed semolina grain, from which pasta is made. The Berbers in Morocco originally created couscous. In recent years it has become very popular in the United States. Couscous can be prepared in a variety of different ways and has an affinity for many different seasonings. I love the combination of the couscous and goat cheese in this recipe. Both flavors are earthy and sensuous. The flan makes a great pairing with game meats and birds.

2 cups instant or precooked couscous, cooked according to directions on package in 2 cups chicken stock (see "Basics")

2 green onions, minced, including green tops

2 canned Roma tomatoes, seeded and cut into tiny dice

5 ounces Texas goat cheese

2 teaspoons minced fresh basil

1 teaspoon chili paste with garlic

4 eggs, beaten

1 cup milk

1 cup whipping cream

Set the cooked couscous aside to cool slightly. Cream the goat cheese in mixer with green onions, tomatoes, basil, and chili paste until fluffy, about 3 minutes. Add the eggs, one at a time, stopping to scrape down side of bowl after each addition. Scald the milk and cream together; cool slightly. Add the milk mixture to the cheese mixture, beating to blend well. Turn the mixture out into the cooked couscous and stir to blend well; set aside.

Preheat oven to 350 degrees. Butter 8 individual 6-ounce ramekins and place them in a large baking dish. Divide the couscous mixture among the prepared ramekins. Add hot water to the baking dish to come halfway up the sides of the ramekins. Bake in preheated oven for 25 to 30 minutes, or until the flans are set and slightly springy when pressed. Remove flans from water bath and unmold onto serving plates. Serve hot or at room temperature.

❧ **Makes 8 flans.**

Sweet Potato Pone

*F*ew *people realize that the South's beloved sweet potato is not a potato at all but a rooted tuber that is first cousin to the morning glory vine. Nevertheless, they've become an institution in the South, where they're boiled, baked, fried, and made into delicious pones. What a bonus that the sweet potato is also very nutritious, containing more than twice the recommended daily allowance of Vitamin A as well as healthy doses of potassium, calcium, and Vitamin C. To retain the greatest possible amount of nutrients, always cook the sweet potato with its skin on, peeling it after it has cooled enough to handle.*

3 large sweet potatoes, about 27 to 30 ounces total

¾ cup unsalted butter, softened and cut into ½-inch cubes

¾ cup sugar

3 eggs, beaten

½ cup evaporated milk

1 tablespoon vanilla extract

½ teaspoon cinnamon

Topping

1½ cups firmly packed light brown sugar

½ cup unsalted butter, softened and cut into ½-inch cubes

½ cup all-purpose flour

1 cup chopped pecans

Fruit stand, Shamrock; Downtown mural, Smithville (pages 218–19).

Preheat oven to 400 degrees. Lightly butter a 13-by-9-inch baking dish; set aside.

Place the sweet potatoes in a second baking dish and bake in preheated oven for about 40 to 45 minutes, or until a fork can be inserted into the flesh with ease. Remove the sweet potatoes and set them aside for a few minutes until they are cool enough to handle. Lower oven temperature to 375 degrees. Peel the skin from the potatoes and place them in a large bowl. Mash the potatoes thoroughly. Add butter, sugar, eggs, evaporated milk, vanilla, and cinnamon, stirring to blend well and melt the butter. Turn mixture out into prepared baking dish.

To make the topping, combine brown sugar, butter, and flour in work bowl of food processor fitted with steel blade. Process until smooth and fluffy. Add the pecans and process just to blend, using the pulse feature and leaving the pecan pieces fairly intact.

Spread topping over potato mixture. Bake in preheated oven until set and lightly browned on top, about 45 minutes. Serve hot.

ର **Serves 6 to 8.**

FRISÉE SWEET POTATOES

*F*risée, of course, is actually a leafy green used in trendy salad mixes called "Spring Mix." It has light green, feathery-lacy fronds that make an attractive addition to salad or as a garnish on the plate. When we first created these potatoes at the lodge, they were crisp-tender and gave the same effect as frisée when piled onto a plate beside an entrée. Hence the nonsensical name, which originated solely in my kitchen. We serve these addictive little potato strings with Slow-Smoked Quail on Savory Bread Pudding with Three-Chili Sauce (see "Things with Wings"). Be sure to cook the potatoes just before serving, so that they remain crisp.

5 sweet potatoes, peeled and cut into thin julienne strips, using a mandoline or julienne blade in food processor

Canola oil for deep-frying, heated to 350 degrees

Salt to taste

Chef Paul's Vegetable Magic seasoning (see "The Texas Cook's Pantry")

Deep-fry the potatoes in batches, taking care not to crowd the pan, until crisp but not browned, about 3 to 4 minutes per batch. Drain on wire racks. Season to taste with salt and vegetable seasoning. Serve hot.

&? **Serves 6 to 8.**

MAPLE AND DILL CARROT SOUFFLÉ

*D*ill is one of my favorite winter herbs. It's so easy to grow that everybody should have a pot of it. Plant a few seeds and you will usually have a bumper crop of dill. The herb has been around for hundreds of years and is a traditional staple in Norwegian cooking. Its feathery leaves impart an astringent flavor to foods. I especially like to pair dill with carrots. They have a special affinity for each other. This dish is not really a "soufflé" by strict definition, but it does rise somewhat and has a light, puffy texture. It's a great winter side dish.

1 pound carrots, peeled and sliced thin

3 eggs, well beaten

⅓ cup good-quality real maple syrup

3 tablespoons unsalted butter, cut into small chunks

½ teaspoon salt

¼ teaspoon freshly ground black pepper

1 tablespoon minced fresh dill

½ cup whipping cream

Using a pastry brush, butter 8 6-ounce ramekins; set aside. Preheat oven to 350 degrees.

Place sliced carrots in a 3-quart saucepan and add water to cover. Boil the carrots until they are very tender, about 10 minutes. Drain well and transfer immediately to work bowl of food processor fitted with steel blade. Process until smooth. Turn carrot puree out into a medium bowl. Add all remaining ingredients except whipping cream; stir until well blended and butter has melted. Whisk in the whipping cream; whisk until mixture is smooth. Divide the carrot mixture among the prepared ramekins, filling each one three-fourths full. Place the ramekins in a large baking dish and set on rack of preheated oven. Add hot water to come halfway up the sides of the ramekins. Bake for about 30 minutes, or until slightly puffed and set. Serve hot.

&? **Serves 8.**

VEGETABLE JAMBALAYA

Jambalaya is a dish of Cajun invention, although many ethnic cuisines have similar dishes made by frying the rice in fat, while still raw, until it is lightly browned, then adding liquid. Nobody is absolutely sure where the Cajuns came up with the word jambalaya, *but the general consensus is that it derives from* jambon, *the French word for ham, and* à la, *meaning "in the style of." This non-meat version of the classic makes a great side dish, or it makes a great meatless meal when combined with a green salad.*

½ cup canola oil

2 small onions, chopped

1 large green bell pepper, chopped

2 celery stalks, chopped

3 medium garlic cloves, minced

⅔ cup finely diced yellow squash

⅔ cup finely diced peeled eggplant

⅔ cup green peas

2 teaspoons sugar

2 cups long-grain white rice

4 Roma tomatoes, peeled (see "Basics"), seeded, and chopped

3 cups vegetable stock (see "Basics")

½ teaspoon minced fresh marjoram

½ teaspoon finely ground black pepper

¼ teaspoon red (cayenne) pepper, or to taste

Salt to taste

4 green onions, sliced, including green tops

2 tablespoons minced flat-leaf parsley

In a heavy, deep, 12-inch skillet, heat the canola oil. When oil is hot, add the onions, bell pepper, celery, garlic, squash, eggplant, peas, and sugar; cook until vegetables are wilted, about 10 minutes. Add the rice and cook, stirring constantly, until grains are lightly and uniformly browned. Add the chopped tomatoes and stir to blend. Cook for 2 minutes. Stir in the vegetable stock, blending well. Add seasonings and reduce heat. Cover the pan and simmer until rice is tender and the liquid is absorbed, about 35 to 45 minutes. Taste for seasonings and adjust if necessary. Stir in the green onions and parsley. Cover and cook an additional 10 minutes. Serve hot.

☙ Serves 4 to 6.

Roast Corn Salsa

Corn is a wonderful vegetable, especially in the summer when you can buy fresh roasting ears at farmer's markets or roadside stands. I love to make this invigorating vegetable salsa and serve it with grilled meat or barbecue.

- 3 large ears of fresh corn
- 1 large onion, finely chopped
- 2 large Roma tomatoes, finely diced
- ⅓ cup minced cilantro, including stems
- 2 serrano chilies, veins and seeds removed, minced
- 1 tablespoon freshly squeezed lime juice
- 1 teaspoon minced lime zest
- ⅓ cup Salsa Chilo (see recipe below)
- 1 teaspoon salt, or to taste
- ½ teaspoon freshly ground black pepper

Salsa Chilo

❧ **Makes about 2 cups.**

- 1 15-ounce can plum tomatoes and their liquid
- 1 cup loosely packed cilantro leaves and stems
- 2 garlic cloves, peeled
- 1 tablespoon chopped chipotle chilies in adobo sauce

Salt to taste

Make the Salsa Chilo. Combine all ingredients in work bowl of food processor fitted with steel blade. Using the pulse feature, process until desired consistency is reached. Refrigerate until ready to use. (It's also great to serve with tortilla chips.)

Preheat oven to 400 degrees. Peel the husks back on the corn, but do not remove them. Remove all of the silk and discard. Pull the husks back around the corn and tie loosely at the top with kitchen twine. Place the corn on a baking sheet and roast in preheated oven for about 40 to 45 minutes, or until the kernels are soft and lightly toasted. Set aside until cool. When the corn is cool, remove and discard the husks. Using a sharp knife, cut the kernels from the cob. Place corn in a bowl and add all remaining ingredients. Stir to blend well. Refrigerate until ready to serve.

❧ **Serves 6 to 8.**

Jalapeño Corn Pudding

Corn has been an integral part of the American diet since it was cultivated by native peoples. We especially love corn in the South, where we use it in many forms—from grinding the dried kernels to make grits, our breakfast staple, to creamed corn, cornbread, hushpuppies, or on the cob. This tasty pudding makes a great side dish to just about any entrée.

- 2 tablespoons unsalted butter
- 2 small French shallots, finely chopped
- 1 fresh jalapeño, seeds and veins removed, minced
- 1 small green bell pepper, finely chopped
- 1 15-ounce can cream-style corn
- ⅔ cup whole-kernel corn
- 2¼ teaspoons sugar
- ½ teaspoon salt
- ¼ teaspoon freshly ground black pepper
- 1 teaspoon Tabasco sauce
- 3 additional tablespoons unsalted butter, melted
- 4 eggs, well beaten
- 1½ cups whipping cream
- 2 tablespoons cornstarch blended into 2 tablespoons cold water

Preheat oven to 350 degrees. Butter 8 4-ounce ramekins and set them in a large baking dish; set aside. Melt the 2 tablespoons of butter in a heavy 10-inch skillet over medium-high heat. Sauté the shallots, jalapeño, and green bell pepper until shallots are wilted and lightly browned, about 10 minutes. Set aside. In a medium bowl, combine all ingredients, including the sautéed vegetables, stirring vigorously to blend well. Ladle the mixture into prepared ramekins. Add hot water to the baking dish to come halfway up the sides of the ramekins. Bake in preheated oven for about 45 minutes, or until custard is firm and a knife inserted in center comes out clean. Unmold the custards onto serving plates. Serve hot.

❧ **Makes 8 ramekins.**

BAKED TOMATOES WITH SPINACH MOUSSE

This colorful and delicious side dish can be put together in advance and baked just in time to serve. The spinach filling for the tomatoes has a note of mystery to the taste, provided by a hint of Pernod, a robust anise-flavored liqueur.

4 large tomatoes

Melted unsalted butter

Salt to taste

SPINACH MOUSSE

15 ounces frozen chopped spinach, thawed

2 tablespoons unsalted butter

2 large garlic cloves, minced

2 green onions, finely chopped

2 tablespoons all-purpose flour

1 cup whipping cream

1 tablespoon Pernod or other anise-flavored liqueur

½ teaspoon salt

¼ teaspoon freshly ground black pepper

¼ teaspoon red (cayenne) pepper

3 eggs, well beaten

Grated Parmesan cheese

Preheat oven to 350 degrees. Halve the tomatoes crosswise. Carefully scoop out and discard pulp and seeds, taking care not to puncture the outside skin. Cut a very thin slice from the bottom of each tomato half so it will sit flat without tipping over. Place the tomatoes in a baking dish. Brush the inside of each tomato shell with some of the melted butter; salt and pepper each to taste. Set dish aside.

Press all moisture out of the spinach. In a heavy 10-inch skillet over medium heat, melt the 2 tablespoons of butter. Add the spinach, garlic, and green onions. Sauté for 5 minutes, then add the flour, stirring to blend well. Cook, stirring constantly, for 3 to 4 minutes. Add the whipping cream, Pernod, and seasonings. Bring to a boil and stir until slightly thickened. Remove from heat and cool slightly. Stir in the beaten eggs. Spoon a portion of the mixture into each tomato half and top with some of the Parmesan cheese. Bake in preheated oven for about 25 to 30 minutes, or until the filling is set. Serve hot.

ᔰ **Serves 8.**

ROASTED RED BELL PEPPER MOUSSE

This is a decidedly different side dish. Its faintly smoky taste makes it a big hit with grilled meats. Many people don't realize that the common bell pepper, both green and red, is in the same botanical family, Capsicum, as chili peppers. They're just milder chilies!

8 small fresh basil leaves

5 large red bell peppers, blistered, peeled, seeded, and diced (see "Basics")

3 tablespoons unsalted butter

3 large garlic cloves, minced

1½ tablespoons minced fresh basil

¾ teaspoon salt

¼ teaspoon freshly ground black pepper

3 eggs

½ cup whipping cream

Preheat oven to 375 degrees. Place oven rack in middle position. Thoroughly butter 8 4-ounce ramekins. Place one of the small basil leaves in the center of the bottom of each ramekin, pressing it into the butter; set aside. Melt the 3 tablespoons of butter in a heavy 10-inch skillet over medium heat. Add the diced bell pepper, garlic, basil, salt, and pepper. Cook, stirring frequently, for 8 minutes. Place the bell pepper mixture in blender and process until smooth; set aside. Combine the eggs and whipping cream in work bowl of food processor fitted with steel blade. Process for about 2 minutes, or until eggs are thickened slightly and light lemon yellow in color. Add the pureed red pepper mixture and process until smooth and well blended. Divide the pepper puree among the prepared ramekins. Place the filled ramekins in a large baking dish and add hot water to come halfway up the sides of the ramekins. Cover the top of the dish with a sheet of buttered parchment paper, buttered side down. Bake for 25 to 30 minutes, or until the mousses are set and feel slightly spongy to the touch. Unmold at once onto serving plates and serve hot. If the basil leaves stick to the bottom of the ramekins, carefully remove them and pat into place on top of the unmolded mousses.

ᔰ **Serves 8.**

GRILLED VEGGIES

*I*n the summer in Texas, when it feels like Hell's not half a mile away and all the fences are down, the last thing you want to be doing is standing in the kitchen over the stove. So during the long Texas summer we cook everything we possibly can outside on the grill—including vegetables. I love grilled veggies. Their flavor seems to intensify when their skins are slowly caramelized by the heat of the grill. And their flavor paired with grilled meats is just ambrosia to my soul. I devised this all-purpose marinade for grilling vegetables several years ago. The recipe makes over a quart of marinade, but it will keep in the refrigerator for several weeks. Just bring it to room temperature and whisk it well before using. When you become hooked on grilled veggies, you'll find it doesn't last all that long!

Whole carrots, peeled and trimmed

Baking potatoes (skin on), cut lengthwise into ½-inch-thick strips, or tiny red new potatoes, cut in half

Eggplant (skin on), cut lengthwise into ½-inch-thick strips

Whole portabello mushrooms

Sliced red or yellow onions

Roma tomatoes, cut in half lengthwise

Small zucchini and yellow squash, halved lengthwise

Beets, peeled and sliced into ¼-inch-thick slices

Green onions, whole, with roots and tender tops removed

Greens (bok choy, collards, mustard, kale, Swiss chard)

MARINADE

❧ **Makes about 1½ quarts.**

1⅓ cups balsamic vinegar

¼ cup Dijon-style mustard

16 large garlic cloves, minced

2 tablespoons plus 2 teaspoons crushed red pepper flakes

¼ cup minced cilantro

¼ cup minced flat-leaf parsley

1 tablespoon plus 1 teaspoon salt

1¼ teaspoons freshly ground black pepper

2 tablespoons sugar

1 quart extra-virgin olive oil

To prepare the marinade, combine all ingredients except olive oil in a medium bowl and whisk to blend well. Whisk in the olive oil in a slow, steady stream until well emulsified. Refrigerate until needed. Bring to room temperature and whisk before using.

Select the vegetables you wish to grill and place them in a single layer in a baking pan. Pour a liberal amount of the marinade on the vegetables, turning them to coat all sides. Marinate for 1 hour at room temperature. Grill the vegetables on gas grill over medium heat. The different vegetables will take various lengths of time to grill. Carrots will take about 20 to 30 minutes, while the zucchini and yellow squash will take about 5 to 8 minutes. Grill until the veggies are browned and caramelized but not charred. Turn often, basting with the marinade left in the pan. Serve hot.

Onion harvesting near Presidio (left); Select-harvest peaches, Gillespie County (facing page).

GRILLED PEACHES

A long about July when the Stonewall peaches are ripe up there in Central Texas, I make my annual peach-buying trip. When I get home with my mother lode of peaches, we eat them with a passion—sliced for breakfast, in cobblers and pies, in turnovers, in sauces. But one of my favorite ways to eat the peaches is grilled. They make a wonderful addition to any summer meal. They're especially great with poultry or fish dishes.

4 ripe Stonewall peaches
6 tablespoons unsalted butter
1 tablespoon freshly squeezed lime juice
1 tablespoon honey

STUFFING

⅓ cup Mexican crema fresca (see "Basics")
3 ounces cream cheese, softened
1 tablespoon sugar
1 teaspoon minced lemon zest

Dip the peaches into rapidly boiling water for 20 seconds. Remove with a slotted spoon and run them under cold water. Slip the skins off the peaches. Slice peaches in half and remove the pits; set aside. Combine the butter, lime juice, and honey in a small saucepan over medium heat. Cook just until butter has melted and mixture is smooth. Preheat gas grill to medium heat.

Brush the peaches all over with the butter and honey mixture. Place them on rack of grill, cut side down. Sear for 3 to 4 minutes, then turn the peaches over and grill an additional 3 to 4 minutes.

To make the stuffing, combine ingredients in work bowl of food processor fitted with steel blade. Process until smooth.

To serve the peaches, spoon a portion of the stuffing mixture into each peach half. Serve hot.

Ↄ **Serves 4 to 6.**

Braised Red Cabbage with Apples, Onions, and Sausage

*B*raised red cabbage is a staple item in the German diet. Eat at a German restaurant in Central Texas and, yep, there it is under the wienerschnitzel or jaegerschnitzel, or alongside the bratwurst, or cuddled up to the sauerbraten. I love red cabbage and I thank the food gods often that this dish survived in the culinary repertoire of the early German settlers.

1 small head of red cabbage

2 small Granny Smith apples, pared, cored, and diced

1 teaspoon salt, or to taste

1 tablespoon freshly squeezed lemon juice

1½ teaspoons light brown sugar

¾ cup chicken stock (see "Basics")

2 tablespoons bacon drippings

1 small onion, chopped

¼ teaspoon freshly ground black pepper

1 tablespoon red wine vinegar

8 ounces kielbasa sausage, sliced into bite-size pieces, or another smoked pork sausage

Quarter the cabbage. With a sharp knife, shred it coarsely, discarding tough center. Rinse the cabbage, then place it in a 6-quart pot with the diced apples, salt, lemon juice, brown sugar, and chicken stock. Bring to a boil, then lower heat and cover the pan. Simmer for 15 minutes, stirring occasionally.

Meanwhile, heat the bacon drippings in a heavy 10-inch skillet over medium-high heat. Sauté the onion until lightly browned, about 10 minutes. Add the onion to the cabbage along with the pepper, vinegar, and sausage pieces. Cook, covered, for about 20 minutes, or until sausage is cooked. Serve hot.

ର Serves 6 to 8.

Mashed Rutabagas

I have loved root vegetables since I was introduced to them by my ex-mother-in-law, who was a marvelous cook and did magic things with rutabagas. A couple of years ago, I decided to add this recipe to our menu at the lodge. Our guests would gobble them up and then ask what they were. When we told them, they wouldn't believe us, saying that their mothers couldn't make them eat rutabagas when they were children. As the late Bert Greene tells us in Greene on Greens, the rutabaga came about through the crossbreeding of a cabbage and a turnip by a Swiss botanist. In 1806, rutabagas first appeared in a U.S. seed catalog, advertised as "South of the Border Turnips." When it comes to taste, rutabagas are sweeter than turnips. When buying rutabagas, select ones that feel weighty. They should be streaked with purple and free of bruises or hoe marks. All rutabagas purchased at the market will have a heavy wax coating to prevent them from drying out. Rutabagas are high in vitamins and minerals, especially Vitamins C and A. Sweet and earthy, rutabagas make the perfect side dish for red meats or roasted birds.

3 rutabagas, about 1 pound each, peeled and cut into 1-inch cubes

3 Knorr vegetable bouillon cubes

12 tablespoons (1½ sticks) unsalted butter, cut into small pieces

Salt and freshly ground black pepper

Combine the chopped rutabagas and vegetable bouillon cubes in a heavy 4-quart saucepan. Add water to cover. Over medium-high heat, bring to a full boil and cook for 45 minutes, or until the rutabagas are very tender. Drain well and return the rutabagas to the saucepan. Mash them with the butter, leaving them slightly lumpy. Season to taste with salt and freshly ground black pepper. Taste for seasoning. If the rutabagas taste a little flat, stir in a bit more salt. Serve hot.

ର Serves 4 to 6.

GERMAN POTATO SALAD

*P*otatoes, in one form or another, were always found on the table among the early German settlers in the Texas Hill Country. This type of potato dish, served hot or warm, is referred to as potato "salad." I like to serve it with barbecue during the colder months when the thought of a cold side dish makes me shiver.

2½ pounds small red new potatoes (unpeeled), scrubbed and sliced into bite-size pieces

6 smoked bacon slices, fried crisp and crumbled, drippings reserved

1 medium onion, chopped

1½ tablespoons all-purpose flour

¼ cup light brown sugar

1 teaspoon paprika

½ teaspoon celery salt

½ teaspoon freshly ground black pepper

⅓ cup apple cider vinegar

⅔ cup hot beef stock (see "Basics")

1½ tablespoons minced flat-leaf parsley

Place potato slices in a 4-quart saucepan and add cold water to cover. Bring the potatoes to a boil, then simmer for 20 minutes, or until potatoes are tender but not mushy. Drain and place in a large bowl. Set aside to keep warm.

Heat the reserved bacon drippings in a heavy 12-inch skillet over medium heat. Add the onion and cook until it is wilted and transparent, about 7 minutes. Stir in the flour all at once, blending well. Cook, stirring, for 3 or 4 minutes. Add the brown sugar, paprika, celery salt, pepper, vinegar, and hot beef broth. Bring to a full boil and stir until thickened. Stir in the crumbled bacon. Pour the dressing over the potatoes, add parsley, and stir to coat the potatoes thoroughly with the dressing. Serve hot or warm.

❧ **Serves 6.**

TEXAS TWO-STEP POTATO SALAD WITH MUSTARD

*P*otato salad is right at the top of the list of quintessentially American foods, even though the potato originated in South America and came to the American South by a circuitous route, stopping first in Europe for a century or so. Every cook has his or her own recipe for making potato salad. For the best taste, use the small red new potatoes and leave the skin on them.

2½ pounds small red new potatoes, unpeeled

1 small onion, chopped

2 small celery stalks, chopped

3 hard-cooked eggs, chopped

4 green onions, chopped, including green tops

2 tablespoons dill relish

2 tablespoons sweet relish

1½ cups mayonnaise

¼ cup French's mustard

½ teaspoon salt

½ teaspoon celery salt

½ teaspoon freshly ground black pepper

1 teaspoon Tabasco sauce

Wash potatoes well. Cut them into ¼-inch-thick slices, cutting larger potatoes in half first. Place the potato slices in a 4-quart saucepan and add cold water to cover. Bring to a boil and cook until tender, about 20 minutes. Do not overcook.

Drain potatoes well and transfer to a large bowl. Add the onion, celery, chopped eggs, green onion, and relishes.

In a separate bowl combine the mayonnaise, mustard, salt, celery salt, black pepper, and Tabasco sauce. Whisk to blend well. Taste for seasoning and adjust as needed. Stir the mayonnaise mixture into the potato mixture, blending thoroughly. Taste again for seasoning, adding salt or black pepper as needed. Refrigerate to chill before serving.

❧ **Serves 6 to 8.**

COUNTRY CORNBREAD DRESSING

I was not raised by a mother who loved to cook. She never taught me to cook. She also never made cornbread dressing. I had never tasted cornbread dressing until I married and inherited a mother-in-law who was a fine country cook. That first Thanksgiving at her table, I couldn't believe my taste buds. After that meal cornbread dressing became a standard side dish at my holiday table.

"To stuff or not to stuff?" The two terms can refer to the same ingredients. The choice becomes whether to bake them alone, in which case the dish is generally referred to a "dressing," or to stuff the mixture inside the bird before roasting, thus making it "stuffing." If you choose to stuff the dressing inside the turkey, be sure that both the turkey and the stuffing have been well chilled and bake the turkey in a moderately hot oven (see "Turkey Talk" in "Basics" for more information on stuffing and baking turkeys). If you are cooking the mixture as "dressing" with a turkey, take advantage of the turkey drippings to add extra flavor and moistness to the dressing.

½ cup unsalted butter

1 large onion, chopped

1 large green bell pepper, chopped

2 large celery stalks, chopped

5 smoked bacon slices, diced

1 tablespoon minced fresh sage

1 tablespoon minced fresh thyme

1 tablespoon minced fresh rosemary

1 teaspoon dried Mexican oregano

1 teaspoon salt, or to taste

½ teaspoon freshly ground black pepper

¼ pound smoked ham, coarsely ground

4 cups crumbled cornbread

6 cups French bread cubes

3 eggs, lightly beaten

About 1¼ cups chicken or turkey stock, or more as needed (see "Basics")

Preheat oven to 350 degrees. Melt the butter in a heavy 12-inch skillet over medium heat. Add onion, bell pepper, celery, bacon, seasonings, and ham. Sauté, stirring often, until vegetables are wilted and bacon is cooked but not browned, about 10 to 15 minutes. Place cornbread and French bread in a large bowl. Pour vegetable mixture over bread; toss to combine. Stir in beaten eggs. Add enough stock or broth to make a moist dressing, stirring to break up cornbread and French bread. Turn the dressing out into a large baking dish or casserole and bake in preheated oven for 1 hour. Drizzle additional stock (or turkey drippings) as needed to keep the dressing moist. Serve hot.

❧ **Serves 8 to 10.**

Rural mailboxes, Lee County

MIXED GREENS WITH SMOKED HOG JOWL

"Greens are good for you." Southerners have heard that since they started eating solid food. But not everybody knows that greens are just plain good, too. A traditional component of soul food, greens have come into the limelight in recent years. When I first discovered greens, I had just married a southern country boy and I weighed ninety-six pounds. After savoring the pleasures of the table in my mother-in-law's home, I knew I would never again weigh ninety-six pounds. One of my favorites was greens. I just couldn't seem to get enough of them or the rich, flavorful broth in which they were cooked—"potlikker."

In defense of the southern spelling of the word, Lieutenant Governor Zell Miller of Georgia sent the following message to the New York Times in response to an article that appeared in a 1982 issue: "I always thought the New York Times knew everything, but obviously your editor knows as little about spelling as he or she does about Appalachian cooking and soul food. Only a culinarily-illiterate damnyankee who can't tell the difference between beans and greens would call the liquid left in the pot after cooking greens 'pot liquor' instead of 'potlikker' as yours did. And don't cite Webster as a defense because he didn't know any better either."

Folks are serious about potlikker in the South, and one of the real reasons to cook greens is so you can drink the potlikker right from the bowl. In this recipe, the choice of seasoning meat is a personal one. You can use plain old bacon, cut into tiny dice, or salt pork, or my personal favorite—smoked hog jowl. You can find it in small-town grocery stores or markets in Mexican or African-American neighborhoods.

2 bunches fresh collard greens

2 bunches fresh mustard greens

2 bunches fresh kale

2 medium onions, halved lengthwise, then sliced

2 small turnips, peeled, halved lengthwise, then thinly sliced

8 ounces smoked hog jowl (rind removed), cut into tiny dice, or other seasoning meat

1½ tablespoons sugar

½ cup picante sauce

1 tablespoon chicken base paste (see "The Texas Cook's Pantry")

1 tablespoon salt, or to taste

2 teaspoons freshly ground black pepper, or to taste

Place all greens in sink and fill to the brim with water. Let the greens stand for 15 minutes. Carefully remove greens from water without disturbing sandy silt that has settled to the bottom. Wash the leaves under running water. Tear leaves into small pieces, removing and discarding tough center ribs. Place torn greens, onions, turnips, and seasoning meat in an 8- to 10-quart pot; add water to cover the greens. Stir in sugar, picante sauce, chicken base paste, salt, and pepper. Bring to a boil over medium-high heat; boil for 5 minutes. Reduce heat and simmer, stirring occasionally, for 2 hours. Taste for seasoning; adjust as necessary. Add additional water if needed. Serve hot in bowls with plenty of potlikker.

∞ **Serves 6 to 8.**

THE GOOD STUFF

Ah, dessert! Visions of sugarplums . . .

What images come to your mind when you think of dessert? Do you see the dessert cart at your favorite restaurant rolling up to your table, laden with gooey, towering confections of chocolate, caramel, fruit and berries, pastries—all peeking out from under mountains of fluffy whipped cream or liqueur-laced sauces, just waiting for you to make your choice? Is it the dessert counter of the gourmet take-out shop where you frequently stop on your way home? Or Martha Stewart whipping up bon-bons on the television?

That image for me is of my grandmother's kitchen. I can see her there in that spotless white room, rolling out pie dough on the enamel counter of the Hoosier cabinet with all of its drawers and bins and racks that pulled out for curious children to play with. Or standing at her ancient Chambers stove, which she refused to replace, making the silken lemon curd that filled her famous lemon pound cake. It's a warm, fuzzy association I have with desserts.

Desserts should do that. They make us happy. When you take that first bite and the sweet flavors begin to burst onto your taste buds, the signal that goes to the brain triggers an "inward smile" that starts way down in the heart of you. "Ah, dessert," it says.

It stands to reason that Texans have always been big on dessert. Cowboys are legendary "meat and potatoes" kind of guys. And what two other things do the "meat and potatoes" bunch request to go along with their favorite meal? You guessed it, bread and dessert—the gooier, the better. The early German and

Czech housewives were masters at pastry cooking, and many opened bakeries in Texas. In the early part of the twentieth century, when the East Texas Piney Woods opened up to the logging industry, boarding houses sprang up by the dozens to house the loggers who came to the area. These boarding houses were known for their good home-cooked meals followed by hearty desserts.

Drugstores in the larger cities opened diner counters; cafeterias proliferated, and major department stores opened lunch counters—all for the convenience of shoppers or local businessmen. And what was the highlight of a meal at one of those down-home eateries? The good stuff you got when you ate all your vegetables.

Often I like to serve dessert to guests in the afternoon, just a small helping of something to tide the tummy over until dinner. I always serve a sweet dessert wine with this afternoon treat. Texas wineries produce some of my favorite dessert wines. Try one of the following: Becker Vineyards Reserve Estate Bottled Port, Fall Creek Vineyards Sweet Jo (Riesling and Muscat), La Buena Vida Vineyards Muscat Dulce or Vintage Port, Messina Hof Angel Late Harvest Riesling, Messina Hof Johannesburg Riesling, Sister Creek Vineyards Muscat Canelli, Spicewood Vineyards Muscat, Texas Hills Vineyard Moscato, or—always wonderful with dessert—Delaney Vineyards Texas Champagne Brut!

Keep alive the Texas tradition and indulge! Remember: "Life is short—eat dessert first."

WHITE CHOCOLATE CHEESECAKE WITH CHOCOLATE-HAZELNUT CRUST

This silken smooth overdose of white chocolate nirvana owes much of its rich depth of flavor to Frangelico. This sweet liqueur is based on hazelnuts (sometimes called "filberts"), one of my favorite nuts. The flavor of the liqueur pairs so well with the taste of white chocolate that one would believe it a match made in heaven. Remember that this cake is very rich, so guests usually appreciate small servings.

12 ounces white chocolate, finely chopped
½ cup whipping cream, slightly warmed
1 pound cream cheese, softened
4 eggs, separated
1 tablespoon vanilla
⅛ teaspoon salt

CHOCOLATE-HAZELNUT CRUST

1½ cups chocolate wafer crumbs
⅔ cup finely ground peeled hazelnuts
6 tablespoons unsalted butter, melted

WHITE CHOCOLATE TOPPING

12 ounces white chocolate, finely chopped
½ cup whipping cream, slightly warmed
6 tablespoons Frangelico liqueur
Grated semi-sweet chocolate as garnish

Prepare the Chocolate-Hazelnut Crust. Thoroughly butter the bottom and sides of a 9-inch springform pan; set aside. Combine the crust ingredients in work bowl of food processor fitted with steel blade and process to blend well. Spread the mixture evenly and firmly over bottom and two-thirds of the way up the side of the buttered pan. Refrigerate while preparing the cheesecake filling.

Preheat oven to 300 degrees. Position oven rack in center position. In top of double boiler, melt half of the white chocolate over hot, not simmering, water, stirring often. Repeat with the remaining chocolate. Combine the two batches of melted chocolate and stir in the whipping cream; continue to stir until mixture is very smooth. Remove pan from hot water and set aside to cool slightly. In bowl of electric mixer, beat the cream cheese at medium speed until smooth, about 3 to 4 minutes. Add the egg yolks, one at a time, beating well and scraping down side of bowl after each addition. Add the cooled white chocolate mixture, vanilla, and salt. Beat for 4 minutes at medium speed, or until smooth and well blended. Set aside.

In a separate, grease-free bowl, beat the egg whites until medium-stiff peaks form, about 2 minutes. Gently but thoroughly fold the beaten whites into the chocolate mixture. Pour the filling into prepared crust. Place the springform pan in a large, deep baking pan and add hot water to come halfway up the side of the springform pan. Bake in preheated oven for 1 hour, or until cake rises and is almost set. The top will still jiggle slightly. Turn oven off and leave the cake inside for 1 hour without opening the door. (The cake will sink during this time.) Remove cake from the water bath and transfer it, still in the springform pan, to wire rack; cool completely.

After cake has cooled, prepare the White Chocolate Topping. In top of double boiler over hot, not simmering, water, melt white chocolate in two batches, stirring often. Combine the two batches and stir in the whipping cream until mixture is smooth. Remove pan from water and stir in Frangelico. Pour the topping over the cake, still in the springform pan. Cover with plastic wrap and refrigerate for at least 4 hours or overnight.

To serve the cheesecake, remove side of springform pan and transfer cake to serving platter. Garnish the top with a liberal amount of grated semi-sweet chocolate. Slice into wedges of desired size.

ଈ **Serves 12 to 14.**

Lamar Boulevard Bridge over Town Lake, Austin (facing page); Wildflower meadow, Llano County (pages 230–31); Papershell pecan crop, Bastrop County (page 232); Peaches, Hill Country (page 233); Blackland Prairie farmland near Uhland (pages 234–35).

WHITE CHOCOLATE

TRUE WHITE CHOCOLATE IS COCOA BUTTER THAT HAS BEEN BLENDED WITH MILK (EITHER POWDERED OR CONDENSED) AND SUGAR AND USUALLY A SMALL AMOUNT OF VANILLA EXTRACT. BEWARE OF PRODUCTS CONTAINING VEGETABLE FATS. THEY ARE NOT THE REAL McCOY, AND CHEMICALLY THEY WILL NOT PERFORM WELL IN RECIPES CALLING FOR WHITE CHOCOLATE. WHITE CHOCOLATE PROVIDES SOME ADVANTAGES TO THE CONSUMER. IT IS THE MOST DURABLE OF ALL NATURAL FATS, RESISTING RANCIDITY FAR LONGER THAN ANY OTHER VEGETABLE OR ANIMAL FAT. AND SINCE CHOCOLATE ALLERGIES ARE ACTUALLY CAUSED BY SENSITIVITY TO COCOA SOLIDS, WHICH ARE OF COURSE ABSENT IN WHITE CHOCOLATE, MOST PEOPLE WHO ARE OTHERWISE ALLERGIC TO CHOCOLATE CAN ENJOY WHITE CHOCOLATE. FOR THOSE CONCERNED WITH CAFFEINE, WHITE CHOCOLATE CONTAINS ONLY A TRACE AMOUNT OF THAT MUCH-MALIGNED SUBSTANCE. BECAUSE OF WHITE CHOCOLATE'S NATURAL CREAM-LIKE QUALITIES, IT WORKS BEST IN RECIPES USING DAIRY PRODUCTS. WHITE CHOCOLATE IS VERY SWEET, SO A LITTLE BIT GOES A LONG WAY.

MELTING WHITE CHOCOLATE REQUIRES EXTREME CARE. THE PRODUCT IS VERY HEAT SENSITIVE DUE TO THE FACT THAT THE FATS—COCOA BUTTER AND MILK SOLID BUTTERFAT—MELT AT DIFFERENT TEMPERATURES, AS DOES THE SUGAR. IF OVERHEATED, THE MILK PROTEINS WILL CLUMP TOGETHER AND SEPARATE FROM THE COCOA BUTTER. TO SUCCESSFULLY MELT WHITE CHOCOLATE, CHOP IT INTO VERY SMALL PIECES AND MELT IT IN THE TOP OF A DOUBLE BOILER OVER HOT, NOT SIMMERING, WATER. SCRAPE DOWN THE SIDE OF THE PAN OFTEN WITH A FLEXIBLE RUBBER SPATULA. DON'T ALLOW DROPS OF WATER OR STEAM FROM THE DOUBLE BOILER TO DROP INTO THE CHOCOLATE, OR IT WILL "SEIZE," WHICH MEANS A POT OF STIFF, GRAINY, RUINED CHOCOLATE. FOR THE BEST RESULTS, MELT NO MORE THAN 8 OUNCES AT A TIME.

WHITE CHOCOLATE–MACADAMIA NUT POUND CAKE
WITH HOJA SANTA SAUCE AND PEPPERED PINEAPPLE

*T*his is a very unusual dessert, combining some very assertive flavors as well as some very delicate ones, but the sum of the parts equals a wonderfully exciting taste experience.

5 ounces white chocolate, chopped fine

1 cup whipping cream

1 tablespoon vanilla extract

1 cup (2 sticks) unsalted butter, softened

3 cups sugar

6 eggs, room temperature

3 cups all-purpose flour

½ teaspoon salt

¼ teaspoon baking soda

½ cup chopped macadamia nuts

Powdered sugar

HOJA SANTA SAUCE

❧ Makes about 3 cups.

3 large Hoja Santa leaves, about 6 to 7 inches in diameter, roughly torn

1¼ cups milk

1¼ cups whipping cream

6 egg yolks, beaten

¾ cup sugar

PEPPERED PINEAPPLE

2 8-ounce cans sliced pineapple, drained and cut into bite-size pieces

Finely ground black pepper

1 cup sugar

½ cup freshly squeezed orange juice

3 tablespoons freshly squeezed lemon juice

½ cup dark crème de cacao

¼ cup browned butter

Minced zest of 1 orange

Preheat oven to 300 degrees. Butter and flour a 10-inch bundt pan. Tap on edge of sink to remove all excess flour; set aside.

Combine the white chocolate and whipping cream in a medium saucepan over medium heat. Cook, stirring often, until chocolate has melted. Stir in the vanilla. Set aside to cool slightly.

In bowl of electric mixer, cream the butter and sugar at medium speed until very light and fluffy, about 5 minutes. Add the eggs, one at a time, scraping down side of bowl and beating to blend after each addition. Blend in the white chocolate mixture. Sift together the flour, salt, and baking soda. Add the dry ingredients to the creamed mixture by thirds, scraping down side of bowl after each addition. Beat just to blend. Add the macadamia nuts and blend. Turn the batter out into prepared pan and bake in preheated oven until a metal skewer inserted near center of cake comes out clean, about 1 hour and 15 minutes. Cool the cake on wire rack for 15 minutes, then invert onto rack and cool completely. When cake is cool, sift a liberal amount of powdered sugar over the top. Place cake on serving platter.

Make the Hoja Santa Sauce. Combine the torn leaves, milk, and cream in a heavy, 2-quart saucepan over medium heat. Bring to a boil, then lower heat and simmer for about 7 minutes. Set the pan aside for 15 minutes to allow the leaves to steep in the milk and cream. Strain into a clean 3-quart saucepan, discarding the leaves. Bring the milk and cream mixture back almost to a boil, and then add about ½ cup of the hot mixture in a slow, steady stream to the egg yolks, whisking vigorously. Whisk the egg yolks into the rest of the milk and cream mixture. Stir constantly over medium heat until the mixture thickens and coats a metal spoon. Do not allow the sauce to boil, or the eggs will scramble and the sauce will break. Remove from heat and whisk for 3 to 4 minutes to cool. Strain through a fine strainer into a bowl set over ice water. Stir until chilled. Refrigerate.

Just before serving, cook the Peppered Pineapple. Place the pineapple chunks in a bowl and toss thoroughly with black pepper; set aside. In a heavy 12-inch skillet over medium-low heat, melt the sugar until it is liquid. Stir gently until it is light golden brown. Add the orange and lemon juices, stirring well.

(continued)

Add the crème de cacao and cook until slightly thickened. Whisk in the browned butter and orange zest. Cook for 1 to 2 minutes. Add the pineapple chunks and cook until pineapple is well glazed, about 4 minutes. Remove from heat.

To serve, slice the cake into thin slices. Spoon a bed of the Hoja Santa Sauce onto each serving plate. Overlap two slices of the cake in the center of the sauce. Spoon a portion of the Peppered Pineapple and its sauce on top of each serving.

ભ **Serves 12 to 14.**

HOJA SANTA

HOJA SANTA (PIPER SANCTUM) IS AN AROMATIC MEMBER OF THE BLACK PEPPER FAMILY WHOSE LARGE, HEART-SHAPED LEAVES HAVE A MARVELOUS SASSAFRAS OR ANISE-LIKE FLAVOR. HOJA SANTA IS USED EXTENSIVELY IN THE CUISINES OF MEXICO AND SOUTH AMERICA, OFTEN AS A WRAPPING AND ALSO AS A FLAVORING. CHEF STEPHAN PYLES, OWNER OF DALLAS'S STAR CANYON AND PERHAPS THE MOST TALENTED AND INNOVATIVE OF ALL THE SOUTHWESTERN CHEFS, WAS ONE OF THE FIRST TO USE THIS STRANGE HERB IN CONTEMPORARY TEXAS CUISINE. I LIKE TO USE IT IN CERTAIN DESSERT PREPARATIONS WHERE IT ADDS AN INTERESTING FLAVOR. THE PLANT IS VERY EASY TO GROW. SEE "A TEXAS COOK'S PANTRY" FOR A SOURCE FOR THE PLANTS.

MRS. POWELL'S POUND CAKE WITH LEMON CURD SAUCE

Yvonne Powell and her husband Reuben were rice farmers outside of West Columbia for over forty years. The first time I tasted Mrs. Powell's pound cake, which is legendary around these parts, it reminded me of my grandmother's lemon pound cake, which was filled with the best lemon curd in the world. I have added a lemon curd sauce to Mrs. Powell's cake. The taste brings back many memories.

1½ cups (3 sticks) unsalted butter, softened
1   8-ounce package cream cheese, softened
3   cups sugar
6   eggs
3   cups all-purpose flour
2   teaspoons each of vanilla, lemon, and almond extracts

LEMON CURD SAUCE

1   cup sugar
½   cup (1 stick) unsalted butter, cut into 1-inch cubes
6   eggs
Minced zest of 2 lemons
Juice of 4 medium lemons

Do not preheat oven. Butter and flour a 10-inch bundt pan; shake out all excess flour. Set aside. Cream the butter and cheese in electric mixer at medium speed until light and fluffy, about 3 minutes. Add the sugar and beat for 5 minutes at medium speed, scraping down side of bowl once or twice. Add the eggs, 2 at a time, alternating with ⅓ of the flour. Scrape down side of bowl and beat just to blend after each addition. Add the extracts and blend well. Turn batter out into prepared bundt pan. Place the pan in a cold oven and set the oven to 325 degrees. Bake for about 1½ hours, or until a metal skewer inserted in center of cake comes out clean. Cool cake in pan on wire rack for 10 minutes, then turn cake out onto rack and cool completely.

While cake is cooling, prepare the Lemon Curd Sauce. Process the sugar in work bowl of food processor fitted with steel blade for 1 minute, or until it is very fine and powdery. Add the butter chunks and process until smooth, stopping to scrape down side of bowl once or twice. Add the eggs and process to blend well. Add lemon zest and juice; process for 20 seconds, or until well blended. Turn mixture out into a heavy, 2-quart, non-aluminum saucepan. (The mixture will appear to be curdled but will smooth out during the cooking process.) Cook over medium-low heat, whisking constantly, until mixture is thickened, about 10 to 12 minutes.

To serve, slice cake and top with a portion of the hot Lemon Curd Sauce.

ର Serves 12 to 14.

Texas Hills Vineyard Moscato Cake

The first time I visited the Tasting Room at Texas Hills Vineyard in Johnson City, I fell in love with the wines, the winery, and the winemakers, Gary Gilstrap and his wife, Kathy. They are among the very few Texas wineries that produce Italian-style wines. One of their wines is a wonderful Italian-style dessert wine called Moscato. The wine contains tones of apricot and lends a light and breezy taste to this cake. This is a good all-occasion cake—great for picnics or other summer meals.

1½ cups (3 sticks) unsalted butter, softened

3 cups sugar

5 eggs

3 cups all-purpose flour

¾ cup Texas Hills Vineyard Moscato wine

Glaze

¾ cup apricot preserves

2 tablespoons sugar

3 tablespoons cognac

Preheat oven to 350 degrees. Using a pastry brush, generously coat the inside of a 10-inch bundt pan with melted butter. Coat the butter with all-purpose flour. Invert the pan and tap sharply to remove all excess flour.

Place softened butter in bowl of electric mixer; beat at medium speed until butter is smooth and fluffy, about 3 minutes. Gradually add the sugar while beating. Continue to beat until the mixture is very light in color and fluffy, about 5 minutes. Add the eggs, one at a time, beating well and scraping

down side of bowl after each addition. Add flour in thirds, alternating with the wine. Scrape down side of bowl and beat just to blend after each addition. Pour the batter into the prepared bundt pan and bake in preheated oven for 1 hour and 15 minutes, or until a skewer inserted in center of cake comes out clean. Allow the cake to cool in the pan for 10 minutes, then invert onto serving plate.

While cake is baking, prepare the glaze. Heat the apricot preserves in a small saucepan over medium heat and add the sugar. Heat until the preserves are thin and the sugar has melted. Strain through a fine strainer, stirring with the back of a wooden spoon to separate all liquid; discard solids. Stir cognac into the liquid and cover; set aside and keep warm.

Brush the hot cake with the warm apricot glaze, covering the cake heavily with the glaze. Allow cake to cool until the glaze sets.

ର Serves 12 to 15.

Spring Creek near Plano

CHOCOHOLIC'S FANTASY CAKE WITH GRAND MARNIER CUSTARD SAUCE

*T*his cake is truly a "Chocoholic's Fantasy." Its very rich texture resembles a cross between a rich cake and fudge. It's a great cake to make when you have to serve a number of guests whom you wish to impress with your culinary prowess. (The cake will make 16 servings.) It is very important that you use good-quality bittersweet chocolate. My personal favorites are Tobler and Lindt, which are available in specialty shops and markets. If you absolutely cannot find bittersweet chocolate, you can substitute cocoa and butter. Rose Beranbaum, in her classic The Cake Bible, recommends the following to replace each ounce of bittersweet chocolate: 1 tablespoon plus 1¾ teaspoons cocoa powder, 1 tablespoon plus ½ teaspoon sugar, and 1½ teaspoons unsalted butter.

1 pound bittersweet chocolate, chopped

2 cups (4 sticks) unsalted butter, cut into small chunks

1¾ cups sugar

11 eggs, room temperature, separated

1½ tablespoons Grand Marnier or other orange-flavored liqueur

1 tablespoon vanilla extract

14 to 16 strawberries with green leafy tops as garnish

12-inch paper cake doily

Powdered sugar in a fine strainer

GRAND MARNIER CUSTARD SAUCE

1 cup milk

1 cup whipping cream

¾ cup sugar

6 egg yolks, slightly beaten

2½ tablespoons Grand Marnier or other orange-flavored liqueur

Butter and flour a 12-inch springform pan; shake out all traces of excess flour. Set aside. Place rack in middle position in oven. Preheat oven to 300 degrees.

In a heavy 3-quart saucepan over medium-low heat, combine the chocolate and butter. Stir until melted and smooth. Cool to room temperature, stirring occasionally. In a large bowl, combine 1½ cups sugar (reserving ¼ cup for the egg whites) and egg yolks. Beat with electric mixer on medium speed until mixture is light, fluffy, and lemon yellow in color, about 5 to 6 minutes. Beat in the cooled chocolate mixture, Grand Marnier, and vanilla. Set aside. In a grease-free, medium bowl,

beat the egg whites until frothy. Beat in the remaining ¼ cup sugar. Continue to beat until medium-stiff peaks form, about 2 minutes on medium speed. Using a rubber spatula, fold a fourth of the beaten whites into the chocolate mixture to lighten it. Fold in the remaining beaten egg whites gently but thoroughly. Pour batter into prepared pan. Bake in preheated oven for 1½ hours, or until a metal skewer inserted in center comes out clean. Cool the cake in the pan on a wire rack for 15 minutes. Remove side of pan and cool completely. When cool, invert the cake onto a large serving platter and remove the bottom of the pan. Refrigerate the cake until well chilled.

To make the Grand Marnier Custard Sauce, combine the milk, cream, and sugar in a heavy, 3-quart, non-aluminum saucepan over medium-high heat. Bring to a full boil. Whisking constantly, add ¼ cup of the hot cream mixture in a slow, steady stream to the beaten egg yolks. Reduce heat to medium. Whisk the warmed egg yolks slowly into the remaining cream mixture. Stirring constantly, cook until mixture thickens and forms a thick coat on the back of a metal spoon, about 5 to 6 minutes. This will happen rapidly; do not overcook and scramble the eggs. Remove sauce from heat and whisk in the Grand Marnier. Strain the sauce through a fine strainer into a bowl. Place the bowl in an ice-water bath and whisk until well chilled. Refrigerate, covered, until ready to use.

To serve the cake, place the paper doily on top of the cake and liberally scatter the powdered sugar over the doily, covering all cutouts in the doily. Carefully remove the doily to expose the pattern on top of the cake. Cut the cake into 14 or 16 slices. Place a bed of the Grand Marnier Custard Sauce on each serving plate. Place a cake slice in the center of each plate and top with a strawberry that has been slit lengthwise to make a fan shape.

ର **Serves 14 to 16.**

Windmill, Brewster County (facing page)

BEATING EGG WHITES

It is actually not as simple as it sounds. To give yourself the best advantage, use the freshest whites you can find. They are more stable (less likely to break down) when beaten. Also, the whites will perform better if they are at room temperature. Be certain that you beat the eggs in a spotlessly clean bowl. Any traces of fat (such as grease on the bowl or the tiniest speck of egg yolk) will play havoc with your efforts to beat the whites. For this reason, don't use plastic bowls, which can absorb and retain fat. Remember that the air you beat into the egg whites may be the only leavening ingredient, as in this cake, which has no flour, baking powder, or baking soda. The beaten whites must be handled gently—not stirred vigorously, slammed around, or overbeaten— or they will break down. Adding sugar to the whites while beating will add stability. Wait until the whites are just beginning to form loose, foamy peaks, then begin adding the sugar. Beat just until stiff peaks form. You can stop the mixer and test by scooping a dollop of the whites onto the beater. Perfectly beaten whites will make a peak that stands proud and tall without flopping over. And if the whites are perfectly beaten, you should be able to turn the bowl completely upside down without the whites sliding out.

Mexican Fresh Apple Cake with Leche Quemada

*T*raditional Mexican apple cake has a very rich and exotic flavor. Top it with the Leche Quemada, or "burnt milk" sauce, and it becomes a cultural link between your happy taste buds and Mexico. Leche quemada *can be bought in the markets in Mexico with various spices and with or without sherry. One of my staff members, Rosalina Ramirez, who is from the state of Guanajuato, coached me on the development of this particular recipe. When she made a trip home to Mexico, she brought back several different varieties of commercially prepared* leche quemada. *I preferred the ones with sherry. The sauce is very intensely sweet and the sharpness of the fortified wine serves to cut the acute sweetness. In this recipe I have used Madeira because I find it to have more depth of flavor than sherry. Apples that are slightly past their prime eating stage are perfect for this recipe. They will break down to the perfect consistency.*

4 medium Granny Smith apples, peeled, cored, and diced

2 tablespoons honey

2 cups water

4 tablespoons unsalted butter

1½ cups sugar

4 eggs

1 tablespoon vanilla extract

2 teaspoons ground cinnamon

2½ cups cake flour, sifted

2 teaspoons baking soda

¼ teaspoon salt

⅔ cup chopped pecans

Vanilla ice cream

Leche Quemada

½ cup sugar

2 cups sweetened condensed milk

¼ teaspoon cinnamon

¼ cup plus 3 tablespoons Madeira wine

2 teaspoons vanilla extract

4 tablespoons unsalted butter, cut into 1-inch cubes

⅔ cup whipping cream

Preheat oven to 375 degrees. Grease a 9-by-13-inch baking dish; set aside. Combine the diced apples, honey, and water in a medium saucepan and cook about 25 minutes, stirring often, or until the water has evaporated and the apples are very pulpy, almost like chunky applesauce. Set aside to cool slightly.

In bowl of electric mixer, cream the butter and sugar at medium speed until light and fluffy, about 5 minutes. Add the eggs, one at a time, scraping down side of bowl after each addition. Add vanilla and cinnamon; beat just to blend. Sift together the cake flour, baking soda, and salt. Add the flour mixture in thirds, stopping to scrape down side of bowl after each addition. Do not overbeat. Add the reserved apple mixture and the pecans; beat just to blend.

Turn the mixture out into prepared baking dish and bake in preheated oven for 25 minutes, or until a metal skewer inserted in middle of cake comes out clean. Remove from oven and set aside to cool.

To make the Leche Quemada, place the sugar in a 6-quart saucepan over medium-high heat. (The large pan size is necessary to prevent overflow when liquid is added to the hot caramel.) Cook until the sugar has melted and a rich, dark caramel has formed, or until a candy thermometer registers about 320 degrees. In a separate bowl, combine the condensed milk, cinnamon, ¼ cup of the wine, and vanilla; add to the caramel all at once. The mixture will spit, sputter, and bubble furiously, and the caramel will harden. Take care that none of the mixture splashes out on you. Lower heat and stir the mixture until it is smooth and the caramel has melted. Remove from heat and cool to lukewarm. Whisk the butter into the lukewarm sauce until well blended. Rapidly whisk in the whipping cream and remaining 3 tablespoons of wine.

To serve, slice the cake into squares. Top each with a scoop of ice cream and drizzle some of the Leche Quemada over the top.

ও **Serves 12 to 14.**

TRES LECHES CAKE

A syrup made with three types of milk forms the rich flavor base for this lighter-than-air confection from south of the border. The Tres Leches Cake, in various incarnations, has become very popular with the advent of several great South American restaurants around the state. When you're looking for a light dessert to provide the perfect ending to a special meal, give this very different cake a try.

1 cup sugar, divided
5 large eggs, separated
⅓ cup whole milk
2 teaspoons vanilla extract
1 cup all-purpose flour
1½ teaspoons baking powder
½ teaspoon cream of tartar

MILK SYRUP

1 12-ounce can evaporated milk
1 cup sweetened condensed milk
1 cup whipping cream
1 teaspoon vanilla extract
2 tablespoons Captain Morgan's Spiced Rum

SWISS MERINGUE

1 cup sugar
¼ cup tepid water
3 egg whites, room temperature
¼ teaspoon cream of tartar

Preheat oven to 350 degrees. Generously butter a 13-by-9-inch baking dish. Combine ¾ cup of the sugar and the egg yolks in bowl of electric mixer. Beat until light and fluffy, about 5 minutes. Fold in the whole milk, vanilla, flour, and baking powder. In a separate, grease-free bowl, beat the egg whites to soft peaks, adding cream of tartar as soon as they become frothy. Gradually add the remaining ¼ cup of sugar and continue beating until whites are glossy and form medium-stiff peaks. Gently, but thoroughly, fold the yolk mixture into the whites using a rubber spatula. Pour the batter into the prepared baking dish.

Bake the cake in preheated oven for 40 minutes, or until it feels firm and a toothpick inserted in center comes out clean. Cool cake completely on wire rack. Unmold cake onto a large, deep platter. Prick cake all over with a metal skewer.

Meanwhile, prepare the Milk Syrup by combining all ingredients in a medium bowl; whisk until well blended.

To make the Swiss Meringue, combine the sugar and water in a heavy saucepan and cook over high heat until the syrup reaches the soft-ball stage, or a candy thermometer registers 230 degrees.

Meanwhile, combine the egg whites with the cream of tartar and beat to soft peaks in electric mixer with wire whisk. Pour the boiling sugar syrup in a thin, steady stream into the whites and continue to beat until the outside of the mixer bowl is cool to the touch. The meringue should be very stiff and glossy.

To assemble, pour the Milk Syrup over the cake. Continue to spoon all overflow back onto the cake until all is absorbed. Using a wet spatula, spread the top and sides of cake with a thick layer of the Swiss Meringue. Refrigerate the cake for at least 2 hours before serving.

☙ **Serves up to 16.**

GAY THOMPSON'S ÉCLAIR CAKE WITH CHOCOLATE GLAZE

Gay Thompson, my ex-sister-in-law from Plainview, up in the Texas High Plains, has been a very accomplished cook for as long as I have known her. Her meals were part of my culinary awakening. She raised three children, led a very active social life, which included much entertaining, and she still loves to cook exciting and innovative meals. After 30 years, it still makes my mouth water to talk to her about what she's been cooking lately.

1 cup water

½ cup (1 stick) unsalted butter

1 cup all-purpose flour

⅛ teaspoon salt

4 eggs

Stiffly beaten whipped cream

PASTRY CREAM

6 egg yolks

¾ cup sugar

¼ teaspoon salt

6 tablespoons cornstarch

2 cups whipping cream, warmed

2 tablespoons vanilla extract

3 tablespoons unsalted butter

8 ounces cream cheese, room temperature

CHOCOLATE GLAZE

CR **Makes 1½ cups.**

6 ounces bittersweet chocolate

¾ cup whipping cream

Preheat oven to 400 degrees. Butter a 9-by-13-inch baking dish; set aside. Bring the water to a rapid boil in a heavy 2-quart saucepan. Add butter and stir until melted. Add the flour and salt all at once, stirring rapidly until mixture forms a smooth, shiny ball that comes away from the side of the pan. Transfer the flour mixture to work bowl of food processor fitted with steel blade. With processor running, add the eggs, one at a time, scraping down side of bowl after each addition. After all eggs have been added, process for about 30 seconds until mixture is smooth. Turn the mixture out into prepared pan, spreading evenly. Bake in preheated oven for 30 minutes. Set aside to cool on wire rack.

Meanwhile, make the Pastry Cream. Place egg yolks in bowl of electric mixer and beat until frothy. Add the sugar and salt. Beat until yolks are light, fluffy, and lemon yellow in color, about 5 minutes. Add the cornstarch, 2 tablespoons at a time, scraping down side of bowl and beating well after each addition. Transfer the egg mixture to a heavy 3-quart saucepan over medium-low heat. Slowly whisk in the warm whipping cream. Increase the heat slightly. Stirring constantly, cook until the mixture is thickened and smooth. Remove from heat and whisk in the vanilla and butter. Strain through a fine strainer into a clean bowl. Set the bowl over an ice-water bath and stir until cool. Place the cream cheese in work bowl of food processor fitted with steel blade. Process until smooth and fluffy, about 2 minutes. When the egg mixture has cooled, fold in the cream cheese, blending well. Spread the Pastry Cream over the cooled cake. Refrigerate for 1 hour before slicing into 12 squares.

To prepare the Chocolate Glaze, combine the chocolate and whipping cream in a heavy 1-quart saucepan over medium heat. Cook, stirring, until chocolate has melted and mixture is very smooth and uniform in color. Remove from heat. Cool to lukewarm.

To serve, place a square of the cake on each serving plate. Top with a portion of the Chocolate Glaze, allowing glaze to drape down the sides. Top each serving with a dollop of the whipped cream and serve.

CR **Makes 12 servings.**

Gypsum veins, Caprock Canyons State Park near Quitaque

Tiramisu with Chocolate Ganache Layer

*T*iramisu is a modern Italian dessert, created in the last 15 or so years and proving that the Italian cuisine is still evolving. The dessert has become very popular in Texas. I've had some excellent renditions in upscale Italian restaurants in both Houston and Dallas. The word tiramisu means "pick me up." Perhaps the confection was so named because, in its traditional version, it is based on the flavor of espresso coffee, which will definitely pick you up. The chocolate ganache layer is not authentic, but I think if we sent a slice or two to Italy, it might become the new standard. I find that the rich chocolate ganache is a very satisfying flavor match to the marsala wine.

3 eggs, separated
⅔ cup sugar
8 ounces mascarpone cheese
1 tablespoon vanilla extract
1 cup espresso coffee, made from instant espresso granules
1 cup marsala wine
2 additional tablespoons sugar
75 soft ladyfingers, or more as needed
Cocoa powder
1¼ cups whipping cream, beaten until stiff

Chocolate Ganache Layer

2 ounces bittersweet chocolate
¼ cup whipping cream

Prepare the Chocolate Ganache Layer. In a heavy 1-quart saucepan, heat the chocolate and cream together, stirring, until chocolate melts and mixture is very smooth and uniform in color. Remove from heat. Refrigerate to chill, stirring 2 or 3 times while chilling to prevent setting.

Spray bottom and side of 9-inch springform pan with non-stick vegetable spray; set aside. Beat the egg whites until they form medium-stiff peaks, about 2 minutes; set aside. In a separate bowl, beat the egg yolks and sugar until they are thick and light lemon yellow in color, about 5 minutes. Beat in the mascarpone cheese and vanilla, blending well. Turn mixture out into large bowl and fold in the egg whites, gently but thoroughly. Set aside.

In a deep dish, blend the espresso coffee, marsala wine, and additional sugar. Dip 25 of the ladyfingers, one at a time, in this mixture; work quickly so they do not become soggy. Line the bottom of the prepared springform pan with a layer of the ladyfingers. Cover the ladyfingers with a layer of the mascarpone mixture. Sprinkle cocoa powder over the cream layer until covered. Repeat the layering one more time, using 25 more ladyfingers and omitting the top layer of cocoa powder. Pour the chilled Chocolate Ganache Layer over the mascarpone layer, spreading evenly. Repeat with the remaining 25 ladyfingers, followed by another mascarpone layer; end with a liberal coat of the cocoa powder.

Cover the pan tightly with plastic wrap and refrigerate overnight. Remove side of springform pan and slice the Tiramisu into 10 wedges. Place the whipped cream in a pastry bag fitted with the star tip and pipe a rosette in the center of each serving.

☙ Serves 10.

Wildflowers at cemetery, Bastrop

WHITE CHOCOLATE BREAD PUDDING
WITH FRANGELICO SAUCE AND RASPBERRY CHANTILLY CREAM

*B*read pudding is kind of a quintessential dessert in Texas. It ranks right up there at the top along with anything chocolate. So what happens when the two are combined? Sky rockets at night, afternoon delight. This delicate-tasting version of the old standard spotlights one of my favorite flavor pairs—white chocolate and hazelnuts, topped off with a decadently rich sauce made of Frangelico, a hazelnut-based liqueur. Frangelico also happens to be the perfect addition to a cup of steaming coffee to wind down a winter's day in front of a cozy, roaring fire.

8 ounces white chocolate, cut into small chunks
2 cups half-and-half, room temperature
½ cup (1 stick) unsalted butter, softened
8 ounces dry French bread, cut into ½-inch cubes
3 eggs
¾ cup sugar
¾ cup golden raisins
½ cup chopped toasted hazelnuts
½ cup flaked coconut
1 tablespoon vanilla extract

FRANGELICO SAUCE

1 cup (2 sticks) unsalted butter, softened
1½ cups sugar
2 eggs, beaten until frothy
½ cup Frangelico liqueur

RASPBERRY CHANTILLY CREAM

1 cup whipping cream, well chilled
2 tablespoons powdered sugar
2 tablespoons sour cream, well chilled
1 tablespoon vanilla extract
1 tablespoon Chambord liqueur or a raspberry brandy such as Framboise

Preheat oven to 325 degrees. Position oven rack in center position. Thoroughly butter a 13-by-9-inch Pyrex baking dish; set aside. In a heavy 2-quart saucepan combine the white chocolate, half-and-half, and butter. Cook over medium-low heat, stirring often, until smooth. Remove from heat and set aside. Place bread cubes in a large bowl and stir in the chocolate mixture, blending well and breaking up the bread cubes. Set aside.

In bowl of electric mixer, combine the eggs and sugar. Beat at medium speed until thickened and light lemon yellow in color, about 7 minutes. Add the raisins, hazelnuts, coconut, and vanilla; beat just to blend. Fold the egg mixture into the bread and chocolate mixture, blending well. Turn the mixture out into prepared baking dish and bake in preheated oven for 45 to 55 minutes, or until a knife inserted in center comes out clean. Set aside to cool.

Prepare the Frangelico Sauce. Using an electric mixer, cream the butter and sugar until it is very light and fluffy, about 7 minutes. Transfer the mixture to the top of a double boiler over simmering water. Cook for 20 minutes, whisking often, or until the mixture is silken smooth and comes away from the side of the pan cleanly when whisked. Whisk ¼ cup of the hot butter mixture into the beaten eggs, then another ¼ cup. Whisk the egg mixture slowly into the remaining butter mixture over the heat. Cook until thickened, about 4 to 5 minutes, whisking constantly. Whisk in the Frangelico, blending well. Sauce may be kept warm over hot water until ready to serve. Whisk vigorously 3 or 4 times before serving to restore the smooth consistency.

To make the Raspberry Chantilly Cream, combine all ingredients in bowl of electric mixer and beat with wire whisk beater until cream has reached the consistency where it holds soft, floppy peaks. Refrigerate, tightly covered, until ready to serve. Cream may need to be rapidly rewhisked before serving if it has become soupy.

To serve, slice the warm pudding into 12 squares. Place a portion of the Frangelico Sauce in the bottom of each serving bowl. Place a square of the pudding on the sauce and top with a generous dollop of the Raspberry Chantilly Cream.

ᛊ Serves 12.

TEXAS TRIFLE WITH RASPBERRIES AND CUSTARD SAUCE

Well, it's not the traditional type of trifle, but in Texas we like to do things our own way. This is the perfect dessert to serve for a fancy occasion. Served in individual brandy snifters on doily-lined plates, the concoction is right impressive.

2 cups all-purpose flour

2 teaspoons baking powder

1 teaspoon salt

1 cup (2 sticks) unsalted butter, softened

2 cups sugar

3 eggs

Minced zest of 1 large lemon

1 cup sour cream

Whipping cream beaten to stiff peaks

Edible flowers or mint sprigs as garnish

Powdered sugar in shaker

RASPBERRIES

3 cups raspberries

¼ cup sugar

1 cup Messina Hof Angel Late Harvest
   Johannesburg Riesling, or other sweet dessert wine

LEMON GLAZE

¼ cup unsalted butter, melted

2 tablespoons freshly squeezed lemon juice

1 cup powdered sugar, sifted

RASPBERRY CUSTARD CREAM

¾ cup milk

¾ cup whipping cream

½ cup plus 1 tablespoon sugar

5 egg yolks, beaten

2 tablespoons Chambord or other raspberry liqueur

Place the raspberries in a medium bowl. Combine the sugar and wine in a heavy 2-quart saucepan over medium heat. Cook just until the sugar has melted, about 5 minutes, stirring once or twice. Remove pan from heat and nest it in a bowl of ice water. Stir until the wine syrup is chilled. Pour the syrup over the berries and stir gently to moisten all berries. Refrigerate until ready to assemble the dessert.

Preheat oven to 325 degrees. Thoroughly butter and flour a 10-inch bundt pan. Set pan aside. Sift flour, baking powder, and salt into a medium bowl; set aside. In bowl of electric mixer, cream the butter and sugar at low speed until well blended, then beat at medium speed until mixture is very fluffy, about 6 minutes. Beat in the eggs, one at a time. Add lemon zest and blend. By thirds, add the flour mixture to the butter and sugar mixture alternately with the sour cream, scraping down side of bowl after each addition. Pour the batter into prepared bundt pan. Bake in preheated oven until a metal skewer inserted in center of cake comes out clean, about 1 hour. Cool in the pan for 10 minutes. Turn cake out onto platter and cool for another 10 minutes.

Meanwhile, prepare the Lemon Glaze. Whisk all ingredients together until smooth. Drizzle the glaze evenly over the top of the cake while it is still moderately hot. Set aside.

Prepare the Raspberry Custard Sauce. In a heavy 3-quart saucepan, combine milk, cream, and sugar; bring to a boil. Add about ¼ cup of the hot milk mixture in a slow, steady stream to the egg yolks, whisking vigorously. Return the remaining milk mixture almost to a boil, and whisk in the egg mixture. Stir constantly until the mixture thickens and coats a metal spoon. Do not allow the sauce to boil, or it will curdle. Remove from heat; whisk for 3 to 4 minutes to cool the sauce. Strain through a fine strainer into a clean bowl set over ice water. Whisk in the Chambord, blending well. Continue to whisk or stir until custard sauce is well chilled.

To assemble the trifles, cut the cake into slices and set aside. (You will only need 6 slices of the cake, so the rest may be kept for later or frozen.) Ladle a portion of the Raspberry Custard Cream into 6 individual 22-ounce brandy snifters. Crumble a slice of the cake on top of the sauce in each snifter. Top each portion of the cake with about ½ cup of the raspberries and their syrup. Top with additional Raspberry Custard Cream. Place the beaten whipping cream in a pastry bag fitted with the star tip and pipe a large rosette on the top of each dessert. Garnish with an edible flower or mint sprig and place on doily-lined plates. Scatter powdered sugar over the dessert and plate.

ભ Serves 6.

TEJANO SUGAR BASKETS

*T*his unique and different dessert is attractive to serve, and the taste is a real sensory experience. To make it, you'll need one of those double wire baskets sold in cookware shops for frying shells for taco salads. The baskets and the sauce can be made up to a day ahead of time. This dessert features a favorite treat—vanilla ice cream from the Blue Bell Creamery in Brenham.

SUGAR BASKETS

6 small (6-inch) flour tortillas, or larger tortillas trimmed down using a 6-inch saucer as a guide

Canola oil for deep-frying, heated to 350 degrees

Blue Bell Homemade Vanilla Ice Cream or other rich vanilla ice cream

Sliced strawberries, bananas, and mangoes

Mint sprigs for garnish

CHOCOLATE-SHERRY SAUCE

4 ounces unsweetened chocolate

1 cup whipping cream

6 tablespoons unsalted butter, softened

4 ounces powdered sugar

¼ cup sherry

CARAMEL SYRUP

1½ pounds light brown sugar

¾ cup water

1 teaspoon ground cinnamon

Prepare the Chocolate-Sherry Sauce. Combine chocolate and whipping cream in a heavy 2-quart saucepan over medium heat. Cook, stirring often, until chocolate has melted and mixture is smooth and creamy. Remove from heat and set aside. In bowl of electric mixer, combine the softened butter and powdered sugar. Beat at low speed until sugar is blended, then increase speed to medium-high. Beat until mixture is very fluffy, about 5 minutes, stopping to scrape down side of bowl once or twice. Transfer sugar mixture to top of double boiler over simmering water. Cook, whisking often, until mixture is silky smooth, about 10 minutes. Whisk the melted chocolate into the sugar mixture. Continue to whisk until sauce is smooth and glossy. Add the sherry and whisk to blend. Refrigerate.

Make the Caramel Syrup by combining all ingredients in a heavy 3-quart saucepan over medium heat. Cook, without stirring, until sugar has dissolved. Then cook, stirring, until syrup is slightly thickened, about 5 minutes. Remove from heat and set aside; keep warm.

Prepare the Sugar Baskets. Working quickly, place a tortilla in the wire frying basket and fry, fully submerged in the hot oil, until crisp and light golden brown. Repeat with remaining tortillas, draining them upside down on a wire rack set over a baking sheet. When all tortillas have been fried, dip them in the warm Caramel Syrup, coating well, inside and out. Place coated baskets on the wire rack to cool. They should become very crisp when cool.

To serve, place 2 scoops of vanilla ice cream in each basket. Top with a portion of the sliced fruit. Drizzle the fruit with the Chocolate-Sherry Sauce, reheated until pourable or allowed to reach room temperature. Garnish with mint sprigs and serve at once.

❧ Serves 6.

Ballet Folklórico dancers, San Antonio

STRAWBERRY SHORTCAKE WITH LEMON VERBENA AND MANGO ICE CREAM

*A*ny part of this sinfully delicious dessert is great on its own, but when combined, the flavors positively explode into something really great for your mouth—like there's a fiesta going on in there. The shortcake as well as the ice cream can be made ahead, so the dessert can be assembled at the last minute when you're ready to serve it. Lemon verbena leaves have a bracing, intense lemon flavor. See "The Texas Cook's Pantry" for a great source for fresh herbs.

 2 cups cake flour

1½ cups all-purpose flour

 ⅔ cup sugar

 1 tablespoon baking powder

 ¾ teaspoon salt

 ½ cup unsalted butter, softened and cut into chunks

 2 eggs, beaten

 ⅓ cup milk

 1 tablespoon vanilla extract

Powdered sugar for dusting

 2 pints strawberries, sliced

Sugar to taste

 1 tablespoon Grand Marnier

Mint sprigs or lemon verbena leaves for garnish, if desired

LEMON VERBENA AND MANGO ICE CREAM

ᗉ **Makes about 2 quarts.**

2¼ cups half-and-half

 2 cups whipping cream

 ⅔ cup sugar

 2 cups coarsely chopped lemon verbena stems and leaves

12 egg yolks

 ½ cup (1 stick) unsalted butter, softened

 1 teaspoon vanilla extract

2 ripe mangoes, peeled and chopped

Prepare the Lemon Verbena and Mango Ice Cream. Combine the half-and-half, whipping cream, ⅓ cup of the sugar, and lemon verbena in a heavy 4-quart saucepan over medium-high heat. Bring the mixture to a full boil, then lower heat and simmer for 10 minutes. Remove pan from heat and set aside until completely cool. Strain the mixture through a fine strainer,

pressing down on the lemon verbena to extract all the flavor. Discard herb. Transfer the cream mixture to a clean saucepan and return to a simmer. While cream is heating, combine the remaining sugar and egg yolks in bowl of electric mixer. Cream until thick and light lemon yellow in color, about 5 minutes.

While whisking vigorously, add ⅓ of the hot cream mixture slowly to the creamed egg yolk mixture, and then slowly return the yolk mixture to the remaining cream while whisking. Cook, whisking constantly, over medium heat to thicken slightly. *Do not allow the mixture to boil.* Remove from heat and whisk in the butter rapidly to blend. Pour the mixture through a fine strainer into a clean bowl. Stir in the mango and vanilla extract. Place the bowl over ice and stir until chilled. Pour into canister of ice cream freezer and process according to manufacturer's directions. Store in freezer until ready to serve.

To make the shortcake, preheat oven to 350 degrees. Line a baking sheet with parchment paper; set aside. Sift the dry ingredients into bowl of electric mixer. Add the butter and beat until it forms crumbs resembling coarse oatmeal. Scrape down side of bowl as needed. Add the beaten eggs, milk, and vanilla. Beat just until a smooth, thick dough is formed; do not overbeat. Turn dough out onto work surface and knead 4 or 5 times to form a smooth dough ball. Wrap in plastic wrap and refrigerate for 30 minutes.

Roll the chilled dough into a ¾-inch-thick circle on a lightly floured work surface. Cut out 4 shortcakes, using a 3-inch round cutter. Place the shortcakes on prepared baking sheet and bake for about 12 to 14 minutes, or until tops are browned. Transfer to wire cooling rack and dust the tops heavily with powdered sugar. Slice in half while warm. Set aside.

To serve, mash half of the strawberries with sugar to taste, then stir in the remaining sliced berries and Grand Marnier. Place the bottom halves of the shortcakes in wide, shallow serving bowls and top with a scoop of the Lemon Verbena and Mango Ice Cream. Spoon a portion of the strawberries over the ice cream and lay the top halves of the shortcakes at an angle on the ice cream. Garnish with mint sprigs or lemon verbena leaves.

ᗉ **Serves 4.**

H. O. Thompson's Lick-the-Bowl-Clean Ice Cream

My ex-father-in-law was a farmer in the Texas High Plains his whole life. He was a simple man whose life was centered around his family and friends in the town of Plainview. My ex-husband Pat loved this ice cream recipe, handed down to him by his father. He used to tell me that when he was a small boy, he knew company was coming when he would see his dad get down the old ice cream freezer. Even though he knew how good the ice cream would be, he knew he'd have to earn it by turning that crank! The recipe is very easy, using an uncooked base, but the ice cream is delicious. The ice cream is very soft when completed. If you want it firmer, transfer the ice cream to a storage container and place in the freezer for about 3 hours before serving.

5   eggs, well beaten

1   14-ounce can sweetened condensed milk

1   12-ounce can evaporated milk

2   cups sugar

2   tablespoons vanilla extract

Whole milk

Combine all ingredients except whole milk in a large bowl. Whisk until smooth and well blended. Pour the mixture into the canister of a 1-gallon ice cream freezer. Add whole milk to fill the container, stirring with a long-handled spoon to blend. Freeze according to manufacturer's directions.

❦ **Makes 1 gallon.**

Tequila and Smoked Mescal Sorbet

Tequila and mescal are both made from the fermented juice of the maguey, or agave. In the production of tequila, the heart of the agave plant is steamed before fermentation. In the making of mescal, the heart is roasted, imparting a smoky flavor to the finished liquor. Mescals come from Oaxaca and the surrounding region, also known for some of Mexico's most exciting foods. The mescals of Del Maguey come from different villages, with each village adding its own signature to the flavor. Mezcal Chicicapa has a front note of deep, sultry smoke, followed by mellow spice, which leaves a glow of subtle warmth all the way down your throat. This sorbet is one of the best desserts ever for ending a summer meal or for cooling off around the pool.

4   cups water

2   cups sugar

1⅓ cups freshly squeezed lime juice

¾   cup Cointreau or other orange-flavored liqueur

½   cup Jose Cuervo Gold tequila

¼   cup Del Maguey's Mezcal Chicicapa

2   teaspoons minced lime zest

Margarita salt, lime juice, and lime wedges

Combine water and sugar in a heavy 4-quart saucepan over medium heat. Cook, stirring, until sugar dissolves. Increase heat to high and bring to a boil. Transfer to a large bowl and stir in the lime juice, Cointreau, tequila, mescal, and lime zest.

Transfer the sorbet to a large baking dish. Cover with plastic wrap and freeze overnight, or until solid.

To serve, scoop the sorbet out into footed dessert glasses that have been dipped in lime juice and margarita salt. Garnish with a lime wedge.

❦ **Serves 8.**

Summer Lemon Mousse with Almond Lace Cookie Rolls

*I*t seems that other than ice cream, there just aren't many really great and bracing desserts suitable for serving in the summer. This light and airy mousse with its thin, crisp cookie companions is one of the few. I equate any food that is rich in lemon flavor with summer. The mousse is very easy and can be prepared in advance. The cookies are a little tricky to roll, but after three or four failed ones, you'll get the hang of it.

¾ cup (1¼ sticks) unsalted butter, softened

¾ cup sugar

5 eggs

½ cup plus 1 tablespoon freshly squeezed lemon juice

Minced zest of 4 lemons

Bowl of ice water

1½ cups whipping cream, beaten until stiff

Mint sprigs and lemon slices as garnish

Almond Lace Cookie Rolls

○₈ **Makes 16 to 20 cookies.**

¾ cup sliced almonds (skin-on)

½ cup sugar

½ cup (1 stick) unsalted butter, room temperature

1 level tablespoon all-purpose flour

2 tablespoons milk

1 teaspoon minced orange zest

Fiesta-bound niña, Del Rio

To make the mousse, cream the butter and sugar together in bowl of electric mixer until light and fluffy, about 5 minutes. Add the eggs, one at a time, beating well and scraping down side of bowl after each addition. Add the lemon juice and zest, beating well. Turn the mixture out into a heavy saucepan over medium-low heat. Cook, stirring constantly with a wooden spoon, until mixture is very thick, about 15 minutes. Remove from heat and nest the pan in the bowl of ice water. Continue to stir until the custard is well chilled.

Turn the lemon mixture out into a large bowl and fold in the beaten cream, incorporating well. Refrigerate until ready to serve.

Make the Almond Lace Cookie Rolls. Preheat oven to 350 degrees. Grind the almonds in food processor until very fine but not pasty. Combine almonds and remaining ingredients in a heavy 12-inch skillet. Stir over low heat with a wooden spoon until butter melts and ingredients are well blended. Remove from heat.

Line a baking sheet with parchment paper. Place heaping tablespoons of the batter on the parchment paper about 5 inches apart. (You can only make 3 or 4 at a time.) Bake in preheated oven for 8 to 10 minutes, or until evenly browned. Remove from oven and set them aside for about 1 minute. Remove with a wide spatula while still warm and pliable. Roll into cigar-shaped rolls. Set on wire rack until cool and crisp. Store in airtight container at room temperature until ready to serve.

To serve, spoon a portion of the mousse into individual footed glass serving bowls. Garnish each serving with a lemon slice and a mint sprig. Set the serving bowls on doily-lined plates and stick an Almond Lace Cookie Roll into each mousse.

○₈ **Serves 6 to 8.**

Rosa's Sweet Potato and Peach Empanadas

*W*e owe so much of our Texas Cuisine to Mexico—some of the very best parts, in fact. Mexican cooks can create such delicious tastes around the most humble ingredients. These addictive little sweets are an example of what I mean. The real boss of the kitchen at Maner Lake Lodge is Rosalina Ramirez, a very wise woman and mother of seven who also happens to be an extraordinary cook. One day she whipped up a batch of these little treats for our staff lunch. Of course, she doesn't measure any of her ingredients so we were following her around the kitchen with measuring cups and spoons to document this great pastry. The recipe makes a lot, but, trust me, they won't last long.

Pastry

3½ cups solid shortening
1 12-ounce can of beer
½ cup powdered sugar
7 cups all-purpose flour, or more as needed
Melted unsalted butter
Powdered sugar in shaker

Filling

4 large unpeeled sweet potatoes (about 3¾ pounds total)
1 18-ounce jar peach preserves

Preheat oven to 325 degrees. Using electric mixer, beat the shortening at medium speed until soft and fluffy, about 5 minutes. Add the beer. Begin beating at the lowest speed, then increase speed to medium as the beer is incorporated. Beat to blend well. Add the powdered sugar and 2 cups of the flour; beat well. Continue to add flour, scraping down the side of the bowl after each addition, until the dough is cohesive and not sticky. Separate the dough into balls about 1½ inches in diameter. Set aside.

To make the filling, microwave the unpeeled sweet potatoes for 12 minutes, or until very soft. Set aside just until they are cool enough to handle. Using your fingers, peel off and discard the skins and place the sweet potatoes in a bowl. Mash the potatoes until smooth, then quickly stir in the peach preserves, blending well.

To assemble the empanadas, roll out each dough ball into a 5-inch circle, then cut out rounds using a 3-inch cutter. Place about 1½ teaspoons of the filling in the center of each round and fold the dough over the filling, creating a half-moon shape. Using the tines of a fork, press along the edge of the pastry to seal it. Turn the pastry over and repeat with the edge on the opposite side. Brush the tops of the pastries with melted butter. Place the completed pastries on baking sheets lined with parchment paper. Bake in preheated oven for 25 minutes, or until lightly browned. Cool on wire racks and dust the pastries heavily with powdered sugar. Serve at room temperature.

Makes about 115 pastries.

Sacristy doorway, Mission San José, San Antonio

STONEWALL PEACH PIE

*T*exans are mighty proud of their peaches. In the summer folks flock to the tiny town of Stonewall, deep in the heart of the Texas Hill Country and a stone's throw from the LBJ Ranch, to buy the ripe, juicy peaches by the bushel. You can buy them just hours off the trees and enjoy eating a few on the way home. One of my favorite uses for peaches, other than just peeling and eating them like God made them, is to make peach pie. This recipe, with its crumbly pecan topping, really borders on being so good it's sinful. Topped with a big scoop of Texas's own Blue Bell Homemade Vanilla Ice Cream, it just defies description.

CRUST

2   cups all-purpose flour
1   cup (2 sticks) chilled unsalted butter, cut into ½-inch cubes
⅛   teaspoon salt
1   teaspoon sugar
About ¼ cup ice water, or more as needed

FILLING

1   cup whipping cream
1   egg, well beaten
¼   cup all-purpose flour
1   cup sugar
½   teaspoon ground cinnamon
½   teaspoon freshly grated nutmeg
6   large peaches, peeled, sliced, and tossed with fresh lemon juice

TOPPING

¼   cup light brown sugar, firmly packed
3   tablespoons all-purpose flour
2   tablespoons unsalted butter
½   cup chopped pecans
Blue Bell Homemade Vanilla Ice Cream

Preheat oven to 350 degrees. Make the pastry by placing flour, butter, salt, and sugar in work bowl of food processor fitted with steel blade. Using the pulse feature, pulse just until the butter is broken into pea-size pieces. With processor running, add enough of the water through the feed tube to form a soft, moist dough. Do not process until the mixture forms a ball. Turn mixture out onto a lightly floured surface; using your hands and a pastry scraper, bring the mixture together and knead 2 or 3 times to form a ball. Do not overwork the dough. Divide the dough in half, forming two round disks. Wrap one disk in plastic wrap and refrigerate. Working in one direction, roll the other disk out on a lightly floured work surface to a thickness of ¹⁄₁₆ inch. Loosely roll the pastry around the rolling pin. Unroll the dough into a 9-inch pie pan, letting the pastry fall into place. Gently ease pastry into bottom of pan by lifting the edges; pat pastry against side of pan. Do not stretch the pastry or it will shrink while baking. Cut away excess pastry, leaving a ½-inch overhang at edge; refrigerate while preparing the filling.

In a medium bowl, whisk the cream and egg together. Add flour, sugar, cinnamon, and nutmeg; whisk until smooth. Pour half of the mixture into prepared pie shell. Add the sliced peaches, spreading evenly; pour remaining cream mixture over the peaches. Roll out the remaining pastry disk and place on top of the pie. Cut off excess pastry, leaving about a 1-inch overhang at edge. Tuck edge of the top pastry securely under edge of bottom pastry. Flute the edges of the pastry, or press pastry against edge of pan using the tines of a fork. Cut 2 rows of steam vents in top of pastry.

To make the topping, combine all ingredients except pecans in work bowl of food processor fitted with steel blade. Pulse to blend until the mixture resembles coarse meal. Add the pecans and pulse just to incorporate; do not chop them beyond recognition.

Scatter topping over the top of the pie and bake in preheated oven for 35 to 40 minutes, or until golden brown and peaches are very soft and mushy when pierced with the tip of a knife. Cool slightly. Slice and serve with a scoop of ice cream.

ର **Makes 1 9-inch pie.**

MADALENE AND GWEN'S PEACH KUCHEN

Mother and daughter Madalene Hill and Gwen Barclay are the state's resident herbal authorities. On special occasions we loan them to the rest of the country where they teach workshops, give lectures, and enlighten folks on the joys of growing and cooking with fresh herbs. Madalene and Gwen, with Madalene's late husband Jim, were the original owners of the Hilltop Herb Farm and Restaurant in Cleveland, about an hour north of Houston. It was one of the best places in Texas to eat, with sometimes a two-month wait for weekend reservations. In 1987 they wrote the classic Southern Herb Growing, *which every serious cook should own. Many more years ago than the three of us care to remember, Madalene and Gwen taught this wonderful peach dessert at the cooking school that I owned at the time. I have loved it ever since. It has a permanent place on the menu at Maner Lake Lodge. I took it off the menu once, and the guests just ordered it anyway!*

4 cups all-purpose flour

2 cups sugar, divided

1 teaspoon salt

½ teaspoon baking powder

1 cup (2 sticks) unsalted butter, cut into ½-inch dice and softened

3 pounds sliced peaches

Freshly squeezed lemon juice

2 teaspoons ground cinnamon

2 teaspoons ground mace

4 egg yolks

1 cup whipping cream

2 18-ounce jars Smucker's peach preserves

4 tablespoons peach schnapps

Blue Bell Homemade Vanilla Ice Cream

Thoroughly butter a 13-by-9-inch baking dish. Preheat the oven to 400 degrees. Combine flour, 4 tablespoons of the sugar, salt, baking powder, and butter. Blend with a pastry blender. Turn out into prepared baking dish and pat down to a smooth crust.

Dip the peach slices in the fresh lemon juice, and then arrange slices on the flour mixture in pan. Combine remaining sugar and spices; scatter over the peaches. Bake for 15 minutes, then remove from oven and lower temperature to 325 degrees.

Beat the egg yolks with whipping cream until smooth. Pour evenly over fruit and bake for about 30 minutes, or until golden brown and custard is set in center. Remove from oven and keep warm.

Meanwhile, melt the preserves in a heavy 2-quart saucepan over medium heat. Press through a fine strainer, extracting all liquid. Discard fruit pulp. Stir in the peach schnapps.

Cut the kuchen into squares and place in individual serving bowls. Top each serving with a scoop of ice cream. Drizzle a portion of the peach glaze over each serving. The glaze can be served hot or warm.

❧ Serves 12.

Peach crop, Fredericksburg

German Chocolate–Meringue Pie

If you're a fan of German chocolate cake and chocolate pie, then this recipe will double your pleasure. It's rich and gooey and scrumptious—manna for the serious chocoholic. If you've often had trouble with meringues, try this Swiss Meringue, made with a cooked sugar syrup. It makes a pretty foolproof meringue that is glossy and fluffy and lasts well.

Crust

1¼ cups finely chopped Oreo cookie crumbs
¼ cup sugar
⅓ cup melted unsalted butter, or more as needed

Filling

4 ounces German sweet chocolate
4 tablespoons unsalted butter
1 cup sugar
3½ tablespoons cornstarch
1⅔ cups milk
4 eggs, separated, room temperature
2 teaspoons vanilla extract
1 cup flaked coconut
1 cup chopped pecans

Meringue

1⅓ cups sugar
¼ cup water, plus 1½ tablespoons
4 egg whites
¾ teaspoon cream of tartar
Flaked coconut as garnish

To make the crust, combine all ingredients in work bowl of food processor fitted with steel blade; process until well blended. Pat the mixture firmly and evenly onto bottom and sides of a 9-inch Pyrex pie pan. Chill while preparing the filling.

In a heavy 3-quart saucepan over medium heat, combine chocolate and butter. Cook, stirring often, to melt the chocolate. When chocolate is completely melted and mixture is smooth, set aside.

In bowl of electric mixer, combine sugar, cornstarch, milk, and egg yolks. Beat at medium speed until well blended, thick, and light lemon yellow in color, about 5 minutes. Gradually add the melted chocolate mixture while beating. When all chocolate has been added and mixture is smooth and well blended, return to saucepan. Cook the mixture over medium heat, stirring constantly, until thick and smooth. Bring the mixture just to the boiling point, and then remove immediately from heat. Stir in the vanilla extract, coconut, and pecans. Pour mixture into chilled pie crust and refrigerate until set.

Preheat oven to 350 degrees. Make the meringue by placing sugar in a heavy saucepan with the water. Cover and cook over high heat until sugar reaches the soft-ball stage, or registers about 230 degrees on a candy thermometer. Do not stir the syrup until sugar has completely dissolved.

Meanwhile, combine egg whites and cream of tartar in bowl of electric mixer fitted with wire whisk beater. Beat until frothy. Pour the sugar syrup into the whites in a thin, steady stream while beating. Continue to beat until the outside of the bowl is cool to the touch.

Spread the meringue over the pie, making sure that no filling is exposed and that meringue touches the crust all the way around. Scatter some of the coconut over the meringue. Bake in preheated oven for 10 minutes, or until meringue is lightly browned and coconut is toasted. Allow meringue to cool before slicing.

∽ **Makes 1 9-inch pie.**

CARAMEL-MERINGUE PIE

*T**exans love anything made from caramel. Perhaps that's because so many of the great Mexican desserts we've always known contain homemade caramel. This rich and gooey pie is the ultimate caramel-lover's treat under its blanket of snowy meringue.*

PASTRY

- 1 cup all-purpose flour
- ¾ teaspoon salt
- 3 tablespoons unsalted butter, softened
- 3 tablespoons lard (or substitute solid shortening)
- 3 to 5 tablespoons ice water

FILLING

- ½ cup sugar
- 1 cup additional sugar
- 4 tablespoons cornstarch
- ¼ teaspoon salt
- 3 eggs, separated
- 2 cups milk, warmed
- 4 tablespoons unsalted butter, softened
- 1 tablespoon vanilla extract

MERINGUE

- 1 cup sugar
- ¼ cup water
- 3 egg whites
- ½ teaspoon cream of tartar

To make the pastry, combine flour, salt, butter, and lard in work bowl of food processor fitted with steel blade. Pulse several times until mixture resembles coarse meal. With the processor running, add just enough water through the feed tube to form a moist, cohesive dough. Turn out onto lightly floured work surface and knead 2 or 3 times. Flatten dough into a disk. Spray a 9-inch pie pan with non-stick vegetable spray; set aside. Roll dough out on lightly floured work surface to a circle about ¹⁄₁₆-inch thick. Loosely roll the dough around the rolling pin and unroll over prepared pie pan. Lift the edge of the dough and allow pastry to fall into bottom of pan. Do not stretch the pastry or it will shrink while baking. Pat onto sides of pie pan. Cut excess pastry from edge, leaving about a ½-inch overhang. Turn the pastry under and flute the edges, or press the pastry against the rim of pie pan with the tines of a fork. Refrigerate until well chilled, about 30 minutes. Preheat oven to 350 degrees.

When the pastry has chilled, line it with aluminum foil. Fill it with uncooked rice or beans. Place the pastry in preheated oven and bake for about 25 minutes. Remove the foil and bake the pastry another 10 minutes, or until the bottom and sides are well browned. Set pastry aside while preparing the filling.

Place the ½ cup of sugar in a heavy 4-quart saucepan and cook until it reaches the light caramel stage, or registers about 320 degrees on a candy thermometer. Stir often. Meanwhile, combine the additional 1 cup of sugar, cornstarch, salt, and egg yolks in bowl of electric mixer. Beat until thick and light lemon yellow in color, about 5 minutes. Slowly add the warmed milk and beat to blend well. Add the egg mixture to the caramel in the saucepan and stir in the butter. When the egg mixture is added, the caramel will foam up and sputter and "clump," but it will melt again while the mixture thickens. Cook, whisking constantly, until mixture thickens, about 5 to 6 minutes. Remove from heat and whisk in the vanilla. Continue to whisk for about 2 minutes. Press the mixture through a fine strainer into the cooled pie crust. Chill thoroughly until set before adding the meringue.

To make the meringue, place sugar in a heavy 1-quart saucepan with the water. Cook over high heat until sugar reaches the soft-ball stage, or registers 230 degrees on a candy thermometer. Do not stir the sugar mixture until all sugar has dissolved. If there are unblended granules of sugar on side of pan, brush them down with a small amount of water on a pastry brush.

While the syrup is cooking, beat the egg whites and cream of tartar to soft peaks in electric mixer with wire whisk beater. Pour the syrup into the whites in a thin, steady stream while beating. Continue to beat the mixture until the bowl is cool to the touch. Preheat oven to 350 degrees.

Spread the meringue over the pie, making sure that it reaches all the way to the crust on all sides and overlaps the crust slightly. Bake in preheated oven for about 8 minutes, or until the tips of the meringue are light golden brown. Chill before serving.

℞ **Makes 1 9-inch pie.**

PECAN BUTTERMILK PIE WITH SOUR CREAM PASTRY

*B*uttermilk pie is a southern institution. It still tastes as good today as it did a hundred years ago or more. The pie originated as a dessert that could be made from inexpensive ingredients that every country cook always had on hand. The pecans are a Texas addition because we like them so much. They add a nice flavor note to the rich pie.

SOUR CREAM PASTRY

 1 cup sifted all-purpose flour
½ teaspoon salt
½ cup (1 stick) unsalted butter, cut into small cubes
 1 egg yolk, beaten
⅓ cup sour cream

FILLING

½ cup (1 stick) unsalted butter, softened
 2 cups sugar
 2 teaspoons vanilla extract
 3 eggs
 3 tablespoons all-purpose flour
¼ teaspoon salt
 1 cup buttermilk
½ cup chopped pecans

To make the pastry, combine flour, salt, and butter in work bowl of food processor fitted with steel blade. Process until butter is broken up into pea-size bits. In a small bowl combine the egg yolk and sour cream, beating to blend well. Add to the flour mixture and process just until blended. Turn dough out onto lightly floured work surface and knead once or twice by hand. Flatten into a round disk, wrap tightly in plastic wrap, and refrigerate for 20 to 30 minutes while preparing the filling.

Preheat oven to 300 degrees. Cream the butter and sugar in electric mixer at medium speed until light and fluffy, about 4 minutes. Add the vanilla and beat to blend. Add eggs, one at a time, beating well and scraping down side of bowl after each addition. Combine the flour and salt. Add to the mixer in thirds, alternating with the buttermilk. Stop to scrape down side of bowl after each addition. Set filling aside.

Roll the chilled pastry out on a floured work surface into a circle about ¹⁄₁₆-inch thick. Roll the pastry loosely around the rolling pin and unroll over 9-inch pie pan. Lift the edges of the pastry, allowing it to fall to bottom of pan. Do not stretch the pastry or it will shrink as it bakes. Pat the pastry onto sides and bottom of pan. Cut off excess pastry, leaving a ½-inch overhang at rim of pan. Fold the excess pastry under and flute the edges, or press against the rim of the pan with the tines of a fork. Scatter the pecans in the bottom of the pastry. Pour the buttermilk mixture over the pecans and bake for 1 hour and 30 minutes in preheated oven. Set on wire rack to cool completely. Refrigerate until well chilled before serving.

ଓ **Makes 1 9-inch pie.**

Maidenhair fern on the Sabinal River (left); Canyonlands of the Upper Medina River (pages 264–65).

SWEET POTATO–PECAN PIE

*T*his rich and gooey dessert fits right in the middle of the category of soul food, which has made its mark on the Texas Cuisine, as in most other regions of the South. The pie combines the sweet potato, so inherent in African-American cooking, with the native pecan. It wouldn't be Christmas at my house without this pie.

PASTRY

- 1 cup all-purpose flour
- ½ cup (1 stick) well-chilled unsalted butter, cut into 1-inch cubes

Pinch of salt

- ½ teaspoon sugar
- 3 to 4 tablespoons ice water

FILLING

- 2 tablespoons unsalted butter, melted
- 1 cup hot mashed sweet potatoes
- 2 eggs, beaten
- ¾ cup firmly packed light brown sugar
- 1 teaspoon ground ginger
- ½ teaspoon ground cinnamon
- ½ teaspoon freshly grated nutmeg
- 1 tablespoon vanilla extract
- ½ teaspoon salt
- ½ cup dark corn syrup
- 1 cup evaporated milk
- 1½ cup chopped pecans

TOPPING

- 1 cup whipping cream
- 2 tablespoons powdered sugar
- 2 tablespoons praline liqueur

To make the pastry, combine flour, butter, and salt in work bowl of food processor fitted with steel blade. Using the pulse button, pulse just until butter is broken into pea-size chunks. With processor running, add just enough of the water through the feed tube to form a soft, moist dough. Do not process until the mixture forms a ball. Turn out onto lightly floured work surface and knead 2 or 3 times by hand. Spray a 9-inch pie pan with non-stick vegetable spray. Roll the pastry out on lightly floured work surface to about ¹⁄₁₆-inch thick. Loosely roll the pastry around the rolling pin and unroll into pie pan. Lift the edges of the pastry, allowing it to fall to the bottom of the pan. Do not stretch the pastry, or it will shrink while baking. Press onto the bottom and sides of the pan. Cut off excess pastry at the edge, leaving about a ½-inch overhang. Turn the pastry under and flute the edge, or press the pastry against the rim of the pan with the tines of a fork. Refrigerate the pastry while making the filling. Preheat oven to 350 degrees.

In a large bowl, stir the butter into the hot sweet potatoes. Add all remaining filling ingredients except pecans; blend well.

Pour the sweet potato filling into prepared pie shell; scatter the pecans evenly over the top. Bake in preheated oven for about 40 to 45 minutes, or until filling is set and knife inserted into center comes out clean. Cool in pan on wire rack before slicing.

To prepare topping, combine the whipping cream, powdered sugar, and praline liqueur in bowl of electric mixer. Beat with wire whisk until stiff peaks form. Refrigerate, tightly covered, until ready to use.

To serve, slice into 8 wedges. Serve each piece with a large dollop of the topping.

෨ Makes 1 9-inch pie.

Crème de Menthe Brownies

This grand recipe has made the party circuit for years. I'm sure that years ago it probably originated on the back of a brownie mix box. Wherever it came from, I predict that it will be around for as long as there are brownies and people who adore them.

1 box of your favorite brownie mix
⅔ cup chopped pecans
¾ cup semi-sweet chocolate chips

Topping

2 cups powdered sugar
½ cup (1 stick) unsalted butter, softened and cut into small chunks
3 tablespoons green crème de menthe

Glaze

1 cup semi-sweet chocolate chips
6 tablespoons unsalted butter

Prepare the brownies according to package directions, adding the pecans and chocolate chips to the batter before baking. Bake and set aside to cool completely.

To prepare the topping, cream the powdered sugar and butter in bowl of electric mixer at medium speed until light and fluffy, about 4 to 5 minutes. Add the crème de menthe and beat just to blend. Spread the topping evenly over the cooled brownies. Refrigerate.

To prepare the glaze, combine the chocolate chips and butter in a heavy 1-quart saucepan over medium-low heat. Cook, stirring often, until chocolate has melted and mixture is smooth. Remove pan from heat and allow to cool until slightly thickened, about 20 minutes. Pour the glaze evenly over the brownies and refrigerate just until the chocolate is set, about 1 hour. Don't allow the glaze to harden completely, or it will crack unevenly when the brownies are sliced. Cut into 1½-inch squares.

❧ **Makes about 20 pieces.**

Jack Daniel's Whiskey Balls

During the Christmas season, I make hundreds of these addictive little confections. They make the perfect hostess gift to take to holiday parties. I like to pack them in the small Chinese food take-out containers, lined with red and green tissue paper, or pack them into decorative tins lined with tissue paper. The take-out containers only hold about 12 to 15 pieces, though. If the hostess sets them out to share with the rest of the guests, you'll probably have to go home for more. Nobody eats just one.

1½ cups vanilla wafer crumbs
1 cup powdered sugar
1 cup finely chopped pecans
2 tablespoons unsweetened cocoa powder
2 tablespoons light corn syrup
¼ cup Jack Daniel's whiskey
Powdered sugar

Combine cookie crumbs, powdered sugar, pecans, cocoa powder, corn syrup, and whiskey in medium bowl, blending well. Roll into 24 balls and dredge in powdered sugar to coat well; shake off excess sugar. Cover and refrigerate until ready to serve.

❧ **Makes about 24 pieces.**

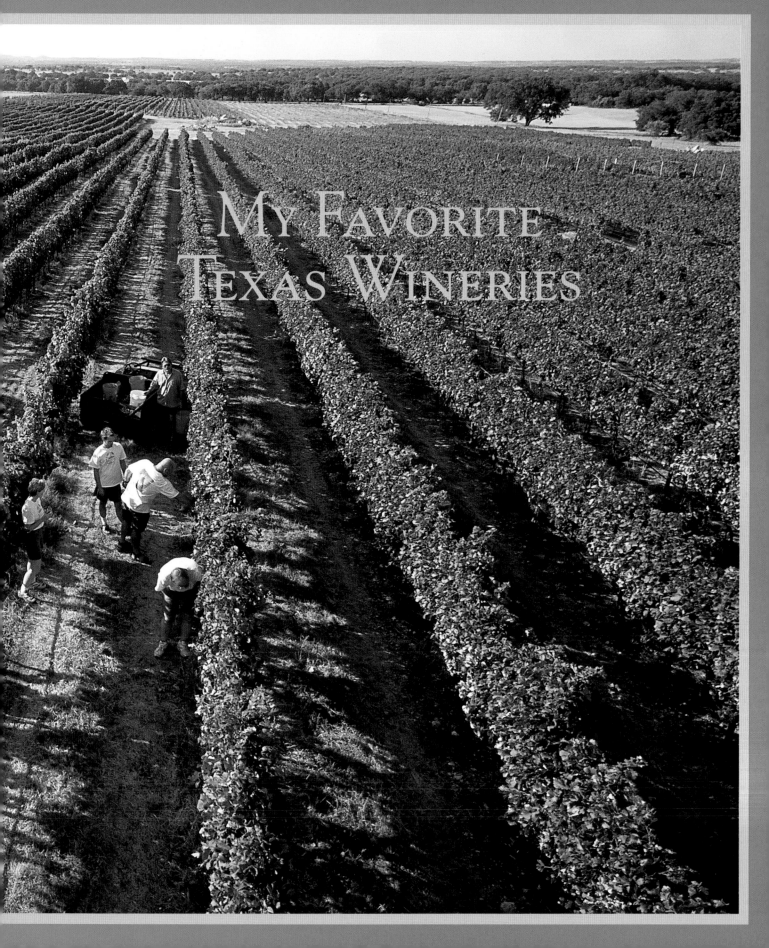

MY FAVORITE
TEXAS WINERIES

Wine is a wonderful creation made from the juice of Mother Nature's grapes. There are those who say that wine is the perfect complement or enhancement to food. There are also real wine lovers who say that good food is the perfect complement to wine!

The Texas wine industry is coming into its own. We now have over forty active wineries in Texas. Many of these wineries are producing award-winning wines. We are also producing wine varietals in Texas that are unique to the state, their tastes formed by our particular soils, elevations, and climates. It's called gout de terroir, "taste of the soil." It refers not only to the earthy flavor of wines as a result of soil type but also to other geographic conditions that might influence the quality and taste of the finished wine. Texas winemakers have taken varietals from France and California and produced wines with completely different tastes than those made from the same grapes in the regions where they originated. Different, unique, and good.

Thirty years ago Texas had one winery, even though the history of Texas grape growing goes back at least to the 1660s when Franciscan monks planted mission grapes adjacent to their missions. In the 1880s a Texan by the name of Thomas Volney Munson became a hero to the French when he shipped thousands of wine rootstocks to European vineyards that had been devastated by phylloxera, a tiny aphid-like insect that attacks the roots of grapevines and slowly starves the plant. Originally Texas wineries used native

American grape varieties. In the late 1970s, wineries began to import European varieties. Today most Texas wineries grow Vitis vinifera grapes from France.

Our wineries are scattered around the state, with a large concentration in the High Plains region around Lubbock. In recent years the Lubbock area has gained international attention as a superb region for vinifera grape growing. At an elevation of 3,400 feet, the region is semi-arid and mild. Cool nights and warm to hot days predominate with a low level of relative humidity. The soil is a deep and well-drained sandy loam suited to growing European varietal grapes. Another noted winemaking area is the Texas Hill Country. We even have a winery with vineyards in Santa Fe, close to Galveston Island on the Gulf Coast!

I have selected my favorite fifteen Texas wineries and asked the winemakers to pair one of their wines with entrées and other dishes in this book. The range of tastes is vast, and I believe each list of recommended wines will include a wine for everyone's taste. Sometimes finding Texas wines can be a problem. Some wineries are so small that their production levels do not make them attractive to liquor distributors. Many of those wines can only be purchased from the winery's tasting room. If you live in a large city, call around to different liquor or wine stores and ask if they carry Texas wines. For information on the Texas wine industry as well as individual wineries, visit www.texaswinetrails.com.

WINE TERMS

*T*he following terms, which appear in the Tasting Notes that follow, are used by eonophiles (people who enjoy wine) to describe the subtle tastes of wine. Browse through these terms for a better understanding of the notes. For everything else you might want to know about wine, consult the excellent and very user-friendly book Wine Lover's Companion by Ron Herbst and Sharon Tyler Herbst. This book is a must for any serious wine lover.

ACIDITY. Acids occur naturally while grapes are growing and again as part of the fermentation process in winemaking. Finished wines show less acid when the growing season for the grapes is hot. Cooler regions produce wines with high levels of acid. Acidity is a desirable component in wines when properly balanced. Too much acid leaves a bitter taste in the mouth. However, without the proper levels of acid, wines would taste flat and boring. The three main acids present in wines are tartaric, malic, and citric, all of which are inherent to the grape. In regions with hotter climates, natural grape acids are often added to wines to achieve a balance of acid and sweetness. Acidity should not be a readily noticeable component in well-made wines.

AROMA. A traditional definition of aroma is the natural fruity smell of the variety of grape. However, in winemaking the definition is extended to include that varietal fragrance along with any changes in the taste that occur during fermentation and aging of the wine. Young wines will have a strong aroma of the grape's varietal fruitiness, while in mature aged wines, varying degrees of the grape's fruitiness are replaced by other aromas, resulting in what is called "bouquet" in these mature wines.

BODY. The texture or weight of a wine in the mouth. Wines with rich, complex, well-rounded tastes are considered to be "full-bodied" while watery, lighter-flavored wines are "light-bodied." Wines ranging between the two are considered "medium-bodied" wines. There are great wines in all categories. Champagne is an example of a light-bodied wine. Dessert wines such as Muscat Canelli and the late-harvest Rieslings are full-bodied wines because the amount of residual sugar inherent in these wines adds weight and texture.

BOUQUET. The complex fragrance that develops in wine during fermentation and bottle aging.

CAP MANAGEMENT. During the fermentation process of wine, the skins, stems, seeds, and pulp from the grapes float on top of the juice. This mass is referred to as the "cap," and it must be continually broken up and pushed down into the juice to help extract color, flavor, and tannins. Furthermore, if allowed to remain intact on top of the juice, the cap would dry out and develop bacteria. Methods of cap management can be as simple as using a long wooden paddle to stir the cap down into the juice. Modern techniques include pumps that constantly turn the mass and specially designed tanks that capture the mass under a screen suspended down into the tank of juice. Some wineries use rotating tanks.

CRISP. A term used to describe a wine that has a lively, fresh level of acidity. The acidity should not be noticeable as a bitter or tart taste, but should give the wine a lively taste instead of a flat one. Crispness is a very desirable characteristic in white wines.

CUVÉE. A term derived from the French word *cuve* (which means "vat") that denoted the "contents of a vat." In the production of Champagne, the term refers to the secret blending of various wines to create the finished product. The term is also used in still wine production to refer to wines blended from different vineyards or even different varieties. If the word *cuvée* is followed by a number, it is used to identify a specific batch of wines blended separately and distinctly from others.

FINING. A stage in the winemaking process in which microscopic protein particles (which would cloud the wine) and compounds like tannins (which would cause bitterness) are removed. Fining agents are used to accomplish this process. The most frequently used fining agents are activated carbon, activated charcoal, casein, egg whites, gelatin, isinglass, nylon, bentonite, and polyvinyl pyrolidone. These agents capture the particles by absorption or coagulation and cause them to settle to the bottom of the tank or barrel where they can be easily removed. Fining agents are also used to remove color from white wines, reduce acids, and neutralize off-odors in wine.

FINISH. The final impression of a wine's flavor and texture that remains on the palate after a wine has been swallowed. The finish is a very important component of the wine's overall taste impression, or balance. Most desirable is a wine that leaves a lingering and pleasant finish.

MALOLACTIC FERMENTATION. A secondary fermentation whereby bacteria is used to convert malic acid into lactic acid and carbon dioxide in wine. No alcohol is produced in this fermentation. This process is not used in all wines, but it is often desirable to create a wine with a softer, smoother taste. With malolactic fermentation, the lactic acid produced is milder than the malic acid inherent in the grapes. The process also produces diacetyl, which has a smell reminiscent of melted butter, adding complexity to the taste of the wine. Most high-quality red wines and some white Burgundies and Chardonnays are produced using this secondary fermentation. The downside of malolactic fermentation is that the inherent fruitiness of the grape is diminished. Some winemakers use the process in half of a batch of Chardonnay, leaving the other portion of the batch with only one fermentation, giving the final blended wine complexity, while retaining the fruitiness and crispness of the malic acid.

MOUTH FILLING. A term describing wines that are big, rich, and intensely flavored. Wines with high alcohol content are generally regarded as "mouth filling." They literally fill the mouth with flavor impressions.

NOSE. The intensity of smell emanating from the surface of the wine when it is swirled rapidly in the glass. The term does not denote the quality of the wine, although the nose does give a preview of the taste.

NV—Non-vintage.

SUR LIE ("on the lees"). Lees is the sediment consisting of dead yeast cells and particles from the grapes that accumulate in wine during fermentation. Certain types of wines benefit from aging with the lees intact. Chardonnays and Sauvignon Blancs gain complexity. Sparkling wines produced according to the French Methode Champenoise are aged sur lie as a matter of natural course. Wines aged in this manner have creamy, yeasty flavors and a touch of carbon dioxide, which gives a slight "spritzy" feeling on the tongue.

TANNIN. Astringents found in the seeds, skins, and stems of grapes as well as in oak barrels, especially new ones. Tannins are important in the production of good red wines because they add flavor, structure, and texture. Tannins also have great antioxidant properties that promote long, graceful aging in red wines. Tannins in young wines can cause a noticeably astringent flavor, but this flavor diminishes with aging and the wine develops character and mellowness. Wines with noticeable levels of astringency, or those that cause a "puckery" sensation in the mouth, are referred to as "tannic."

TAR. A desirable quality, used to describe the smell of hot tar sometimes found in cabernets and zinfandels.

TOASTY. A term that refers to the appealing taste of toasted bread. This characteristic is particularly desirable in some Chardonnays and sparkling wines. The taste is produced by aging the wines in oak barrels that have been charred on the inside.

ALAMOSA WINE CELLARS

677 County Road 430, Bend, Texas 76824
(915) 628-3313
www.alamosawinecellars.com

Alamosa Wine Cellars is owned and operated by Jim and Karen Johnson. Jim is realizing a dream he has had nearly all his adult life. He left Houston in 1989 to pursue a degree in fermentation science at the University of California at Davis. After graduating, he gained practical experience at three of California's most prominent wineries, Iron Horse Vineyards, St. Francis Winery & Vineyards, and Heitz Cellars. Jim returned to Texas in 1993 to be the winemaker at Slaughter-Leftwich Vineyards in Austin and later at Becker Vineyards in Stonewall.

The Alamosa Wine Cellars winery was built in time for the 1999 harvest. It is a 2,400-square-foot production facility consisting of a crush pad, tank room, climate-controlled barrel room, office, and lab. Due to the local option, wines cannot be sold at the winery, so there is no formal tasting room. Call for an appointment to tour the facility and taste the wines.

Alamosa Wine Cellars wines are produced with the belief that blending makes more complex, interesting, and lasting wines. The vineyard was planted with the intention of picking the fruit and blending prior to fermentation when possible.

TASTING NOTES

El Guapo, Tio Pancho Ranch, Texas Hill Country—92% Tempranillo, 5% Cabernet Sauvignon, 3% Garnacha. This long-awaited release of the state's first Tempranillo is getting rave reviews. A big blueberry nose with spice and chocolate and a hint of mint. Will pair with the biggest, juiciest steak or a delicate lamb chop or a wild game dish.

Fumé Blanc—an interesting blend of High Plains Sauvignon Blanc and Viognier. Citrus, fig, apricot, and melon notes.

Rosato di Sangiovese—a lighter Italian-style red, dry and crisp. Complex cherry and dark fruit nose with a very light touch of oak. Very versatile. Great with anything smoked; will stand up to Thanksgiving dinner's many flavors.

Sangiovese—82% Sangiovese, 15% Cabernet Sauvignon, 3% Ruby Cabernet. Cherry and vanilla, rose petals, and mushrooms. Continues to improve as it acquires bottle age. Serve with duck, lamb, salmon, and pork with a variety of sauces. Also great with Italian dishes.

Viognier—100% Viognier grapes. Dried apricots, figs, and honey. Mouth feel and structure enhanced by extended sur lie aging in mostly neutral French oak barrels. Great with oysters and smoked quail, apricot sauces.

BECKER VINEYARDS

Jenschke Lane, Stonewall, Texas 78671
(830) 644-2681
www.beckervineyards.com

Becker Vineyards, owned by Richard and Bunny Becker, is located in the Texas Hill Country between Fredericksburg and Stonewall. Becker Vineyards was established in 1992. The vineyard was planted on a site of native Mustang grapes much prized by German neighbors and their ancestors for its wine. Thirty-six acres of French vinifera vines with sixteen different varietals, including Viognier, Mouvedre, Syrah, Chardonnay, and Merlot, were planted in a mixture of deep sand and Precambrian granitic soils at 1,500 feet above sea level.

Becker Vineyards' first harvest was 1995. All vintages are aged in both new French and American oak and stored in the largest underground wine cellar in Texas. The winery is housed in a replica of a nineteenth-century German stone barn and surrounded by grazing quarterhorses, peach orchards, and fields of Provincial lavender, native wildflowers, and coastal Bermuda. The winery is approximately 10,040 square feet with a storage capacity of 64,000 gallons and fermenting capacity of 35,000 gallons.

The winery's tasting room, which opened in June of 1996, includes a large stone fireplace and an antique bar originally from the Green Tree Saloon, established in San Antonio in the nineteenth century.

TASTING NOTES

Cabernet Sauvignon Estate Bottled—85% Cabernet Sauvignon, 10% Cabernet Franc, 5% Syrah. A favorite of those who enjoy the "big reds." Round, spicy, and earthy, with complexity in the finish. Aged 20 months in American oak.

Cabernet Sauvignon Reserve Estate Bottled—92% Cabernet Sauvignon, 5% Syrah, 3% Merlot. Warm days and cool nights in the estate vineyard yield wines of depth and richness. Carefully matured in new American oak barrels. Essences of chocolate, dried cherries, espresso, and spice.

Chardonnay Estate Bottled—delicious and clean, with a slight toastiness. Aged 5 to 6 months in French oak.

Chenin Blanc—an award-winning white wine produced in the style of France's Loire Valley. Aged in French oak, sur lie, for 6 months. A wonderful balance of acid, soft vanilla tannin, minerals, and tropical fruit flavors of peach and pear.

Claret Estate Bottled—the first Texas wine to contain all five red Bordeaux varietals; 50% Cabernet Franc, 36% Cabernet Sauvignon, 8% Merlot, 4% Malbec, and 2% Petite

Verdot. Carefully matured in French and American oak barrels for 18 months. Rich and complex, with essences of raspberries, blackberries, cassis, chocolate, and spice.

Fumé Blanc Estate Bottled—lively white wine aged 4 months in French oak. Juicy and full of flavor. Spicy nose with tastes of honeysuckle and green apples. Crisp, with a subtle hint of lemon on the finish. Good with Texas barbecue or grilled chicken.

Merlot—75% Merlot, 20% Cabernet Sauvignon, and 5% Ruby Cabernet. Strawberry jam and cloves, with nice toastiness resulting from 15 months in French oak. Delicious.

Provence (Mourvedre, Syrah, Grenache) Estate Bottled— dry rosé is replicated in the Tavel, France, style of dry rosés where the rosé is considered a "summertime" red. Bright strawberry notes and rose petals. A nice fruitiness, yet light.

Riesling (Becker Vineyards' Ballinger vineyard)—A nice honey bouquet with hints of cantaloupe, mint, licorice, lime, and orange peel. The finish has both a great balance of acidity and is reminiscent of peach syrup. Residual sugar: 1.25%.

Viognier—an esteemed white wine grape considered very rare because of the limited acreage planted throughout the world. An intense, dry white wine with vibrant floral qualities and an intriguing bouquet of apricots, peaches, and pears.

Cap*Rock Winery

408 Woodrow, Lubbock, Texas 79423
1-800-546-WINE
www.caprockwinery.com

In 1992 a new vision emerged in the Texas wine industry with the debut of wine from Cap*Rock Winery in Lubbock. Out of the flatness of the Texas High Plains rises one of the most beautiful winemaking facilities in the country. The stunning southwestern mission-style winery is outfitted with the finest quality equipment available. The building is 23,000 square feet with the capacity to produce 45,000 cases at present and space for additional tanks and barrels to reach a capacity of approximately 90,000 cases. The fermentation rooms have 40-foot ceilings to accommodate the American-made stainless steel tanks, which range in size from 1,000 to 13,000 gallons and the barrel racks containing both French and American oak barrels. Visitors from all over the country enjoy the beauty and style of the winery's tasting room with its 14-foot ceiling, stone fireplace, and green marble-topped bar.

The grapes for Cap*Rock wines come from 98 acres of estate vineyards and from a few carefully selected growers in the surrounding Lubbock area. Both the estate and contracted vineyards are farmed with exacting attention to excellence. The vineyards maximize modern growing techniques and utilize drip irrigation and carefully constructed trellis systems. Valves are located within each vineyard block so that individual varieties can be watered as needed. There is an adherence to traditional farming values, such as hand harvesting of grapes, when this method improves overall quality; exacting modern methods are used when they are most beneficial. The wine grape varietals currently being grown include Cabernet Sauvignon, Merlot, Cabernet Franc, Malbec, Sangiovese, Barbera, Chardonnay, Sauvignon Blanc, Chenin Blanc, and Orange Muscat.

Tasting Notes

Cabernet Royale, Rosé of Cabernet Sauvignon—this rosé of Cabernet Sauvignon has a beautiful, deep reddish pink color and great varietal character. Heavy cherry, strawberry, raspberry, and cranberry aromas and flavors with a perfect balance of sweetness and acidity for a clean finish. Great for Tex-Mex and barbecue.

Cabernet Sauvignon—this Bordeaux blend of Cabernet Sauvignon, Cabernet Franc, and Malbec is specially fermented and barrel aged for 12 months to produce its smooth, friendly style. Medium-bodied and dry with firm tannins and nicely woven aromas and flavors of black cherry, berry, plum, and currant.

Cap*Rock Sparkling Blanc de Noir—a cuvée made from both the great Burgundy grapes, Pinot Noir and Chardonnay, produces this methode champenoise sparkling wine.

Chardonnay—a judicious blend of Chardonnay aged in oak (50%) and stainless steel (50%) allows this wine to retain all the fruit character of the grape, especially citrus, apple, and pear, with light, desirable layers of oak, vanilla, and butter. Pleasantly dry, medium in body, and wonderful by itself or with food.

Merlot, Texas High Plains—soft tannins and excellent fruit but by no means a "shy" Merlot. A dry red with good body and a nice oaky undertone balancing the aromas and flavors of ripe cherry, plum, and spice.

Reserve Cabernet Sauvignon, Texas High Plains, Newsom Vineyards—soft and velvety, deep purple wine aged in French oak barrels for 18 months; 100% Cabernet Sauvignon grapes. Characteristic black cherry/raspberry aromas and flavors of High Plains Cabernet grapes, along with layers of plum, spice, tobacco, herbs, and a seductive chocolate edge that eases in after a little breathing time.

Reserve Chardonnay, Texas High Plains—a full-bodied wine, 100% barrel fermented and aged in medium toast French/American hybrid oak barrels for 10 months. Green apple, citrus, and pear qualities with a light but distinct floral character, a pronounced but not dominating oakiness, and the high acidity typical of a Burgundian-style Chardonnay.

Reserve Merlot, Texas High Plains, Newsom Vineyards—a nice layer of oak complements the deep aromas and flavors of ripe cherry, berry, plum, and cassis. Aged in French and American oak for 18 months. Medium-bodied with full but very soft tannins.

Reserve Orange Muscat, Texas High Plains, Newsom Vineyards—a dessert wine in every sense; pleasing, deliciously sweet, fortified wine with the light citrus, ripe apricot, deep floral, and delicate orange flower characteristics of the distinctive and unique Muscat grape variety. Fruit and rich sweetness perfectly balanced by acidity and alcohol.

Reserve Toscano Rosso, Texas High Plains—Tuscan-style blend of Sangiovese, Barbera, and Cabernet Sauvignon. Soft and supple in texture with smooth tannins and pleasant dryness. Abundance of aromas and flavor, notably black cherry, plum, berry, clove, and cedar.

Topaz Royale—a combination of three grape varietals known for lush fruit character: Chenin Blanc, Riesling, and Muscat Canelli. The result is a wine filled with apricot, pear, melon, apple, and fresh floral aromas and flavors, but done in an off-dry, delicate style with only a touch of sweetness, balanced by excellent acidity.

Vintner's Red, Texas Table Wine—smooth and flavorful; can be enjoyed by both red and non-red wine drinkers because of its softness and abundant varietal fruit character.

Vintner's White, Texas Table Wine—an all-occasion wine that is off-dry but loaded with peach, pear, apple, and floral aromas and flavors with nice acidity for a refreshing, pleasing finish.

COMFORT CELLARS WINERY

723 Front Street, Comfort, Texas 78013
(830) 995-3274

While pondering what to do after retirement from the military, Cathie Winmill, now owner of Comfort Cellars Winery, had two key criteria: something that would keep her busy and that would allow her to work outside. Growing grapes fulfilled both these criteria.

Home winemaking was a family affair while Cathie was growing up in northern Illinois, and she never forgot those fond memories. Work on a master's degree in dietetics and nutrition in southern Arizona offered her an opportunity to learn about growing grapes in arid climates. Many years later, after her retirement from the Army Medical Specialist Corps and the death of her husband, Cathie started the vineyard, with the help of her brother, Bob.

In 1997, land was purchased in the Texas Hill Country between Comfort and Sisterdale and grapevines were planted. Building the winery in Comfort was a natural development after the vineyard was established.

TASTING NOTES

Chenin Blanc—a light, dry, crisp wine that complements rich but light sauces.

Comfort Blush—a slightly sweet blend of Merlot, Muscat Canelli, and White Zinfandel that complements spicy, hot Texan cuisine.

Merlot—a very full-bodied, berry-flavored red wine that complements hearty, red-meat dishes.

Orange Chardonnay—an unusual white wine that complements any type of poultry with fruity sauces. Also a great patio wine served well chilled and straight or blended with club soda over ice.

Pinot Noir—a light, dry red wine that complements red wine sauces and roasted meats and game.

Raisin Wine—a light, sweet, dry, sherry-like wine that complements spicy, smoky, salty appetizer or snack foods. Named for Cathie's dog, Raisin, who greets visitors to the tasting room.

DELANEY VINEYARDS AND WINERY

2000 Champagne Boulevard, Grapevine, Texas 76051
(816) 481-5668

In the heart of Grapevine, just minutes from the Dallas–Fort Worth International Airport, sits the Delaney Vineyards and Winery. Nestled comfortably near groves of century-old live oaks, Delaney Vineyards is a working winery, styled after an eighteenth-century French vineyard. Features include a 5,200-square-foot Grand Barrel Room with soaring vaulted ceilings, warm wood architecture, and beautiful vintage French oak casks.

TASTING NOTES

Barrel-Fermented Chardonnay—Grapevine-grown, -aged, and -bottled. Fermented to dryness in French oak barrels and also matured sur lies. A creamy, buttery-flavored Chardonnay that will appeal even to the red wine drinker. Great with white meats or seafood.

Cabernet Franc—a High Plains, estate-bottled blend of 90% Cabernet Franc and 10% Cabernet Sauvignon. Oak-aged following the tradition of the Loire Valley of France. A slightly rustic wine with a delightful fruity nose and mellow feel. The perfect accompaniment to cheese, meat, or venison.

Estate Cabernet Sauvignon (Lamesa Vineyard)—80% Cabernet Sauvignon, 10% Merlot, and 10% Cabernet Franc. Oak-aged for more than 18 months and fined using traditional Bordeaux methods.

Merlot—80% Merlot and 20% Cabernet Sauvignon grapes from the Grapevine vineyard. The first Merlot produced by Delaney Vineyards. Grown, fermented, aged, and bottled in

Grapevine. Aged for more than 18 months in French oak barrels. A superb bouquet, very smooth on the palate. Good with any type of meat.

Muscat Canelli—a late-harvest type of wine, generally a dessert wine. Because of its residual sweetness and powerful aroma, it may be appealing as an after-dinner drink. Muscat wines have been appreciated since antiquity for their typical fragrant character. The wine was a favorite of Thomas Jefferson, who brought it back from Frontignan in southern France.

Sauvignon Blanc—a light, fresh wine that is milder than a Chardonnay. Totally dry, this wine captures the wild flowery and vegetal character of the Sauvignon Blanc grape, a grape traditionally grown in the Loire Valley and in some parts of the Bordeaux region of France. Served cool, it is a perfect complement to fish.

Texas Champagne Brut (NV)—made by the traditional bottle-fermented method with the same varieties of grapes as grown in the Champagne region of France. Bottle-fermented and aged for 24 months. Can be served with any type of food and throughout the meal.

Texas Claret—a typical French Claret made from 90% Cabernet Sauvignon and 10% Cabernet Franc grapes according to traditions dating back as far as the seventeenth century. A favorite with the English who brought it to the American colonies. Fruitiness and fresh nose, peppery finish. Keeps its qualities even with spicy dishes, such as peppered steak, Mexican and Italian foods, even Texas barbecue.

Vintner's Reserve Cabernet Sauvignon—85% Cabernet Sauvignon, 15% Merlot. Produced exclusively from grapes from the Grapevine vineyard, aged for 14 months in French oak using traditional Bordeaux methods. A soft wine with a delicate bouquet confirmed by its silky yet well-balanced texture. Complements red meats.

DRY COMAL CREEK VINEYARDS

1741 Herbelin Road, New Braunfels, Texas 78132
(830) 885-4121

Dry Comal Creek Vineyard, owned by Franklin D. Houser, is located in a small protected valley nestled in the Texas Hill Country. The rich alluvial soil, laced with limestone, flint, and shale chips, provides ideal growing conditions for grapes.

Dry Comal Creek Vineyards is a small boutique wine producer. Its goal is to make small lots of wine that are the very best that can be attained. Climate and soil primarily dictate what can be accomplished. The winery does not make French-style or California-style wines but rather "Texas-style" wines! Franklin Houser describes this style as wines that feature fruit and, where applicable, "flower." Particular emphasis is placed on mouth feel and smoothness from beginning to end, especially on the finish. The wines and vines receive personal care and tending, combined with a labor-intensive handmade approach to picking, fermentation, winemaking, and bottling. This produces a very personal result in the wines, unmatched in character and uncompromised in quality. The winery strives to make wines as unique as Texas itself!

TASTING NOTES

Cabernet Sauvignon—aged for 16 months in new French oak barrels; big, bold, and smooth. Hints of oak, fruit, tobacco, leather, and spice.

Chardonnay—extremely smooth and brisk, with vanilla overtones and understated oak, flowers, and fruit. A Texas-style Chardonnay, barrel-fermented and aged in French oak.

Sauvignon Blanc—a Texas-style Sauvignon Blanc with crisp fruit and spice overtones.

White Veritage—extremely light, crisp, and smooth. Proprietary select white wine with zero sugar. Perfect for Texas summers.

FALL CREEK VINEYARDS

County Road 222, Tow, Texas 78624
(915) 379-5361
www.fcv.com

Fall Creek Vineyards began in 1975 as an ambitious project by Ed and Susan Auler to determine whether high-quality wine grapes could be grown on their Fall Creek Ranch in the Texas Hill Country. The Aulers' curiosity for the project was sparked when they noticed that the soil, terrain, and microclimate surrounding the ranch were remarkably similar to parts of the French wine country. After a few short years it became very clear that the high caliber of Fall Creek grapes could result in the production of top-quality wines. Fall Creek Vineyards was formed as a small, completely integrated vineyard and winery operation separate from Fall Creek Ranch. It has continued to grow dramatically in size, quality, production, and recognition.

TASTING NOTES

Cascade Semillon/Sauvignon Blanc—blends spiciness with a little more fruitiness; a good match for spicy shellfish dishes.

Chardonnay—good fruit flavors that will complement oysters and smoke flavors.

Chenin Blanc—mouth-filling fruit and body sufficient to balance the heat and flavors of spicy Texas foods.

Granite Reserve Cabernet Sauvignon—full-bodied, fruit-flavored wine that stands up to smoky, spicy foods made with chilies.

Merlot—has the weight and fruitiness to balance heavy sauces. Soft tannins are mitigated by fatty meats.

Reserve Cabernet Sauvignon—flavors of coffee and tar, which marry well with big, bold sauces and red meat.

Reserve Chardonnay—elegant fruit softened with oak, a classic match for oysters and delicate cream sauces.

Sauvignon Blanc—slightly herbaceous citrus flavor with good flavor balance.

"Sweet Jo" Johannesburg Riesling—a late-harvest wine that will stand up to rich meats such as foie gras.

Haak Vineyards and Winery

6310 Avenue T, Santa Fe, Texas 77510
(409) 925-1401

Raymond and Gladys Haak established Haak Vineyards in 1980. The two have lived all their lives in Galveston County, including over 46 years in Santa Fe. The Haaks' vineyard is located on their 12-acre estate. Currently, there are two varieties grown: Blanc du Bois, a white grape, and Black Spanish/Lenoir, a red grape. Most of the wines produced are made from grapes grown in premium growing regions in Texas, California, and New Mexico. The vineyards and winery are located on the original homestead where the Haaks built their home in 1963 and raised their five daughters.

Construction for the winery began in January 2000, after more than 25 years of winemaking research and study by Raymond Haak. The winery is a state-of-the-art facility with jacketed stainless steel tanks equipped with automatic temperature control, propylene glycol chiller, and refrigerated winemaking facilities.

The tasting room offers tours and tastings on a daily basis. The winery has a unique 1,800-square-foot cellar located over 9 feet below the tasting room floor. It was engineered and constructed of concrete and steel with 18-inch-thick concrete walls throughout the cellar, where wines are stored, fermented, and aged in their oak barrels.

Tasting Notes

Barrel-Fermented Chardonnay—notes of honey, walnut, smoke, and butter.

Blanc du Bois—notes of citrus, grapefruit, and figs.

Cabernet Sauvignon—notes of blackberry with pepper and plums. Good red-meat wine that stands up to heavy sauces.

Chardonnay—spicy tropical fruit and banana notes.

Sauvignon Blanc—notes of citrus and figs with a crisp, clean palate feel. Great with spicy seafood dishes.

Zinfandel—notes of raspberry, strawberry, pear, and plum. A rough-and-tumble wine for full-flavored red-meat dishes.

Hidden Springs Winery

256 N. Hwy. 377, Pilot Point, Texas 76258
(940) 686-2782
www.hiddenspringswinery.com

Lela Banks, winemaker and co-owner, was an amateur winemaker for years prior to her formal education at Grayson County College. She was then awarded a scholarship at Clos du Vougeot in France to complete her studies for an Associate of Applied Science in viticulture and enology. She and her husband established the vineyard in Whitesboro before the opening of the winery. The winery officially opened in 1996 with 18 acres of its own grapes. The winery is known for producing lighter wines, using primarily stainless-steel fermentation for Chardonnay, resulting in a very fruity nose. The red wines use only a short oak fermentation to avoid a heavy tannin flavor.

Tasting Notes

Blush—created from premium grapes. A soft appealing color and exceptional flavor. Good with light fish entrées or simply enjoy drinking it with friends.

Cabernet Sauvignon—gently aged in French oak barrels for one year with traces of berries and peppers. Great with beef, veal, and venison.

Chardonnay—careful cold fermentation produces a true Chablis style, with tropical nuances, both in nose and taste. Slightly oaked, delightful served with light poultry and fish entrées with light cream sauces.

Crystal Red Table Wine—a blend of superb-quality grapes producing a smooth, soft, truly elegant wine with a color reminiscent of candlelight and sparkling crystal. A taste treat with beef, veal, and soft Italian entrées. Best served slightly chilled.

Merlot (Lone Oak Vineyards, Cooke County)—Merlot grown to a very high standard. Smooth, yet intriguing texture, forward fruit, and lingering velvet. Carefully aged in French oak for one year. Fruits that feature red currants and ripe raspberries.

Muscat Canelli—a truly unique wine and an excellent table wine. Delightful bouquet of fruit and flowers. Serve well chilled with spicy, Oriental, Indian, Tex-Mex foods as well as strawberries, peaches, and melon.

Ruby Glow—the winery's signature wine with just a touch of sweetness. A fine Texas red wine similar to a claret, with a splash of Ruby Cabernet. Enjoy with barbecue, Tex-Mex, and hearty pasta dishes.

Sauvignon Blanc—made from grapes of abundant varietal character and intense flavor. Careful fermentation at cold temperatures has resulted in the capture and enhancement of the fresh grassy quality of the Sauvignon Blanc fruit. A clean, crisp wine that stands up to spicy foods.

Vintner's White—made from a blend of carefully fermented premium grapes (Chenin Blanc, Sauvignon Blanc, Semillon, Riesling, Muscat Canelli, and Chardonnay). A crisp, clean taste to be enjoyed with poultry and fish.

La Buena Vida Vineyards

416 East College Street, Grapevine, Texas 76051
(817) 481-9463
www.labuenavida.com

Bobby Smith, founder of La Buena Vida Vineyards, is a pioneer in the modern-day Texas wine industry. A native of Alabama, Bobby is the son of a grape farmer. In 1972, while in family practice in Arlington, he fulfilled his longtime desire to plant a vineyard. He bought an abandoned dairy farm in Springtown, Parker County, a location with the perfect soil and climate. Today La Buena Vida is one of the state's oldest and most re- spected wineries, and the entire vineyard is farmed with or- ganic techniques. Bobby Smith has also been instrumental in bringing about the enactment of many laws that have allowed the Texas wine industry to grow and prosper.

The winery's tasting room is located in Grapevine near the Dallas–Fort Worth International Airport. Situated in a charming limestone church in the historic district, La Buena Vida takes pride in being Grapevine's first winery and tasting room. An antique tasting bar, native Texas gardens, an herb garden, fountains, and a winery museum are featured, along with a friendly and knowledgeable staff. Wine 101, a course in wine appreciation, is taught in the winter months.

La Buena Vida Vineyards produces tables wines under the brands Springtown, Grapevine, and La Buena Vida. Champagne is produced under the brand Smith Estate. The ports are named after a local stream near the vineyard, Walnut Creek Cellars. Two specialty wines, Texmas Blush, a holiday favorite, and Scarborough Mead, a wine made from honey, are popular choices.

Tasting Notes

SPRINGTOWN

Cabernet Sauvignon—75% Cabernet Sauvignon and 25% Merlot. Aged in American oak, heavy toast, yielding rich flavors to the mouth with a lingering black pepper finish.

Chardonnay—a full-bodied, fruity white wine with a round mouth feel. Aged in half American oak and half French oak barrels with malolactic fermentation, yielding a buttery, vanilla finish. Great with herbed cream sauces over chicken.

Merlot l'elegance—a beautiful blush wine produced from the juice of the Merlot grape and fermented cold to retain the fresh, fruity flavors. Soft, off-dry with a velvet finish. Great with anything spicy or just poolside sipping.

Merlot—80% Merlot and 20% Cabernet Sauvignon. Aged in half American oak and half French oak, with a berry nose. Cap management by gentle shower effect, providing soft tannins and intense hue. Will age well for 10 to 20 years.

Mist—a beautiful mix of Zinfandel, Cabernet Sauvignon, Merlot, Chardonnay, and Chenin Blanc. Fermented in stainless steel tanks, providing crispness and spritz. Great for Texas spicy foods.

Muscat Canelli—the beautiful, floral nose of this wine is very characteristic of this grape. Honeysuckle sweetness and round mouth feel, perfect for spicy foods, fruits, and dessert.

Muscat Dulce—sweet, floral Muscat Canelli fortified with brandy; smooth, rich texture. Try this on the veranda either after dinner on a summer night with a light dessert or as an aperitif over ice with an orange slice.

Red (NV)—a blend of Cabernet Sauvignon, Cabernet Franc, and Merlot. A Bordeaux-style wine that is perfect for pasta with light sauces.

Sauvignon Blanc—a good fruity wine with a nose of herbs and grass. Pairs well with salmon or wild game with mango salsa.

WALNUT CREEK CELLARS

Reserve Port—a mature wine made from the Chambourcin grape, a French-American hybrid, and fortified with brandy. Immense, delightfully overwhelming nutty flavor that calls for walnuts, pecans, and English Stilton cheese.

Vida del Sol Port (NV)—rich berry flavors with lush mouth feel; a tawny port that is perfect with chocolate. Blended from Cabernet Sauvignon and Merlot, fortified with brandy.

Vintage Port—made from the Tinta Madeira grape, a true Portuguese variety. Rich with berry flavors. Winner of six international medals in tastings of ports from all over the United States and Portugal. Try this fortified wine with chocolate and raspberries.

SPECIALTY WINE

Scarborough Mead—produced from Texas honey. A great accompaniment for spicy foods and also great to cook with.

LLANO ESTACADO WINERY

Farm Road 1585, Lubbock, Texas 79404
(806) 745-2258
www.llanowine.com

Since its inception in 1976, the simple mission of Llano Estacado has been to embody the fabulous potential of Texas wines. Llano Estacado began as the passion of a group of Texas investors, including a Texas Tech horticulturist and chemist who believed West Texas held the potential to become a source of quality wine grapes. To convince local farmers to invest in vineyards and experiment in growing grapes, Llano Estacado's original winemaking facility was constructed. The construction of the new winery encouraged new grape growers, and vineyards began to dot the Texas High Plains. Llano Estacado planted its first vineyard in 1978. It initially released 1,300 cases of wine.

In 1983 Llano Estacado replaced all its equipment, installing state-of-the-art tanks, crushers, and other equipment in order to continue to expand and make better wines. As more and more wines were produced, word spread that a small, upstart winery in West Texas was producing quality wine. Texans took to the venture and by 1985 production had increased to 15,000 cases. It was in 1986 that Llano made a real mark on the American wine scene when it walked away from the prestigious San Francisco Fair Wine Competition with a Double Gold award for its 1984 Chardonnay.

By 1993 Llano Estacado had increased its production to over 50,000 cases of wine. In this same year, Greg Bruni, an experienced and award-winning California winemaker, was persuaded by the company to relocate to Lubbock and take over winemaking responsibilities as Vice President of Winemaking. In 1997 Llano embarked on an ambitious project to expand the winery to accommodate production of 125,000 cases.

TASTING NOTES

Cabernet Sauvignon, Signature Red Meritage, and Cellar Select Cabernet Sauvignon—these wines are almost interchangeable. Generally speaking, the Cellar Select Cabernet will be richer. Signature Red is a blend of Cabernet Sauvignon, Merlot, and Cabernet Franc. It has a very nice peppercorn aroma with a soft tannic structure. Cabernet Sauvignon from the High Plains is similar in many ways to fine Chilean Cabernets. Cassis-cherry fruit, Spanish cedar tones, moderate tannin level, not astringent or bitter. Rounder feeling in mouth, complex, and ready to drink and enjoy as compared to heavy-bodied wines needing "bottle age" to develop. The main difference between the two Cabernets is the amount of oak aging (16 months for Cellar Select versus 12 months); the Cellar Select is richer and heavier-bodied. Good with peppercorns, smoked meats, chocolate, wild game meats, and domestic game (more fat), lamb, and wild turkey.

Cellar Select Chardonnay—centered around pear fruit, with a much more complex aroma and bouquet and mouth structure. Aged 10 months in French oak with malolactic fermentation, which contributes to the complexity of the aroma and bouquet and adds toasty oak and tannic structure to mouth flavor. Good with saffron, almonds, cumin, tarragon, ripe cheese, citrus, and pork loin herb rubs.

Chardonnay—an "everyday" Chardonnay centered on pear fruit in the aroma and bouquet. The fruit follows in the mouth. Very little oak aging. Very bright fruit when paired with palate-rich sauces containing lemon, ginger, and tomato.

Chenin Blanc—aroma and bouquet center on green-fleshed melons, very fruity. The melon fruit carries into the mouth with a nice balance of acid. The 2.5% residual sugar makes this wine perfect to put out the fire of hot spicy dishes. Good with all fresh fruit.

Passionelle, Texas Rhone-Style Red—a blend of three Rhone varieties: Carignane, Syrah, and Viognier. Very spicy in aroma and bouquet with cinnamon and nutmeg. Much of the spice is derived from the Carignane/Syrah components. Light-bodied, very fruity on the palate (blackberry), noticeable overtones of oak. Pairs well with anything from the spicy Mexican Southwest, Italian foods, light game or fowl. Good with cinnamon, chocolate, range spices, nuts and berries, dry cheese.

Sauvignon Blanc—a focus on fruit aroma and bouquet, with flavors ranging more toward green olive, celery-dill, and citrus. A dry wine, with a crisp, refreshing acid component. Complementary pairing with most range herbs (dill, sage, etc.). Great with fresh chilies with green pepper flavor. Good with citrus, black pepper, and seafood/herb combinations; acid balance is nice with fatty fish and shellfish.

Signature White—a fun food wine, a blend of Chenin Blanc, Sauvignon Blanc, and Chardonnay. The 0.5% residual sugar makes it great with hot spicy foods. The heritage of the Sauvignon Blanc and Chenin Blanc fruit results in a very appealing southwestern food wine. Great with fish prepared and cooked almost any way—with fresh, fleshy chilies, dried chilies, range herbs. Especially good with garlic, lime, citrus, cilantro.

Zinfandel—currant jam in the aroma and bouquet. Complex American oak, toasty in mouth. Medium-bodied, not astringent or bitter. A great all-around wine. Good with dill, sage, hearty meat sauces, game (domestic and wild), smoked meat and fish, dark meat fowl, ripe cheeses.

Messina Hof Wine Cellars

4545 Old Reliance Road, Bryan, Texas 77808
(979) 778-9463
www.messinahof.com

Founded by Paul and Merrill Bonarrigo in 1977, Messina Hof was named after their respective ancestral homelands. Paul's family is from Messina, Sicily, and Merrill's family is from Hof, Germany.

In Paul's family, the first-born male is always named Paul, and at the age of 16, he begins to learn the 200-year-old family tradition of winemaking. Thus, during the reign of Napoleon, Paul Bonarrigo's ancestors were making award-winning wines. Those skills have been passed down to each generation. The newest family winemaker, Paul Mitchell Bonarrigo, is already involved in the day-to-day operations of Messina Hof and has now begun his five-year apprenticeship in learning the art of winemaking.

In 1983, Messina Hof's first year of producing commercial wines, the Bonarrigos produced 1,300 gallons, all from grapevines on their 100-acre estate, of which 42 acres are planted in vines. Now Messina Hof produces 265,000 gallons of wine per year.

Tasting Notes

Angel Late Harvest Johannesburg Riesling—a delectable dessert wine. Crisp and sweet with incredible nectar aromas. Delicious by itself but perfect paired with fruit, cheesecakes, and light chocolate dishes.

Barrel Reserve Cabernet Sauvignon—a classically rich and full-bodied Bordeaux-style red with luscious berry flavors and hints of oak. Perfect with beef, lamb, venison, and rich and spicy sauces.

Barrel Reserve Chardonnay—aged and fermented in French oak barrels. Crisp and soft, yet rich, creamy, and buttery. Great with lobster, shrimp, chicken, turkey, and rich buttery sauces.

Barrel Reserve Merlot—known for its berry aromas and silky smooth elegance. A blend of Merlot and Cabernet Sauvignon that is great with beef, lamb, pizza, and rich, red sauces.

Barrel Reserve Pinot Noir—an earthy Burgundian red. Very fruity and aged in French and American oak casks. Great with light meats, pasta, and grilled seafood.

Barrel Reserve Sauvignon Blanc—aged in small French oak casks. Like its French counterparts, this wine is surprisingly crisp, clean, and herbal. Brings out the best in seafood, especially Gulf Coast seafood. Great with chicken, pasta, and other light dishes. Serve chilled at 45 degrees.

Barrel Reserve Shiraz—a hearty, complex, full-bodied red wine. Perfect with wild game, beef, lamb, and tomato sauces. Serve at room temperature.

Barrel Reserve "Tex-Zin" Zinfandel—a Texas-size Zinfandel; big and bold, yet soft and full of berries. Perfectly aged in American oak barrels. Wonderful with almost any meal, but particularly good with Texas beef, game, and zesty red sauces.

Chenin Blanc—very fruity and slightly sweet with floral aromas. Pairs perfectly with Cajun and other spicy seafood and chicken dishes, strong-flavored cheeses, and low-fat dishes. Serve well chilled.

Gamay Beaujolais—the perfect red wine for white-wine palates. Lighter than most reds, this Gamay is soft, light, and fruity with just a hint of sweetness. Delicious with hamburgers, barbecue, or pork chops. Serve at 60 degrees for best flavor.

Gewürztraminer—slightly sweet, crisp, and fruity with spicy flavors and floral aromas. Great with Asian or spicy foods, seafood, and poultry; or delicious by itself. Serve chilled at 45 degrees.

Johannesburg Riesling—fresh and delicate. Great with many cuisines, particularly German or Asian dishes, even Tex-Mex.

Mama Rosa Rosé—semi-sweet with hints of cherries and raspberries. A very smooth, light wine. Great with spice.

Muscat Canelli—an excitingly fruity and crisp wine with just a touch of sweetness. Wonderful by itself but also great with seafood, spicy dishes, pasta, and German or Asian dishes.

Pinot Grigio—a crisp, clean wine and a great warm-weather wine. Wonderful floral and citrus aromas that complement light cheeses, fish, poultry, and lemony sauces. Serve chilled at 45 degrees.

Private Reserve Chardonnay—a very high-quality Chardonnay. Dry, crisp, and creamy with a wonderful balance of fruit and oak. Great with seafood, poultry, and buttery sauces.

White Zinfandel—fruity and spicy, yet slightly sweet. Great with light meats and cheeses, melon, shrimp, pasta, and tomato sauces. Serve slightly chilled.

Sister Creek Vineyards

1142 Sisterdale Road (F.M. 1376)
Sisterdale, Texas 78006
(830) 324-6704 or (830) 324-6682

Sister Creek Vineyards is located in the heart of the Texas Hill Country in Sisterdale (population 25). The traditional French vines (Chardonnay, Pinot Noir, Cabernet Sauvignon, Cabernet Franc, and Merlot) are planted in the vineyard, which is located between the cypress-lined East and West Sister Creeks.

A century-old cotton gin, built in 1885 by German settlers, has been restored to house the winery and tasting room. Some of the cotton gin equipment is still present in the tasting room. French (Bordeaux and Burgundy) winemaking techniques are employed. Wines are aged in French oak barrels. Minimum filtration and fining allows the wines to retain their fullest flavors. In addition to French-style wines, an Italian-style Muscat Canelli is also produced.

Perhaps the most notable aspect of winemaking at Sister Creek is the attitude toward ripeness. Sister Creek has set its sights on leaner French prototypes. The winemaker, Danny Hernandez, was stationed in Germany during his military career, and there he took an interest in the local wines. With additional study and hard work, he now discusses vineyard and winemaking procedures with a depth of understanding rare even to a winery veteran.

The five acres that constitute the vineyard were originally planted on the California model of 8-by-12-foot spacing. This was converted to the 4-by-12-foot model, allowing 800 vines per acre.

The vineyards were planted in 1985 and in 1988 the winery was opened to the public. Its growth continues to increase annually.

Tasting Notes

Cabernet Sauvignon Blend—40% Cabernet Sauvignon, 45% Merlot, and 15% Petite Syrah. Red Meritage French Bordeaux. Blended and lightly filtered before bottling. Aged 14 months in oak barrels. Rich black currant, blackberry, black cherry, spicy, vanilla, and toasty flavors.

Cabernet Sauvignon—a red Meritage French Bordeaux. Aged separately in traditional 60-gallon French and American oak barrels for 18 months. Blended and lightly filtered before bottling. Rich black currant, blackberry, vanilla, and toasty flavors.

Chardonnay—a French white Burgundy. Fermented in stainless steel tanks. No secondary malolactic fermentation. Pleasant, clean, and medium-bodied with pear, tropical, and honey flavors.

Merlot—red French Bordeaux. Lightly filtered before bottling. Aged 13 months in oak barrels. Smoky, blackberry, black cherry, bell pepper, vanilla, and toast flavors.

Muscat Canelli—white Italian-style wine fermented and aged in stainless steel tanks. Chilled and filtered to retain residual sugar of 7%. Slightly carbonated with carbon dioxide to add crispness and spritz. Sweet and balanced with intense peach, apricot, and floral aromas.

Pinot Noir—red French Burgundy. Lightly filtered before bottling. Aged 14 months in oak barrels. Nutmeg and cherry-like aromas, raspberry, cinnamon, vanilla, and toast.

Spicewood Vineyards

Spicewood, Texas 78669
(830) 693-5328

Spicewood Vineyards is located 35 miles north of Austin in the middle of nowhere, so be sure to call for directions. The winery is built on a hillside 900 feet above sea level and has 17.5 acres of planted vineyards, terraced down the hill in front of the winery. Owned by Ed and Madeleine Manigold, the winery was bonded in 1995 and has since been dedicated to producing quality Hill Country wines.

Tasting Notes

Cabernet Claret—a sweet red, oak-aged in barrels for 10 months. Great with Texas brisket.

Cabernet Sauvignon—produced by the sur lie method and aged in French oak for 18 months. Pairs well with dishes containing cumin, which brings out the spiciness of the wine.

Chardonnay—an unfiltered wine that has won several awards since its release, including the Grand Harvest Award and a silver medal in the Lone Star Competition in 1996. Pairs well with grilled foods with spices and butter.

Merlot—produced by the sur lie method and aged in French oak for 18 months. Wonderful with pork, sauces with cherries, and anything with cumin.

Sauvignon Blanc—the crisp acidity of the wine matches the richness of breaded fish. The natural spiciness of the wine matches spicy flavorings used in various seafood dishes.

Texas Hills Vineyard

Ranch Road 2766, Johnson City, Texas 78363
(830) 868-2321
www.texashillsvineyard.com

Texas Hills Vineyard is located east of Johnson City near Pedernales Falls State Park. The rolling hills and the soil are much like that of the hill country of the Tuscan countryside in Italy. Once Kathy and Gary Gilstrap saw the location where they established their winery, they decided to make Italian-style wines. They even planted vines that are thought of as Italian: Pinot Grigio, Sangiovese, and Moscato. They also have plantings of Cabernet Sauvignon, Chardonnay, Merlot, and Chenin Blanc. "Wines from Texas in the Style of Italy" is their motto.

Gary and Kathy are both pharmacists and owned a pharmacy in Kansas for a number of years. While traveling in Europe, they became interested in wine and winemaking and started to study wine production, applying their knowledge of chemistry and biochemistry. After much study and product testing, they decided to "look for dirt" to grow grapes to make wine. Their son, Dale Rassett, who had always loved gardening, decided to join the venture.

The vineyard is now in its sixth year of production, and the quality of the grapes improves each year. After the initial planting of 12 acres, a few more vines have been added each year. Soon there will be 35 acres in cultivation. Texas Hills Vineyards also has contracts with four vineyards in the Hill Country that grow the same grapes that they do, adding to their volume and allowing them to maintain their appellation designation. Texas Hills Vineyard advocates "sustainable organic" growing techniques, which involve using the least amount of chemicals possible. The vineyard uses turkey compost to fertilize, and weeds are removed with a mechanical device called a Clemens.

The rammed-earth method was used to construct the winery and tasting room, a unique facility that includes a cozy and inviting tasting bar as well as a gift shop.

TASTING NOTES

Cabernet Sauvignon—Cabernet Sauvignon grown in the Texas Hill Country is truly a class-act grape. A rich, full flavor with a pleasant feel in the mouth. Nice blackberry domination with a little black cherry on the finish.

Chardonnay—a dry white wine with a wonderful flavor and a nice finish. Swirl the glass to push up the buttery aroma from the fermentation in the French oak barrels, then savor the spicy touch provided by the American oak. The Chardonnay has enough fruit and character to be the perfect companion for a meal accented with rosemary.

Due Bianco ("two white")—a blend of a dry, Italian-style Pinot Grigio and estate Chardonnay. A distinctive and food-friendly wine, especially with cheese. A very popular blend in Italy and a refreshing change of pace for the white-wine lover.

Merlot—for the red-wine lover; a wine with a perfect blend of fruit and flavor. The tannins require longer aging than the other wines; aged in American oak for the first year, then up to two years in the bottle. Dark color, with the pleasant strength of a dominant plum taste.

Moscato—a great classic Italian-style wine made from the Muscat Canelli grape. Winner of four awards. Aroma of fresh pear, passion fruit, and guava. The nice acid balance makes it a good complement to spicy foods or sweet foods. Great as a dessert wine or with first courses. Try it with chocolate for a real treat.

Pinot Grigio—most of the Pinot Grigio sold in the United States comes from Italy. Most of us have tried the light, white wine, but few have had the pleasure of trying one of this caliber. A dry yet fruity white wine.

Sangiovese—wine with a beautiful color and balanced taste. Mild and pleasant to drink. The perfect wine for people who are trying to cultivate a taste for red wines. Referred to as a "Super Texan" style Tuscan wine because it is blended with 10% to 12% Cabernet or Merlot.

Tre Paesano ("three countrymen")—an estate-blended wine containing 52% Cabernet Sauvignon, 18% Merlot, and 30% Syrah with the flavors of blackberry, mulberry, plum, and white pepper. Shows each of the varietals from which it is blended.

Texas Hills Winery vineyard, Johnson City (pages 270-71); Merlot grapes at Texas Hills Winery, Johnson City (page 272); Becker Winery vintages, Stonewall (page 273); Tasting room at Texas Hills Winery, Johnson City (page 274); Batching grapes at Sister Creek Winery, Sisterdale (page 275).

BASICS

BEURRE MANIÉ

My kitchens, both at work and at home, are never without this magic French thickener (*beurre manié* means "kneaded butter"). To make beurre manié, combine equal portions, by volume, of softened unsalted butter and all-purpose flour in the work bowl of a food processor fitted with a steel blade. Process until mixture is smooth and no unblended traces of flour remain. Scrape down the side of the bowl as needed. Form the paste into cylinders, wrap in plastic wrap, and freeze. When you need to thicken a sauce or a soup, bring the liquid to a boil. Cut off about a tablespoon of the frozen beurre manié and vigorously stir it into the rapidly boiling liquid. Add additional pieces until the desired consistency is reached. Beurre manié is also handy for fixing broken sauces or soups with broken roux. It cannot, however, salvage broken emulsified egg-based sauces like hollandaise or Cajun-style (gumbo) roux.

BLISTERING CHILIES

You can use any one of several methods to blister or roast chilies, but all of them require the use of a flame or another source of very high heat. Be very cautious when blistering chilies to avoid a nasty burn.

Place the chilies directly over the flame of a gas burner or light the gas grill and turn the temperature control to high. (Or turn on the broiler of an electric oven and set the rack about 3 to 4 inches below heat source. There are also special culinary blowtorches available at gourmet shops for this purpose.) Cook, turning often with chef's tongs, until the chilies are blackened and blistered all over. Place the well-blistered chilies in a metal bowl and seal the top with plastic wrap. Set aside for about 20 minutes, or until the chilies are cool enough to handle comfortably, then peel off all traces of the blistered skin. Remove and discard the veins and seeds from inside the chili. Use as directed in recipe.

CREMA FRESCA

The equivalent of crème fraîche, crema fresca is often used in modern Texas and Mexican cooking, either alone or as a base sauce with various flavorings. It provides a cooling countertaste to the spice of chilies. It can be found in Mexican markets in the southern portion of the state as well as in H-E-B and Fiesta markets all over the state. Crema fresca is also very easy to make. When well chilled, it can be whipped and used in desserts.

1 cup heavy whipping cream
1 tablespoon buttermilk

Heat the whipping cream over medium heat until warm, about 70 degrees, but no higher. Remove from heat and transfer to clean storage container. Whisk in the buttermilk. Cover the container with a clean cloth and set aside in a warm place (no higher than 80 degrees) for 24 hours. The crema fresca should be slightly thinner than sour cream. Chill, tightly covered, before using. May be refrigerated for up to one week.

CRÈME FRAÎCHE

Crème fraîche is acidulated (thickened) cow's milk cream that has been allowed to "incubate" briefly until it achieves a velvety thickness and rich, tangy taste. Crème fraîche is available from speciality markets, or you can culture your own. It will keep for about a week in the refrigerator.

1 cup whipping cream
1 tablespoon sour cream

Whisk the sour cream into the whipping cream in a non-aluminum bowl. Cover the bowl with plastic wrap and set aside. Keep the temperature between 78 and 80 degrees. Do not expose it to higher temperatures. Allow the mixture to sit unrefrigerated for 24 hours before using. Refrigerate until needed.

POACHING EGGS

Poaching the perfect egg is easy if you know a few simple guidelines. First start with eggs at room temperature. Use eggs that are very fresh. The white of an egg becomes looser as the egg ages and it will not poach well. Fill a deep skillet about ⅔ full of water. Add 1 tablespoon of vinegar per quart of water used. Do not add salt to the water. Salt will toughen the egg whites.

Bring the water to a simmer and break an egg into the water. Cook the egg for 3 minutes, or just until the white is firm. Remove egg carefully with a slotted spoon. If any of the white has made thread-like strings on the edges, use a large round cutter to cut the egg into a perfect round shape.

A restaurant trick for poaching large quantities of eggs is to poach them for 2 minutes, then remove the eggs to an ice-water bath. Leave the poaching water simmering. When the eggs are needed, simply spoon out as many as you need and poach them for the final 1 minute. Serve hot.

SELECTING FISH AND SEAFOOD

FISH

First and foremost, buy only the freshest! Select from whole fish whenever possible and have the market fillet your selection, if desired. Look for eyes that are clear and bulging, not cloudy and sunken. The gills should be bright red. The skin should be shiny and moist but never slimy to the touch. Avoid fish with dull, dry skin. A most reliable test for freshness is the sniff test. If it smells overtly "fishy," it's not fresh. Really fresh fish has a slight odor, which I call "faintly marine." If you are choosing from fish fillets, select those that feel firm when pressed with a fingertip, not soft and mushy. Avoid overly dry fillets. If you purchase fresh fish and don't get around to cooking it until it has begun to smell a bit over the hill, try soaking it in whole milk for about an hour. This simple trick will often take away the offensive odor. But don't leave the fish in the milk for longer than about an hour. The lactic acid in the milk acts as a tenderizer, and fish don't need tenderizing. The connective tissue will break down and the fish will fall apart when you cook it.

SCALLOPS

Scallops should be cream- or ivory-colored, never grayish. They should be slightly rounded with smooth edges and should never have a "stamped-out" appearance. Scallops have a very delicate, slightly sweetish aroma and taste. They should be cooked very briefly, only until they lose their translucency. Scallops are equally delicious sautéed, broiled, fried, or skewered and grilled. Overcooking makes them rubbery and unpleasantly chewy. Overcooking is the reason many people think they don't like scallops! Grilled scallops are positively divine. When purchasing scallops to grill, seek out the large ones, designated as "U-10's" in the fish markets.

SHRIMP

When buying fresh shrimp, look for those that are light gray in color and firm-fleshed and sweet-smelling. Fresh shrimp should never have an ammonia odor, which indicates decomposition. If you buy shrimp with heads on, the heads should be firmly attached, not dried out. If you purchase shrimp with their heads, which contain the fat, cook them the same day you purchase them because they deteriorate much more quickly than do those with the heads removed. Head-on shrimp are best for boiling because the fat is also very tasty. Whatever the cooking method, be sure that you don't overcook them. As soon as their flesh turns opaque throughout with a coral tint on the outside, they are done. Overcooking makes them tough and chewy. Extreme overcooking turns them to mush.

OYSTERS

When purchasing oysters in the shells, be sure they're alive. The shell should be tightly closed or close rapidly if tapped. When you open an oyster, it should be shiny and full of its viscous liquor. If the oyster is dry, with no liquor present, discard it. If there is an off-odor, don't use the oyster. When buying shucked oysters, be sure they're packed in their own liquor, which should be clear and viscous, never cloudy or thin and runny. The oysters and liquor should have a pleasant aroma. The oyster itself should be plump and a light, creamy tan.

CRABS

When buying whole blue crabs, be sure they are alive. If they are dead when you cook them, they will have very little meat and a strong, unpleasant taste. Crabs start to decompose rapidly the longer they are held out of water, literally consuming their own flesh. Live, fresh crabs should have only that "faintly marine" aroma.

SEASONED FLOUR FOR FRYING

The art of frying food is not necessarily a simple one. Two of the most important factors in frying are the type of oil used and its temperature. Select an oil with a mild flavor, such as canola or peanut oil. Both of these oils also have high smoking points, so you can fry safely with little fear of combustion. For best results, use a fryer with a thermostat so you can regulate the temperature of the oil, which must remain constant. A good temperature for deep-frying is 350 degrees. Be careful not to crowd the pan, or the temperature of the oil will plummet. When this happens, the delicate barrier of the breading or batter does not get crisp enough quickly enough. Oil seeps in through the breading and the juices of the food seep out. The result is a greasy, limp, and generally tasteless product.

The breading process is also important. Most professional chefs use a three-step breading process. First coat the food with seasoned flour. (Be sure to shake off all excess flour.) Next dip it in an egg wash made by beating 3 eggs into 4 or 5 cups of milk. Finally, dredge the food in a final coating, which can be seasoned cornmeal, dry breadcrumbs, Japanese (panko) breadcrumbs, or even the seasoned flour again. The choice of the final breading should be one compatible with the food being breaded. If you are using a beer or tempura-style batter on the food, omit the egg wash. Simply start with the seasoned flour, shake off all excess, and then dip the food in the batter.

The following recipe makes a large quantity, but it's convenient to have on hand. After using the flour, you can sift it through a fine strainer and reuse it.

2½ pounds all-purpose flour

2 tablespoons each of salt and finely ground black pepper

2 tablespoons red (cayenne) pepper

2 tablespoons granulated onion

2 tablespoons granulated garlic

2 tablespoons Hungarian (sweet) paprika

Place flour in a large bowl. Add all seasonings; whisk to blend well, distributing seasonings evenly throughout flour. Store in a zip-sealing bag.

ROASTING GARLIC

Garlic is one of nature's finest ingredients. The flavor is bold and assertive. But there's a way to make it even better. Roasting whole garlic cloves will take away some of the bite and mellow out the flavor. In fact, the roasted cloves taste very much like toasted nuts. To roast garlic, slice the top ⅜-inch off a whole head of garlic. Place it in a small baking dish and drizzle olive oil over the top. Salt and pepper the garlic. Cover the dish with aluminum foil and roast at 350 degrees for about 45 minutes, or until the cloves are lightly browned and very soft. Set aside to cool. To use the garlic, pull off the desired number of cloves and simply squeeze the bottom of the clove. The pulpy garlic should squeeze out easily. A great way to serve hot, homemade bread is to serve 3 or 4 roasted garlic cloves with some olive oil to each guest. Squeeze the garlic pulp onto the bread slices and dip the slices in the olive oil.

GAS GRILLS VERSUS CHARCOAL GRILLS

In Texas cookery the selection of outdoor cookers is not only a serious subject; it's also big business. The state is dotted with shops which sell only outdoor cookers and their attendant paraphernalia. First, let me clarify the difference between "barbecue pits" and "grills." A barbecue pit is a large outdoor cooker that generally has a separate firebox in which a large wood fire is built and an attached chamber where the meat is cooked slowly over a long period of time by the indirect heat and smoke from the firebox. A grill, either gas or charcoal, is a smaller unit on which the food is cooked over a direct heat source for shorter periods. Gas grills are considerably more expensive than charcoal grills. For grilling, I generally prefer a gas grill, but a charcoal-fired grill may be substituted in any of my recipes. Charcoal is made from wood and will add the dimension of wood taste to your food. Often this taste is desirable, as in grilled hamburgers. The bottom line is that the choice is a personal one.

MEASURING CUPS

When measuring ingredients, it is important to use the proper type of measuring cup. One type is for measuring dry ingredients, such as flour and sugar. The other is for measuring wet ingredients, such as water, cream, or stock. The dry measuring cups can be made of metal, plastic, or glass and come in various sizes, ranging from 1 cup to several quarts. Dry measuring cups, on the other hand, come in sets with each graduated cup being a different size—usually ¼ cup, ⅓ cup, ½ cup, and 1 cup. If you try to measure dry ingredients in a cup meant for wet ingredients, you could get an erroneous measurement. In some delicate pastry and bread recipes, this small difference in quantity could affect the outcome of the recipe. To give yourself every advantage in preparing successful recipes, invest in both types of measuring cups.

GREAT COOKED RICE

Perfect rice consists of slightly firm grains that don't stick together, even when reheated. Here are a few handy pointers about cooking rice. Always use one part rice to two parts liquid. If you're serving rice with a chicken dish, use chicken stock as the cooking liquid, beef stock for a beef dish, and so on. Add a little salt and melted butter to the cooking liquid. When you come across a recipe that calls for a certain amount of cooked rice and you need to know how much raw rice to start with, use this simple formula: divide the amount of cooked rice indicated in the recipe by three. This will give you the amount of raw rice that you need. The remaining portion will be your liquid. For example, if a recipe calls for 6 cups of cooked rice, you'll need 2 cups of raw rice and 4 cups of liquid. In other words, 1 cup of raw rice produces 3 cups of cooked rice.

This recipe will give perfect results in cooking rice. However, when rice is used in certain dishes like jambalayas, Mexican-style rices, or Spanish paella, the rice is actually sautéed in its raw state. This process reduces the amount of liquid that the rice can absorb. Therefore, in recipes for those dishes, a lesser quantity of liquid is specified.

℞ **Makes 3 cups.**

2 cups water or stock

1 tablespoon unsalted butter

½ teaspoon salt

1 cup long-grain white rice

Combine the liquid, butter, and salt in a heavy, 2-quart saucepan over high heat. Bring to a full boil, and then stir in the rice. Cover the pan and reduce heat to the lowest setting. Set a timer for exactly 15 minutes. When the timer goes off, transfer the rice to a serving dish and cover until ready to serve, even if there is still a small portion of liquid remaining. By the time you have put the rest of the meal together, the rice will be perfect.

Use the same procedure for brown rice, but increase cooking time to 45 minutes. Allow 50 minutes for wild rice. The aromatic strains of rice—such as basmati, Texmati, pecan rice, popcorn rice, jasmine rice—are actually long-grain white rice strains. They should be cooked the same as plain long-grain white rice.

GUMBO ROUX

To make really good gumbo, one must start with a really good roux. A real roux—not the stuff in a jar or dried in a package, no browning the flour in the oven, or, heaven forbid, cooking roux in the microwave. You have to invest some sweat equity to make a real roux. The choice of fat is a personal one. Of course, the Cajuns, who invented gumbo, use lard. It will produce a roux with the best taste. If you just can't bear the saturated fat content, then you can substitute solid vegetable shortening or canola oil. (Coconut oil, which is used in most convenience foods and fast foods, contains 87 percent saturated fat, while pure pork lard contains only 42 percent.) When you're considering sacrificing the great taste of lard, keep in mind that gumbo is a lot of work. I personally want the optimum amount of taste when I expend that much effort.

My advice on the tedious process of making roux is to get your flour and fat measured, take the phone off the hook (because once you start a roux, you can't stop whisking for even a second), pull a tall stool up to the stove, and pour yourself a nice glass of wine—then whisk away. If you wish to increase or decrease the amount of roux you make, always use equal portions (by volume) of fat and flour.

Makes 3 cups.

3 cups lard or vegetable shortening
3 cups all-purpose flour

Melt the shortening or lard in a large, deep skillet over medium heat. When the fat is hot, add the flour all at once and whisk rapidly to form a smooth paste. Continue to whisk constantly until the roux reaches a deep mahogany color, about 30 to 45 minutes. *Do not stop whisking even for a second!*

As the roux gets darker, it will become thicker. As soon as it reaches the proper color, you may use the roux at once, or store it in the refrigerator or freezer for later use. To store the roux, turn it out into a large metal bowl set on a heatproof surface. Continue to stir the roux as it is cooling to prevent separation of fat and flour. When the roux is completely cool and solidified, it may be stored.

STOCKS

These full, robust-flavored stocks are what I like to use in the two-fisted cuisine of Texas. If you make stocks from scratch, it is important to give as much time and thought to their preparation as you do to the finished dish itself. The stocks freeze well, so freeze them in the container sizes that you will most often use. After you make the stock and strain it, transfer it to clean containers. Put the containers in ice-water baths to cool them as rapidly as possible. As soon as they are cold, freeze at once. Here are a few additional tips for making stock:

- Never use internal organs such as liver, hearts, or kidneys. They contain blood, which gives stock a very strong, unpleasant taste.
- Don't make stock on a day when you plan to have guests. Fat from the bones will smoke during browning and produce a strong smell.
- Bring your stock to a full boil and skim the surface before adding your seasonings so that you don't skim them away.
- Remove all traces of fat after stock is chilled and fat has solidified on the surface. Stock stored with fat remaining in it will have a fatty, oily taste. Fat will also become rancid quickly, rendering the stock unusable.
- To avoid the risk of bacterial growth, do not leave prepared stock in the refrigerator longer than two days. Freeze for longer storage. Do not freeze stocks longer than three months. After that length of time, poultry and beef stocks begin to lose their flavor, and the seafood stocks get "fishier."
- When preparing seafood stock, remove the heads of any fish carcasses and rinse the entire bony carcass under running water to remove every last trace of blood from the bones. Use only lean, non-oily fish. Avoid all deep-sea fish when making stock.
- When straining stocks, be sure to press firmly on the bones and vegetables to release all their intense flavors.
- If you use fresh herbs, save all your herb stems—even those of parsley—in a bag in the freezer and use them for making stocks. They contain even more flavor than the leaves.

CHICKEN STOCK

Makes about 8 quarts.

10 to 12 pounds uncooked mixed poultry bones and carcasses (chicken, turkey, duck, game hen, quail, and dove)
2 large carrots, coarsely chopped

2 large onions, unpeeled, coarsely chopped

1 large leek, stem and green top discarded, halved lengthwise and washed under running water, then coarsely chopped

2 celery stalks with leafy tops, coarsely chopped

6 flat-leaf parsley sprigs

6 fresh thyme sprigs

3 fresh bay leaves

Canola oil

2 teaspoons whole black peppercorns

Preheat oven to 425 degrees. Place all bones and carcasses in a large roasting pan. Scatter the vegetables and herbs over them. Add about 3 tablespoons of canola oil and toss the bones and vegetables with your hands to coat well. Brown in preheated oven until very dark, but *not burned*, turning often, or about 1 hour. Place the browned bones in a 20-quart stockpot. Pour off all fat from the roasting pan. Place the pan on the burner over high heat. Add two cups of water to deglaze the pan, scraping up all browned bits of meat glaze from the bottom of the pan with a flat-edged spatula. Add to the stockpot. Add enough cold water to the stockpot to completely cover the bones and vegetables by about 2 inches. Bring to a rapid boil; skim off the gray foam that rises to the surface. Continue to boil and skim until no more of the foam appears.

Reduce heat to a low simmer and add the black peppercorns. Simmer for 8 hours. Skim the fat from the surface often. Strain the stock through a fine strainer, pressing down on the bones and vegetables to release all flavors. Strain the stock two more times. Pour into shallow pans and cool quickly over ice-water baths. Refrigerate until well chilled. Remove all fat from surface. Use as directed in recipe or freeze for up to three months.

SEAFOOD STOCK

Use this stock with any recipe in the book that calls for fish or seafood stock.

❧ **Makes about 10 quarts.**

¼ cup canola oil

3 large live blue crabs

10 pounds mixed shellfish shells and fish carcasses and bones, skinned

5 unpeeled onions, quartered

1 tablespoon whole cloves

2 celery stalks, coarsely chopped

5 medium unpeeled garlic cloves, crushed

1 large lemon, sliced

1 3-ounce box Zatarin's Shrimp and Crab Boil in bag

1 tablespoon whole black peppercorns

Heat the canola oil in a heavy 20-quart saucepan over medium-high heat. When the oil is very hot, add the live crabs and sauté until they turn bright orange. Remove the pan from the heat and add the remaining ingredients. Add cold water to cover the bones, shellfish, and vegetables by 2 inches. Bring the stock to a rapid boil. Skim off the gray foam that rises to the surface. Continue to boil the stock until until no more foam appears. Lower heat to a simmer and cook the stock for 3 hours. Strain through a fine strainer, pressing down on bones and shellfish to extract every drop of flavor. Discard bones, shellfish, and vegetables. Strain the stock two more times. Pour the stock into shallow containers and chill quickly over ice-water baths. Refrigerate to chill completely. Use as directed in recipe or freeze for up to three months.

BEEF STOCK

❧ **Makes about 10 quarts.**

8 pounds beef bones and knuckles

4 pounds veal shoulder and shanks

5 pig's feet, sliced in half

2 pounds pork neck bones

6 unpeeled onions, coarsely chopped

3 carrots, coarsely chopped

3 celery stalks, coarsely chopped

6 fresh thyme sprigs

3 fresh bay leaves

6 flat-leaf parsley sprigs

Canola oil

1 6-ounce can tomato paste

1 tablespoon whole black peppercorns

Preheat oven to 425 degrees. Place all bones and meats in a large roasting pan. Add vegetables and herbs. Drizzle about 3 tablespoons of canola oil over the bones, meats, and vegetables. Toss with your hands to distribute the oil. Place pan in preheated oven and roast the bones, meats, and vegetables until well browned, turning often, about 1 hour. *Do not burn the bones.* Transfer contents of pan, except fat, to a 20-quart stockpot. Set aside. Drain off all fat from the roasting pan and place pan on a burner over high heat. Add 2 cups of water to deglaze the pan. Use a metal spatula to scrape up all the browned bits of meat glaze from the bottom of the pan. Pour the browned water into the stockpot. Add the tomato paste and cold water to cover the bones by about 2 inches. Bring the stock to a rapid boil. Skim off the gray foam that rises to the surface. Add peppercorns. Continue to boil the stock until no more foam appears. Lower heat and simmer the stock for 10 to 12 hours. Skim the fat from the surface of the stock often. Strain the stock through a fine strainer, pressing down on the bones and vegetables to extract all the flavor. Strain the stock two more times. Pour into shallow pans and cool over ice-water baths until cool. Refrigerate until well chilled. Remove and discard any fat that congeals on the surface. Use as directed in recipe or freeze for up to three months.

Blistering and Peeling Tomatoes

Blistering

Often a recipe will call for smoked or "blistered" tomatoes. This process adds an exciting, intensely tomato taste to the dish. Blister tomatoes by placing them directly on the burner over a gas flame (or use a gas grill). Cook the tomatoes, turning them often, until skins are completely black and charred. Place the tomatoes in a bowl and cover the bowl with plastic wrap. When the tomatoes are cool enough to handle, peel off and discard the charred skins.

Peeling

To peel tomatoes easily, drop the whole tomato into a deep pot of rapidly boiling water for about 20 seconds. Remove with a slotted spoon and run under cold water. The skin will slip off quite easily.

Turkey Talk

∞ When selecting your turkey, allow 1 pound per person, if buying a turkey weighing 12 pounds or less. If buying a larger turkey, allow ½ to ¾ pound per pound.

∞ Should you buy a hen or a tom? There is virtually no difference in today's market. Modern processed turkeys reach a ready market weight quite young, which means both sexes are juicy and tender. A hen will weigh up to 14 pounds, a tom 12 pounds and up.

∞ Whether you buy a hen or a tom, the larger bird is the best buy for your money. The skeletal structure is the same in a 12-pound turkey as it is in a 16-pound turkey. The difference in weight is all meat, so think big when you buy.

∞ Fresh or frozen? With today's modern processing and flash-freezing methods, there is a very thin line of difference. If there is very little difference in price, opt for a fresh turkey. But don't pay a premium price for a "fresh" turkey expecting a miraculous difference in quality and taste. You'll be sadly disappointed and dollars poorer.

∞ When thawing the frozen turkey, thaw it slowly in the refrigerator to prevent bacterial growth. Allow one to three days for thawing, depending on the size of the bird. When pressed for time, you may place the bird, still securely sealed in its wrappings, in a large bowl under trickling *cold* water for 2 to 6 hours, depending on size. Keep the water trickling. *Never* thaw the bird at room temperature.

∞ Natural or "self-basting"? Here's where we draw the bold red line. Buy a natural bird and baste it yourself, using its own wonderful drippings. You'll have a better-tasting turkey at a much lower price.

∞ Never cook the turkey at temperatures lower than 325 degrees. Lower temperatures do not get the inside of the bird hot enough, quickly enough, to kill the growth of potentially harmful bacteria. The popular method of putting the bird in the oven to roast the night before at 200 degrees could result in the proud hostess carrying a ptomaine turkey to her holiday table.

∞ Roast the turkey at 325 degrees until a meat thermometer inserted in the center of the inner thigh muscle registers 180 to 185 degrees. To help test for doneness, move the leg. The fowl is done if the leg joints move easily. Softness of the flesh on drumstick and thigh are additional indicators of doneness.

∞ Time the roasting so that the turkey is done 20 to 30 minutes before you wish to carve it. Cover turkey loosely with foil and allow it to rest for 20 to 30 minutes before carving. The resting period allows the juices to redistribute throughout the meat.

∞ To stuff or not to stuff? Your choice, but if you do stuff, never put hot dressing inside the raw bird. In doing so, you create the perfect environment for the growth of potentially harmful bacteria. Always chill the dressing before stuffing the turkey. To be on the safe side, stuff the bird as close to the roasting time as possible and always keep the stuffed bird refrigerated until it goes into the preheated oven. Remove stuffing from cavity of turkey after roasting. Allow ½ cup of stuffing per pound to stuff the bird. Stuff loosely.

∞ After the feast is over, refrigerate leftover turkey and dressing, covered loosely, as soon as possible. Don't be tempted to leave it on the table for late-afternoon snacking lest you risk sponsoring those prolific little bacteria again. Make the evening turkey sandwiches chilled ones and zap the dressing in the microwave for that après-feast snack.

THE TEXAS COOK'S PANTRY

*B*ecause Texas Cuisine involves so many regional and ethnic types of foods, the Texas cook's pantry can be quite large. Some of the ingredients for the various types of dishes encompassed in the state's cuisine may be difficult to obtain in some areas of the state or out of state.

Following is a source guide for ingredients used in this book that may not be readily available. Wherever possible, Texas products have been listed. These are generally products produced by small companies using a "hand-made" approach. They are also products that are made by folks who have a "Texas Taste Tongue" from which they develop their products. In other words, they're especially developed to taste good in Texas Cuisine. Many of the products are available on the Internet. Website addresses are listed for these products.

APPLEWOOD-SMOKED BACON

෯ Nueske's Hillcrest Farm
Rural Route 2
P.O. Box D
Wittenberg, Wisconsin 54499-0904
1-800-392-2266

I love to use this bacon in cooking (or just to eat) because it has a pleasantly sweet, deep smoky flavor. I prefer the Nueske brand. It is available at all Central Market stores, or you may purchase it directly from Nueske's.

CHEESE

෯ The Mozzarella Company
2944 Elm Street, Dallas, Texas 75226
1-800-798-2954
e-mail: mozzco@aol.com
www.mozzco.com.

Cheeses from the Mozzarella Company may also be found at Cooke's Gourmet Market, Central Market, Whole Foods Market, Simon David, Tom Thumb, and Marty's. The product line includes fresh Texas goat cheese, fresh cow's milk mozzarella, Capriella (fresh goat's milk mozzarella), smoked scamorza (fresh mozzarella cheese smoked over pecan shells), caciotta (a delicious Texas version of Monterey Jack), cream cheese, crème fraîche, mascarpone, and goat's milk feta.

෯ Cheesemakers, Inc.
2266 South Walker Road
Cleveland, Texas 77327
www.cheesemakers.com

Products include fresh chèvre (goat's milk cheese) under the Yellow Rose Dairy and Lone Star Chevre labels and a line of Mexican cheeses under the name Jaimito. Cheesemakers cheeses can be found at Central Market, Whole Foods Market, the Kroger Signature stores, and Rice Epicurean Markets.

CHILIES

DRIED CHILIES

Many types of dried chilies are used in the recipes in this book. To use dried chilies, first soak them in hot water until they are softened and pliable. Remove the stems, seeds, and white veins on the inside of the chilies. Use as directed in the recipe. Dried chilies are available throughout Texas in ethnic and specialty markets or from the following sources:

෯ Casados Farms
P.O. Box 1269, San Juan Pueblo, New Mexico 87566
(505) 852-2433

෯ The Chili Guy
206 Frontage Road, Rio Rancho, New Mexico 87124
1-800-869-9218
fax: (505) 891-0197

෯ Josie's
1130 Agua Fria, Santa Fe, New Mexico 87501
(505) 983-6520

෯ The Spice House
1031 N. Old World Third Street
Milwaukee, Wisconsin 53203
(414) 272-0977
fax: (414) 272-1271

FRESH CHILIES

The varieties of fresh chilies used in the recipes in this book are available in most markets throughout the state. Many recipes call for blistering or roasting fresh chilies, especially red bell peppers and poblano chilies, which are always blistered before using. This roasting process sweetens and mellows the taste of the chilies, in addition to giving them a subtly smoky flavor (see "Basics" for the procedures for blistering and roasting chilies). When using fresh chilies, keep in mind that several chilies of the same type may vary in their hotness. For example, the poblano chili, which is used to make chilies rellenos, can vary dramatically from just pleasantly spicy to very spicy.

COUNTRY HAM

The best American country hams come from Smithfield County, Virginia. To purchase authentic Smithfield hams, ask your butcher to order one for you, or place an order with the following purveyors:

- E. M. Todd Company
  1-800-368-5026

- Luther Smithfield Packing Company
  1-800-444-9180

- Johnson County Country Hams (recommended)
  (919) 934-8054

FOIE GRAS

Technically, foie gras ("fat liver") is the term used for the liver from geese or ducks that have been force-fed and fattened over a period of months. Foie gras is used in the making of excellent pâtés or is sliced and simply seared. Although it is quite expensive, foie gras is one of the ultimate culinary pleasures, and there is no substitute for the real thing.

- Central Market (all locations)
  Orders taken at the meat counter.

- D'Artagnan
  280 Wilson Avenue, Newark, New Jersey 07105
  1-800-DARTAGN
  www.dartagnan.com

- Hudson Valley Foie Gras
  80 Ferndale Road, Ferndale, New York 12734
  1-877-BUY-FOIE (toll-free)
  fax: (914) 292-3009

- Sonoma Foie Gras
  P.O. Box 2007, Sonoma, California 95476
  1-800-427-4559
  fax: (707) 938-0496

GAME BIRDS

Game birds such as Muscovy duck, Pekin duck, duck breast, quail, pheasant, and free-range chickens are often available at markets such as all Central Market stores and all Whole Foods Market stores. Often you might have to ask the butcher to order these items for you. They are also available from the following sources:

- D'Artagnan
  280 Wilson Avenue, Newark, New Jersey 07105
  1-800-DARTAGN
  www.dartagnan.com

Moulard duck breast, whole Muscovy duck hens or drakes, whole Pekin ducks, Pekin duck breasts, and whole Mallard ducks; whole free-range chickens, geese, and turkeys; farm-raised quail; free-range pheasant; whole rabbits.

- Prairie Harvest Specialty Foods
  1-800-350-7166
  www.prairieharvest.com

Various game birds are available.

GAME MEATS

- Broken Arrow Ranch
  P.O. Box 530, Ingram, Texas 78025
  1-800-962-4263
  www.brokenarrowranch.com

Texas wild boar, venison (axis, sika, and fallow), antelope, and various game sausages. These free-range game meats are killed under conditions that produce no stress in the animal, resulting in a tender meat product.

- Central Market (all locations)

Butchers at the meat counter can special-order most game meats, including rattlesnake.

- D'Artagnan
  280 Wilson Avenue, Newark. New Jersey 07105
  1-800-DARTAGN
  www.dartagnan.com

Cervena venison tenderloin from New Zealand and wild boar racks from Texas.

- Prairie Harvest Specialty Foods
  P.O. Box 1013
  Spearfish, South Dakota 57783
  1-800-350-7166
  www.prairieharvest.com

Hard-to-obtain game meats and specialty foods, including boneless rattlesnake meat.

GRAINS

Couscous, polenta, quinoa, and blue cornmeal are widely available at health food stores or at specialty markets in large cities. Arrowhead Mills in Hereford, in the heart of the Panhandle Plains grain-growing region, produces some of the country's finest grains—both common and exotic. Arrowhead Mills grains are available at health food and specialty grocery stores. Specialty grains are also available from the following source:

႙ Dean & DeLuca
560 Broadway, New York, New York 10012
1-800-221-7714
www.dean-deluca.com.

HERBS

Fresh-cut herbs are available year-round in most specialty markets. The best thing, though, is to grow your own. Even if you don't have yard space, you can grow the basics (basil, thyme, sage, rosemary, flat-leaf parsley, and perhaps some dill) in pots. If you grow your own herbs, use them often. The more you cut them, the fuller they will grow. There are some really special herbs used in a few recipes in this book which you most likely can only obtain by growing them. These include lemon verbena, hoja santa, lemongrass, and Mexican oregano. (Mexican oregano is one of the few herbs which I will use in its dried form.) I am also passionate about fresh bay leaves. Sweet bay laurel is easy to grow. In fact, it grows to tree size. I've grown them in oak barrels so I could take them indoors when a serious freeze threatened. In the semi-tropical regions of South Texas, they can be grown outdoors. Here is a great source for top-quality herb plants:

႙ It's About Thyme
11726 Manchaca Road, Austin, Texas 78748
(512) 280-1192

Healthy plants, grown without harsh pesticides or chemicals, are shipped in 4-inch pots.

If you grow your own herbs, here's a method for making herb oils that you can use like fresh herbs year round. At the end of the growing season (before the first frost), harvest all remaining herbs. Remove the leaves and very tender topmost stems. Wash and dry them well, keeping the different varieties separate. Place one variety at a time in work bowl of food processor fitted with steel blade. Fill the bowl to the brim. Add just enough mild-flavored oil (I use canola oil) to make a paste. Process the herb and oil mixture until it is smooth. Label, store in plastic containers with tight-fitting lids, and freeze. When a recipe calls for the herb, spoon out just the amount you need.

All of the recipes in this book call for fresh herbs. If you absolutely can't get them, be advised that the substitution of dried for fresh is not equal. For every tablespoon of fresh herbs called for in a recipe, use only 1 teaspoon of the herb in its dried form (i.e., ⅓ the amount). When you dry a fresh substance, you sharply concentrate its flavor, making it stronger. Also note that dried herbs retain their peak flavor for only about six months.

MUSHROOMS

Wild mushrooms are available in their dried form in most specialty markets. Morels, chanterelles, Shiitake, and porcini are all wonderful woodland mushrooms and delicious when rehydrated from their dried state. For the ultimate mushroom experience, however, buy the fresh ones whenever possible. Here are two reliable sources for fresh, exotic mushrooms:

႙ Fresh and Wild
P.O. Box 2981, Vancouver, Washington 98668
1-800-222-5578
fax: (360) 737-3657

႙ Mr. Mushroom
273 Meserole Street, Brooklyn, New York 11206
1-888-821-9895 (toll-free)
www.mrmushroom.com

ORIENTAL INGREDIENTS

A number of Oriental ingredients are used in the recipes in this book: chili sauce (or paste) with garlic, Japanese (panko) breadcrumbs, wasabi (Japanese) horseradish, pickled ginger, hoisin sauce, lemongrass, and Thai or Vietnamese fish sauce. These ingredients can be found in Oriental markets as well as most specialty markets with ethnic food sections. Cut lemongrass stalks are available in the produce section of ethnic markets. Or you can plant a pot of it if you like the taste. In any recipe that calls for grated gingerroot, I prefer to use pickled ginger, the same ginger that is served with sushi or sashimi in Japanese restaurants or sushi bars. Its flavor is not as biting or harsh as that of fresh gingerroot.

RICE

The Texas rice industry, concentrated in Fort Bend, Galveston, and Brazoria counties, is becoming more specialized in the varieties of rice being grown. This diversity is in response to the demands of the "fusion-style" of cooking that is so popular in our state today. The specialty aromatic rices that were previously imported—like basmati, used in Indian cuisine; jasmine, used in Thai cuisine; and Arborio, used to make the delicious Italian risotto—are now being grown by a Texas rice producer. RiceTec, Inc., in Alvin markets its rices under the brand name RiceSelect. The company's Texmati rice is great in any recipe where you would normally use basmati rice. RiceTec also grows a Texmati brown rice. Or, if you want a more intensely basmati taste, the company produces a rice called Kasmati, which is a dead ringer for imported Indian basmati. All RiceSelect products, which are grown from non-GMO, proprietary seed, are widely available in most of the state's major markets, or you can visit RiceTec's on-line store at www.riceselect.com.

SPICES

Chef Paul's Magic Seasonings are a collection of wonderful spice blends that Chef Paul Prudhomme created many years ago to use in his landmark New Orleans restaurant, K-Paul's Louisiana Kitchen. I especially love Seafood Magic, Meat Magic, Poultry Magic, and Vegetable Magic. The spices are available in the spice sections of most grocery stores or specialty stores. Or they can be ordered direct:

○ Chef Paul Prudhomme's Magic Seasoning Blends, Inc.
   824 Distributor's Row
   Harahan, Louisiana 70123
   (504) 731-3590

The Spice House is one of my favorite food suppliers. This second-generation, family-owned spice business purchases spices from the finest sources worldwide and grinds them on the premises. The Spice House was among the first to import the wonderful Saigon cinnamon, the most aromatic of all the cinnamons. In addition to marvelous spice blends, the company also carries first-quality dried woodland mushrooms, the finest dried Mexican oregano I've found on the retail level, and many types of salt: curing salt (marketed under the name Prague Powder No. 1), kosher salt, and the finest grades of sea salt available, including the purest of all salts, the French Malandel Fleur de Sel.

○ The Spice House
   1031 North Old World Third Street
   Milwaukee, Wisconsin 53203
   (414) 272-0977
   fax: (414) 272-1271
   www.thespicehouse.com

STOCKS

Stocks are one of the most important components of fine cooking. Nothing can substitute for the flavor of a well-made stock in a recipe. Since most of us rarely have a couple of days a month to dedicate to the making of fine stocks to fill our freezers, today's retail market has responded, thankfully, to the demand for fine-quality products with which to make good stock. A number of options are available to the home cook.

The Swanson's brand (owned by Campbell's Soup) markets great canned beef stock and chicken stock. Swanson's also markets a low-sodium chicken stock under the name Natural Goodness. This product is especially good because it keeps a stock-based sauce or soup from becoming too salty as it cooks and reduces. If you are using a commercial stock product, it's a good idea not to add any salt until the end of the cooking process. At that time, taste and add salt as needed.

In addition, Knorr markets an excellent fish bouillon cube. For fish stock, you can also substitute bottled clam broth, which is available in most markets. Knorr also make a great vegetable bouillon cube.

The best product for making stocks, if not making them from scratch, is base paste. These pastes are the end products of stocks that are slowly reduced until they form thickened pastes. Most gourmet shops and specialty markets carry the beef and chicken base pastes. Central Market even carries a lamb base paste. These products can be expensive, but a teaspoon of the paste will make a cup of rich stock. Keep the base pastes in the freezer, tightly covered, for an unlimited shelf life.

○ More Than Gourmet Company
   1-800-860-9385
   www.morethangourmet.com

This company produces the best-quality base pastes available to the consumer. They include demi-glace, chicken stock, brown (beef) stock, seafood/fish stock, duck stock, and vegetable stock.

INDEX

ROUTE 66

AMARILLO

LUBBOCK
Llano Estacado Winery
Cap Rock Winery

SWEETWATER

BIG SPRING

ABILENE

EL PASO

MIDLAND •

ODESSA

SAN ANGELO

FORT DAVIS

TERLINGUA

DEL RIO

N

W

E

S

JOHN A WILSON